Using LibGuides to Enhance Library Services

Using LibGuides to Enhance Library Services

A LITA Guide

Edited by

Aaron W. Dobbs,
Ryan L. Sittler, and
Douglas Cook

An imprint of the American Library Association

CHICAGO   2013

Printed in the United States of America

17 16 15 14 13   5 4 3 2 1

Extensive effort has gone into ensuring the reliability of the information in this book; however, the publisher makes no warranty, express or implied, with respect to the material contained herein.

ISBNs: 978-1-55570-880-1 (paper); 978-1-55570-903-7 (PDF). For more information on digital formats, visit the ALA Store at alastore.ala.org and select eEditions.

Library of Congress Cataloging-in-Publication Data

Using LibGuides to Enhance Library Services : A LITA Guide / Edited by Aaron W. Dobbs, Ryan L. Sittler, and Douglas Cook For the Library and Information Technology Association.
    pages   cm
  Includes bibliographical references and index.
  ISBN 978-1-55570-880-1
  1. Library Web sites—Design. 2. Digital libraries—Design. 3. Libraries—Special collections—Computer network resources. 4. Library information networks. 5. Electronic information resource literacy. I. Dobbs, Aaron W., 1968—editor of compilation. II. Sittler, Ryan, editor of compilation. III. Cook, Douglas, editor of compilation. IV. Library and Information Technology Association (U.S.)
Z674.75.W67U85 2013
025.0422—dc23   2012040830

Book design in Berkeley and Avenir. Cover images © gualtiero boffi/Shutterstock, Inc.

⊗ This paper meets the requirements of ANSI/NISO Z39.48-1992 (Permanence of Paper).

Contents

■ PART 3 ■
Creating LibGuides—For Guide Creators

■ PART 4 ■
Making Better Use of LibGuides

■ **PART 5** ■

Technological and Pedagogical Exemplars from Academic, K–12, Public, and Special Libraries

Preface

LibGuides is a product that has filled a timely need with librarians. Faced with rapid change in the more complex Web 2.0 expectations of our patrons, librarians, particularly at smaller institutions without dedicated web personnel, have struggled to keep up. Library functions that had previously been physical or face-to-face have moved to the Web. Digital collections are a good example of this. Patrons no longer expect to come to the library to search for information. Students expect, rightly so, to go to one place for library resources for their information needs—the library's web space. We librarians have moved rapidly to fill this need by spending considerable amounts of time and effort creating and maintaining large bodies of informational and instructive content to assist patrons at the point of need on their websites.

LibGuides—a simple-to-use, cloud-based, web-content management system—provides easy-to-use tools for the librarian to improve patrons' experience in finding information. LibGuides has many virtues. Providing numerous templates and help guides, LibGuides offers an easy method for the time-strapped librarian to create a workable web presence. As it resides on a server off-campus, it solves some of the web-branding and campus standardization issues that have recently cropped up on university campuses that look at the Web as a billboard rather than as a teaching tool. Librarians who would like to use Web 2.0 technology to reach clients have those capabilities in LibGuides, as well.

So if LibGuides is so easy to use why should you read this book? Probably the best answer is to get a quick overview of the potential, the setup and maintenance routines, and the potential uses of LibGuides in one readable and hopefully interesting format. LibGuides has been the subject of many recent articles in professional journals, as well as the topic of numerous workshops and conference presentations. However, this book is the first attempt at putting into a single published volume the broad issues that need to be discussed, the decisions that need to be made, and the specific steps that need to be undertaken to set up, use, and maintain LibGuides effectively. This book is meant to be a handy user guide for LibGuides; thus it is written in simple, straightforward language and features plenty of examples and accompanying illustrations.

Like any new software, LibGuides has its own vocabulary, so chapters 1, 4, and 8 include definitions of LibGuide terminology. We have included checklists of implementation and assessment procedures. For example, chapter 3 includes a checklist of steps/decisions that need to be made through the planning and implementation process. Chapter 11 includes a rubric that will help you to assess your use of LibGuides and attempt to place a monetary value on your LibGuides usage. Chapter 14 includes a checklist of major criteria for technical design evaluation of LibGuides and a checklist of major criteria for reference/educational evaluation of LibGuides.

Our expert authors have chosen outstanding examples of LibGuides from the huge cadre of LibGuide users out there in LibraryLand who have contributed to the best use of LibGuides. These librarians have created pages that are educationally sound, designed well, and are worth lauding in such a tome as this. Viewing these exemplars will provide you with numerous ideas to put into place at your own institution.

Although academic libraries have been the largest users of LibGuides, public libraries, K–12 libraries, and special libraries have been referenced here as well. Chapter 14, in particular, highlights good examples of technical design and pedagogical instruction from all four library types. We have chosen numerous LibGuide instances as good examples to follow in each of these categories. We have highlighted twelve sites for technological excellence—three academic libraries, three public libraries, three K–12 libraries, and three special libraries. We have also chosen three exemplars from each of the four library types to represent good instructional design. (So far that is twenty-four awesome LibGuides sites discussed in chapter 14.) Finally we have named an academic library LibGuides site as the best overall technological and instructional designer of a LibGuide. We have done the same with a public library, a K–12 library, and a special library. (That is four more so we have a total of twenty-eight amazing websites discussed in chapter 14.)

We will be dealing with all matters LibGuide in the following fashion. The book is divided into five parts.

PART 1
A BRIEF INTRODUCTION TO LIBRARIES AND THE INTERNET

This is an introductory chapter that starts with the history of library guides and ends with the importance of using a flexible and easy-to-use content management system, which meets patrons' needs.

Chapter 1
A Short History of Library Guides and Their Usefulness to Librarians and Patrons

Jennifer Emanuel

This chapter begins by chronicling the long historical use of library guides in instruction. Various options available currently for creating library web guides are presented—HTML and other free and open source options. Finally, LibGuides by Springshare is presented as a viable software package to create and organize your web platform.

PART 2
ADMINISTERING AND MAINTAINING LIBGUIDES— FOR SYSTEMS LIBRARIANS

As with all content management systems, some tech-savvy person needs to implement the local platform. This part provides valuable information to convince managers that LibGuides is a worthy purchase, to implement and roll out LibGuides, to maintain the platform, and to train library staff in the creation of LibGuides. We have also included a chapter that will cover your initial setup and continuing maintenance of the LibGuides software.

Chapter 2
Making the Case Campus-wide for Purchasing LibGuides

Stephanie DeLano Davis

This chapter begins by identifying the various organizational stakeholders involved in making the initial decision to purchase LibGuides—students, faculty, librarians, library administrators, information technology managers, and institutional marketing managers. The various viewpoints of each group are examined, clearly outlining some of the marketing that you must do campus-wide before expending money for the project. Finally, the chapter explores decisions made by three actual implementations of LibGuides. Michigan State University replaced a previous web-based system with LibGuides. Northwestern Michigan College replaced the library portion of its campus HTML server with LibGuides. And Kellogg Community College had no web-based guides before setting up LibGuides.

Chapter 3
Administering LibGuides: Planning, Implementation, and Beyond

Beth Larkee Kumar and Tabatha Farney

This chapter builds upon chapter 2 by describing the options for setting up and administering LibGuides after it is purchased. Various administrative styles and workflows are explained, which will help you to decide how to best maintain your own installation, including appointing a single LibGuides administrator, setting up a large administrative team based on workflow issues, or creating a loosely structured system where a LibGuides administrator and an author/librarian work together. The remainder of the chapter is equally specific in discussing such concepts as deciding what types of guides your library can create, marketing your initial LibGuides launch, and maintaining LibGuides after it is implemented.

Chapter 4
Strategies and Techniques for Administrators

Aaron W. Dobbs and Rich Gause

Chapter 3 discusses decisions that need to be made while implementing LibGuides. Chapter 4 provides advice for the system administrator assigned to maintain LibGuides. Provided is a detailed explanation of the complex components of LibGuides which a LibGuide's administrator can enact to provide specialized functionality to the platform. This very practical chapter steps through the menu that allows LibGuides customization. Administrative menu choices and their consequences are explained. The LibGuides administrative menu—Admin Stuff—has two functions: customizing the formatting of the LibGuides site and managing and maintaining the various components of the site. Both these functions are explained in a step-by-step fashion.

Chapter 5
Developing LibGuides Training: A Blended-Learning Approach
*Laura Westmoreland Gariepy, Emily S. Mazure, Jennifer A. McDaniel,
and Erin R. White*

One implementation step often overlooked or treated haphazardly is training staff to take advantage of LibGuides. Chapter 5 presents a strategy for setting up organized training based on the needs of your personnel. The chapter begins with a discussion of factors to consider when determining whether training is necessary for software implementation. Building on their experience of training staff at Virginia Commonwealth University to use LibGuides, the authors discuss numerous formats for providing training, including creating a style and training manual, face-to-face workshops, personalized support and training, and continuing support after initial training. Finally, the chapter suggests what content might be covered in your LibGuides staff training.

PART 3
CREATING LIBGUIDES—FOR GUIDE CREATORS

This part is for readers who are responsible for creating LibGuides. Although LibGuides are physically very simple to create, we have included a chapter on pedagogy and a chapter on effective design that will inform librarians as they create a LibGuide. We have included two step-by-step chapters on the actual creation of a LibGuide: a chapter that explains in simple language how to create a LibGuide, and an advanced chapter for those of you who want to explore LibGuides' creative potential.

Chapter 6
Design: Why It Is Important and How to Get It Right
Nedda H. Ahmed

This chapter discusses the overall design issues that need to be considered when creating a LibGuide. The author clearly states that a poorly designed LibGuide will be ignored by your library patrons. Beginning with broad guidelines of graphic design, this chapter quickly moves to practical application. Such simple but often misused components as color, image placement, text blocks, and font style are applied to the creation of attractive LibGuides. The author specifically explores one often overlooked piece of web design—writing for the Web.

Chapter 7
Integrating LibGuides into the Teaching-Learning Process
Veronica Bielat, Rebeca Befus, and Judith Arnold

Web aesthetics is a first step toward creating useful LibGuides. Guide creators also need to understand how students learn in order to create effective LibGuides. Chapter 7 takes you through some basic learning theory and describes the practical application of these theories in designing LibGuides that support independent student learning. First, the authors apply various learning theories to LibGuide creation—scaffolding, metacognition, and cognitive load. The authors then display the usefulness of these principles by applying them to the creation and design of LibGuides for two specific courses at Wayne State University.

Chapter 8
Creating Your First LibGuide
Kenneth Liss

Chapters 6 and 7 provide some theory and examples as a basis for chapters 8 and 9. Chapter 8 provides you with a step-by-step guide to the actual creation of a LibGuide. LibGuide components—guides, pages, columns, and content boxes—are illustrated to explain how each is related to the other. The LibGuide creation menu—the Dashboard—is presented in a step-by-step fashion. The author provides examples of the various basic LibGuide components he discusses—creating a guide, setting up the column widths, and adding basic content boxes to a guide.

Chapter 9
Adding Some Pizzazz to Your Guides
Kathy Gaynor

Chapter 9 builds on chapter 8. In the same very practical menu-based format, this chapter covers some of the more complex functionality of the Dashboard menu. Although librarians with little technical experience can easily navigate the creation of a guide, there are many advanced tools and techniques that can enhance the appeal of your LibGuide to a patron. This chapter will explain how to use these more advanced components of the software, such as adding to a guide RSS feeds, podcasts, videos, and items from your catalog. The author goes on to explain the use of several types of user feedback boxes which are components of LibGuides. Examples in actual use on the Internet are provided for each box type discussed.

PART 4
MAKING BETTER USE OF LIBGUIDES

Part 4 provides you with information regarding several specialized situations that frequently face us as we begin to make a broader use of LibGuides. We have included a chapter on LibAnswers—a popular add-on to LibGuides—which acts as a searchable FAQ databasefor patrons, as well as a console for librarians to handle e-mail and phone-texting queries. LibGuides has numerous built-in assessment and statistical tools that can provide information regarding effectiveness and accountability, which are discussed in chapter 11. Two special settings are covered with a chapter. LibGuides' integration with distance education is discussed first pedagogically and then very practically with suggestions for formatting LibGuides for use with course management systems. The final chapter in this part deals with the recent advent of mobile devices to access library content. This chapter provides advice for producing LibGuides for the small screens of devices such as smartphones.

Chapter 10
Helping Users Help Themselves:
Maximizing LibAnswers Usage

Aaron Tay

LibAnswers is an integrated add-on component of LibGuides which acts as a searchable FAQ database, as well as a console that handles e-mail and text queries from patrons. This chapter explains how to maximize this software to most effectively provide answers to oft-asked questions. Based on his expertise in setting up and assessing LibAnswers at the National University of Singapore, the author provides insight into user behavior when searching for factual information about the library as well as examples of fine-tuning the LibAnswer settings to best match user needs.

Chapter 11
Using Statistical Gathering Tools to Determine Effectiveness and Accountability

Lora Baldwin and Sue A. McFadden

The need for assessment is always with us. This chapter discusses a variety of assessment tools that are easily implemented with LibGuides. Beginning with a rubric for gauging LibGuides' effective use, the chapter continues by discussing the built-in analysis components of LibGuides. The rubric created by the authors attempts to objectify numerous very qualitative goals typically discussed when assessing a product. Much of the chapter consists of displaying how you can make best use of the data that can be gathered from LibGuides' statistical component. The use of Google Analytics with LibGuides is also discussed. Finally they use a fictional university to explain how their rubric can be used to determine the overall objective value of LibGuides to a library.

Chapter 12
Using LibGuides to Promote Information Literacy in a Distance Education Environment

Barbara J. Mann, Julie Lee Arnold, and Joseph Rawson

Using LibGuides within the environment of a course management system can provide special challenges. This chapter will explain the types of LibGuides that work most effectively for distance students. Using examples of specific courses in online degree programs at the University of Maryland University College, the authors give examples of the four LibGuide types that they find can most effectively help online students: (1) embedded stand-alone library instruction modules, (2) course resources guides, (3) subject-specific guides, and (4) tutorials. Finally the authors discuss the use of LibGuides with various popular online learning systems—Blackboard, Angel, Moodle, and Desire2Learn.

Chapter 13
Why Go Mobile?

Mark Ellis, Leslie Adebonojo, and Kathy Campbell

Smartphones have become increasingly popular with our students. Unfortunately, all web content does not display well on a phone screen. This chapter will discuss the various technical issues that cause this problem—screen size, device memory, telecommunication barriers, authentication in proprietary databases, and so on. The authors go on to outline a plan for overcoming these technical problems so that students can access your website via smartphone. The authors explain their plan with examples from their LibGuides site at East Tennessee State University.

PART 5

TECHNOLOGICAL AND PEDAGOGICAL EXEMPLARS FROM ACADEMIC, K–12, PUBLIC, AND SPECIAL LIBRARIES

People learn by viewing the examples of others. This final chapter will tackle the difficult question of what makes an effective LibGuide by presenting a rubric for appropriate instructional methodology and a rubric for effective technical helpfulness. This chapter then showcases twenty-eight exemplars of highly exceptional LibGuides which display the positive characteristics discussed in this book.

xvii

Chapter 14
Showcase of Exceptional LibGuides

Sharon Whitfield and Claire Clemens

It is often difficult to ascertain if a LibGuide has been created with the greatest potential for usefulness. Using a rubric for pedagogical effectiveness and one for technical effectiveness, this chapter explains the overall components of useful web content and then provides exemplars of LibGuides in actual use. Three outstanding examples of LibGuide pedagogical design are presented from each library type—academic, public, K–12, and special. As well, three exemplars of LibGuides technical design and effectiveness are discussed from each of the four library types. Finally, truly outstanding sites are presented that combine expertise in both technical and instructional design—one academic library, one public library, one K–12 library, and one special library. These twenty-eight LibGuides will inspire you to make use of the best of the concepts in this book that contribute to excellent web design.

Acknowledgments

S pecial thanks go to the Springshare team. We hope they will keep improving the platform and the related product family. All Springshare images have been used with the permission of the organization. Please note that none of the editors or authors of this book had any fiduciary connection to Springshare as it was being written and sent to the publishers. We are just fans of LibGuides.

Thanks go to Marta Deyrup for helping us through the project. We also want to thank all of our chapter authors. We truly could not have put the book together without their hard work and expertise.

Thanks go to the "Three Amigos"—your illustrious editors. Thanks to Aaron W. Dobbs for the original idea for the book and for his extensive knowledge of LibGuides' inner workings. Aaron is the LibGuides site administrator at Shippensburg University of Pennsylvania and grokked LibGuides as soon as he gained access. Aaron is all about making it easy for content authors to manage their own guides. The second amigo, Ryan L. Sittler, is the instructional technology/ information literacy librarian at California University of Pennsylvania. Ryan is a LibGuides user and a mighty instructor. Ryan, rightly so, is of the opinion that to use LibGuides to its fullest you, dear reader, need to know a bit about designing good-looking and educationally sound web space. And finally your third editor, Doug Cook, is the graybeard of the group. Doug is an instruction librarian at Shippensburg University of Pennsylvania and considers himself a pedagogue. Doug has been teaching library skills since 1975. Every day he believes more and more that it really does matter what you say to your students and how you say it. Special thanks to Doug for being the project trail boss—keeping all the spreadsheets up-to-date and for herding the cats. (Editorial note from Ryan: Doug is the glue that kept this book together. This is my third book with him—and I continue to marvel at his patience, intellect, and encouragement during these projects. He is not just a colleague, but also a very valued friend. So an extra special personal thank you, Doug, for your work on this project. We never would have finished it without you—Ryan.) (Ryan said it best, ditto his comments—Aaron.) (Thanks guys!—Doug.)

We trust that sharing our mistakes will keep you from repeating them. And we trust that our exemplary uses of LibGuides will inspire your emulation. By the way, please show your adulation of our prowess by purchasing a copy of this book—and maybe a copy for each of your library friends. (Maybe your Mom would like one for her birthday . . .)

■ ■ ■

Feel free to e-mail us if you have any questions.

The Three Amigos
Aaron W. Dobbs, Ryan L. Sittler, and Doug Cook
September 2012

PART 1

A Brief Introduction to Libraries and the Internet

A Short History of Library Guides and Their Usefulness to Librarians and Patrons

Jennifer Emanuel

L ibrary guides have had various incarnations over the years, starting from the paper pathfinders of the 1960s and 1970s to the more elaborate online guides of today; yet they all strive to connect users with library resources, no matter the format. In our increasingly online environment for library resources, services, and assistance, several options have developed for creating online guides, with Lib-Guides just being one option; others include open source, content management systems (CMS), and basic HTML web pages. Selecting a platform to create library guides involves examining individual institutional needs and then matching them with the resources and knowledge available to the implementing library. Understanding that patrons often do not turn first to library guides, but instead to search engines makes it important to have a web presence that encourages sharing and improves discoverability. This chapter will provide you with a short history of the use of library guides in instruction. Computer- and Internet-based guide creation options will be overviewed. Finally, LibGuides by Springshare will be presented as a viable software package to create and organize a library's web platform.

A SHORT HISTORY OF LIBRARY GUIDES

Roughly defined, library guides have had various names and different formats throughout the history of modern librarianship. These include bibliographies, pathfinders, subject guides, online tutorials, online guides, and web guides, among others. Early guides, some dating back to the late nineteenth century, can be simply described as subject-specific essays and bibliographies of relevant library materials (Smith, 2008). These lists and bibliographies were produced in paper format, often as brochures, and allowed researchers to efficiently find relevant resources within a specific subject area without having to look through multiple print indexes, which was a time-consuming and tedious practice. These resources were strictly lists of various library materials created by a librarian who had already performed an appropriate search. These bibliographies, however, did not provide guidance as to the actual process of conducting research. It was common for libraries to only allow librarians or serious researchers physical access to library collections, which meant little instruction was given as to how to actually conduct research and properly utilize library materials. When instruction was given, it was generally in the form of orientation tours or class-specific instruction on the use of the library (Cipolla, 1980).

The late 1960s and early 1970s brought changes to libraries, and the now familiar "pathfinder" was created. During this period, the number of print publications proliferated and at the same time computers began to find their way into the library world. As a result, the Massachusetts Institute of Technology (MIT) started a research program called INTREX, or Information Transfer Experiments, to create an online "model experimental library" (Shera, 1965: 359). One part of INTREX was the Modern Library Program, which was included as an instructional module comprised of an analog slide and taped audio tutorial on how to access, use, and search for networked library information (Overhage and Reintjes, 1974; Smith, 2008). These point-of-need instructional materials were named "pathfinders" and were considered "organized introductory checklists for a variety of sources of information on specific topics" and were "structured to save time by aiding [the user] in systematically locating materials within a subject literature" (Harbeson, 1972: 111).

Harbeson (1972) helped to initially develop pathfinders, and believed that they fell into a twelve-step pattern with adaptations based on the individual guide. These steps included, among others, a definition of the scope of the guide itself, a discussion of the topic, resources such as relevant subject headings, call numbers, reference books, indexes, journals, conference proceedings, and bibliographies. Harbeson also noted that pathfinders have much in common with bibliographies, but place more emphasis on the process of searching and are better teaching tools. Pathfinders give researchers an awareness of what resources are available, help them gain expertise with a variety of library resources, and allow researchers to individually choose which resources are best for their project.

As evidenced above, pathfinders were initially very structured, with somewhat rigid formatting and content. However, they soon became more flexible as librarians began to utilize them in new and innovative ways. During this time, MIT established a repository to share and cooperatively develop pathfinders across multiple institutions. This repository was marketed by the Addison-Wesley Publishing Company and, though frequent technical problems and limitations precluded it from gaining popularity, the repository showed that the pathfinder was a valuable tool and efforts for cooperative pathfinder development were important (Smith, 2008).

Starting in the late 1980s and early 1990s, libraries began building text- and graphic- based websites (Smith, 2008). Since printed pathfinders were heavily used research aids, they became one of the first things that libraries put online. Over time, online pathfinders evolved into a variety of formats that showed the diverse capabilities of the Internet, including (but not limited to) PDF copies of print pathfinders, HTML (hypertext)-based pathfinders, interactive tutorials, and multimedia presentations on both subject-specific resources and how to use the library (Large, 1996). During this period, the term *pathfinder* began to be deemed as antiquated since it was linked too closely to the fading print format. The names "research guide," "subject guide," or "online tutorial" were more commonly being used throughout library literature and colloquially (Glassman and Sorensen, 2010). A lack of web design and HTML coding skills were (and continue to be) a frequent barrier for librarians to create online point-of-need instruction materials. As a result, web design and content often became the work area of a specialized web services librarian or even campus-level information technology specialists. Some web services librarians created online subject guide templates for their colleagues to make use of, but these also required similar high-level technical skills to use and update. Eventually this led to the development of both commercial and open source software for library guides and tutorials. Before reviewing some of these software packages, I will discuss patron perceptions of library guides on the Web.

PERCEPTIONS OF LIBRARY GUIDES

Much research has been done concerning library guides. Not all librarians are in agreement about the use and utility of guides on the Web. There are librarians who feel that the time spent to input content into a web guide is better spent on other tasks, including devoting time to making library interfaces easier to use so that guides are not necessary. There is also a widespread belief that tutorials and guides should be stored in a central repository so that each institution does not need to duplicate their efforts (Jackson and Pellack, 2004).

In "Students, Librarians, and Subject Guides: Improving a Poor Rate of Return," Reeb and Gibbons examined several studies of student usage of various library guides, and combined this outside data with results of several user studies they performed at Rochester University. Reeb and Gibbons are especially critical of the basic analytics used to evaluate online guides; they feel that the number of hits a page gets is not a good indicator of how long users spend looking over the page, what they thought of the content, or if they considered the content useful. These authors also noted that many of the guides identified in various studies had very few hits and were probably not generating enough traffic to justify the librarian time spent in order to create them. User studies conducted by Reeb and Gibbons and similar studies at other institutions also showed that students, when they needed to complete a specific assignment, usually first performed a search and did not attempt to look for guides that may have been relevant to their assignments. Even though some students acknowledged that their library provided such online assistance, they did not take the time to explore the library website for research help.

Reeb and Gibbons's (2004) analysis of library guide usage led them to develop new guidelines and to create new and different types of library guides at their institution. They stress that librarians should only create guides that relate directly to students' point of need. Guides should be contextual to a student's specific assignment, and not attempt to cover a broad subject area. Guides, they argue, should relate directly to student coursework and specific assignments and be located inside course management systems and alongside specific library resources and products. Reeb and Gibbons stress that content, not necessarily the container, is the most important factor determining if a library guide will be used and if the user considers it a useful tool.

CONTEMPORARY LIBRARY ONLINE GUIDES

The complexity of maintaining a library website (plus such data from user research regarding why patrons do or do not use guides when searching for information) nudged technologically oriented librarians into experimenting with Web 2.0 technologies to address these issues. A consensus began to form that library guides should reflect the new attention to interactivity, participation, and design that was emerging on the Internet (Coombs, 2007). Librarians looked to Web 2.0 tools to deliver content to library users in new and innovative ways, and experimented first with tools such as online bookmarking and tagging applications such as Delicious (http://delicious.com), as well as wiki applications such as PBwiki (now Pbworks, http://pbworks.com) and MediaWiki (www.mediawiki.org). These tools allowed multiple librarians to edit guides and also did not require extensive technological skills to maintain because all material was input with a "what you see is what you get" (WYSIWYG) interface. These platforms simplified the skills needed to create library web guides so that all librarians, regardless of their technological savvy, could create and edit a customized guide for library patrons without the aid of a technology or systems librarian.

However, social bookmarking and wiki applications still lacked features of the Web 2.0 movement that appealed to librarians, such as the ability to easily add widgets (a widget is a small icon or search box which opens a session in a different software application from the one in which the widget resides) from other online services, the integration of library virtual reference services, and the ability for users to add comments or rate the site, or to share with various online bookmarking and social media applications. Some librarians even started to develop and integrate homegrown, open source, and/or content management systems to accommodate this need.

OPEN SOURCE ALTERNATIVES

Several libraries have sponsored the development of popular open source programs that allow librarians to create customized guides. ("Open source" software is freely available for anyone to use without a license.) The two tools that are best known in the library community are SubjectsPlus from Ithaca College (www.subjectsplus .com) and Library à la Carte from Oregon State University (http://alacarte.library .oregonstate.edu). Both require that the software be run on a local server, so there is considerable technical expertise needed to get both products up and running. However, in exchange for this work, both open source products are technically free. The only costs are human capital and server space. Some libraries have the technological expertise to easily provide this support. The libraries using these open source projects are able to customize the software to fit their needs.

SubjectsPlus

SubjectsPlus is an open source software package that supports course guides, an A-Z database list, FAQs, a suggestion box, and a staff list. It was fully developed at Ithaca College, but traces its roots to East Carolina University. Its technical requirements are a local server and MySQL database software. Systems librarians generally have at least a basic familiarity with MySQL.

SubjectsPlus is a widget-based environment that allows for the creation of a customized course, subject, or topic guide. It allows the librarian to create a single page with multiple, flexible-content boxes. Content can be entered in a WYSIWYG format, brought in from other Web 2.0 applications such as Delicious, flickr, or RSS feeds, or can also come from the other modules that SubjectsPlus supports. It can also be modified using Cascading Style Sheets (CSS) to fit seamlessly into a library template without looking like a different product than the library's website. As of July 2011, SubjectsPlus had been implemented in a total of thirty-four small and midsize colleges and universities. Since it is open source, librarians with MySQL and PHP skills can add to the code and the main developer is willing to take suggestions for improvements and features. However, there is one primary developer and while the developer is responsive, it can take time to implement updates.

Examples of various guides created with SubjectsPlus are available at www .ithacalibrary.com/subjects. The home for SubjectsPlus is at www.subjectsplus .com.

Library à la Carte

Library à la Carte is an open source application developed at the Oregon State University Libraries. Since it is open source, there are technical skills needed to install and maintain the software. Library à la Carte utilizes Ruby and MySQL for its structure. Since Ruby is not a commonly used programming language in libraries, fewer libraries have adopted Library à la Carte. As of July 2011, the project website listed nineteen academic libraries of all sizes utilizing the software. Since this group is small, there is not a large community to provide technical assistance. As sometimes happens with open source products, the primary programmer left the project in March 2011 and even though the project has continued, there have not been any updates to the Library à la Carte website since then and the project appears stalled.

One important thing to note about Library à la Carte is that it was designed with usability and accessibility in mind. It allows for complete customization so that individual libraries can make the software look like the rest of their website. Like SubjectsPlus, librarians can create tip pages, tutorials, and subject or course guides using a variety of module types including links, videos, profile information, quizzes, and web links. Additionally, Library à la Carte can integrate some Web 2.0 features that are lacking in SubjectsPlus, including creating RSS feeds, adding third-party widgets to individual guides, comments, tagging, and options to share.

The project page for Library à la Carte is http://alacarte.library.oregonstate.edu and an example of a guide created with the software is http://guides.library.reed.edu/course-guide/52-Anth344.

Static HTML and Campus Content Management Systems

There are some libraries that do not have a dedicated system for creating guides, and instead simply create new web pages. A web page in the library's content management system or a static HTML page gives librarians as much flexibility in guide creation as they are comfortable with. There is frequently a high learning curve based on what platform the library uses for its website. Some CMSs are very easy to use and offer the same WYSIWYG formatting that dedicated guide software provides, while some sites employ HTML and other web-scripting languages, such as ASP and PHP, which means content can only be created by librarians with highly technical skills or by campus computer staff

However, creating pages within a library's website does have significant advantages that dedicated library guide software does not. Web pages are endlessly expandable, from static content to interactive sites with multiple widgets and custom functionality. They can also seamlessly blend into the library's online identity because they use the same templates as the library as a whole. Creating a web page is ideal for content that may not fit neatly in a subject guide, such as when a long narrative is necessary or when the guide takes users through a sequence of events that require clicking on a new page.

LIBGUIDES

Although open source programs, campus-wide CMS solutions, and HTML each have advantages and disadvantages, many librarians have turned to another solution—LibGuides by Springshare. LibGuides is a commercially available software package that allows librarians to create dynamic library guides. Creating a guide in LibGuides has a low learning curve. Additionally, there are numerous templates available to display library information. LibGuides does need to be customized by a technologically aware librarian before its use, consisting of setting default parameters, and so on.

In early 2007 Springshare released LibGuides to the library market, with Temple University and Cedarville University being the first implementers. The aim for the development of LibGuides was, and still is, to give librarians a simple-to-use platform to enable them to easily publish their own web content. The simplicity brought about by the user-friendly interface also incorporates the endless formatting possibilities provided by HTML. What librarians can do with LibGuides is only limited by what the interface allows and what content they decide to place within the platform.

LibGuides has an extensive user community made up of librarians in more than 2,000 (www.springshare.com/libguides) libraries worldwide. This extensive community is what sets LibGuides apart from open source library guides, as they tend to have a small user base mostly comprised of web and systems librarians. LibGuides are constantly being improved upon by Springshare in response to community needs, and the product is constantly evolving without needing to submit code as would be the case with open source products. Springshare does all the server hosting work, maintenance, and code updating, which can be less expensive when compared to a library employee doing these tasks locally.

LibGuides are very easy to use. The simplicity of the interface, utilizing a WYSIWYG editor that can be customized with knowledge of basic HTML, and the inclusion of third-party widgets, makes it appealing for librarians with a wide range of technology skills. The guides also enable librarians to share and copy information from one guide to another, allowing content to be replicated, saving a great deal of time in creating new guides. Additionally, LibGuides can include widgets and RSS feeds, which can expand their content significantly, allowing for integration with library resources such as online catalogs, electronic resources, virtual reference services, course management systems, social media, and other embeddable media. LibGuides also provides built-in user statistics so that librarians can assess the use of their guides as well as get user comments and check to make sure content is up-to-date and accurate. Not only is the content of a LibGuide customizable, but libraries can take steps to modify the default installation of LibGuides with unique headers and Cascading Style Sheets, changing aspects such as the color scheme, font, and link characteristics.

Naturally, there is no such thing as a perfect system, and there are some items about which LibGuides users need to be aware. For example, some initial training is needed for librarians to make the utmost use of this software. LibGuides can easily appear crowded and confusing for the patron to use. The most common and obvious way to organize content in a LibGuide web page is through the use of tabs, which also have accessibility concerns because screen readers can confuse their order. (See the "LibGuides Vocabulary Lesson.") However, LibGuides is taking steps to minimize accessibility concerns, working towards bringing the product in line with 508 standards, the details of which are explained at http://help.springshare.com/accessibility. Including more than four or five tabs in one guide can easily complicate a guide's layout. Additionally, the number of boxes, columns, and widgets can quickly make even a single-paged LibGuide too busy and too complicated for the end user. The flexibility of LibGuides also can create

LibGuide Vocabulary Lesson

LibGuides, as is true of many software programs, uses terminology that can be confusing at first. Here are some basics:

LibGuides—the name of the program itself. Since it is the name of a program, it is singular. *"LibGuides is a great program."*

LibGuide or Guide—the term used for a web page on one general subject. *"I created a LibGuide for the English class with which I am working tomorrow."*

Page or Tab—a LibGuide can have numerous "pages." Each page has differing content and is accessed by clicking on a "tab" icon at the top of the LibGuide. *"My ENG101 LibGuide has a page for searching EBSCOhost databases, one for searching CQ Researcher, and a page explaining MLA Citation Style."*

Box—each page has numerous "boxes." A box is the content area of a page. *"My ENG101 Guide's MLA citation style page has a box with a link to an MLA handout in PDF, another box with a link to Purdue's MLA website, and several boxes in which I have keyed examples of common mistakes students make in MLA."*

accessibility and functionality issues when libraries try to insert their own CSS code or Google Analytics code into their library's guides.

USES FOR LIBGUIDES

In total, there are over 125,000 LibGuides which have been created by more than 25,000 librarians at more than 2,000 libraries of varying types (though the majority are academic). These LibGuides receive 50 million views per month (www .springshare.com/libguides). Since LibGuides are easy to create and maintain, libraries use them for purposes other than subject guides, which was the original intent of the product. Librarians create LibGuides for various reasons that include class-specific instruction, topical subjects, library resources, research assistance, training, and some even function as the library home page. Some of the more common purposes that librarians have utilized LibGuides for are discussed below.

Since LibGuides Are Easy to Create and Maintain, Libraries Use Them for Purposes Other Than Subject Guides:

- Specific classes—ENGL 1410
- Subject resources—Hip Hop Research Guide
- Highlighting library collections—E-Books
- How-tos—The Research Process
- Highlighting new technologies—Using RSS
- Training—Better Customer Service
- Library home pages

Specific Classes

Librarians use LibGuides to create guides specific to certain classes, highlighting relevant resources and instruction to help students achieve success in a specific class or for a specific assignment. (See figure 1.1 for an example.) Since LibGuides are easy to create and content can be copied from one guide to another, librarians opt to have very specific guides that they can use as a presentation aid when they perform instruction. Students can later refer to these guides in order to reinforce

FIGURE 1.1

United States History: 20th and 21st Centuries, Boyden Library, Deerfield Academy, http://libguides.library.deerfield.edu/history

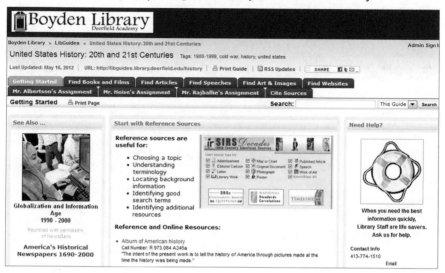

Image courtesy of Boyden Library, Deerfield Academy

concepts discussed in the instruction session. Another example is AP Literature and Composition, Mesa (Arizona) Public Schools (http://libguides.mpsaz.net/mhsap).

Subject Resources

LibGuides can also be used to highlight resources within a particular subject area. (See figure 1.2 for an example.) These guides can take numerous forms, such as having different tabs for different material formats, or using tabs to highlight different subject resources. Subject resources can also take the form of guides for specific current events. LibGuides are a good platform with which to highlight current event resources because they can be created quickly and do not require a lot of time to maintain or update.

Other good examples are:

- Hip Hop Research Guide at Cornell University (http://guides.library .cornell.edu/content.php?pid=21640&sid=153929)
- African American Studies by Northwestern University Library (http://libguides.northwestern.edu/content.php?pid=39921)

FIGURE 1.2
International Affairs, Georgia Tech, http://libguides.gatech.edu/intatop

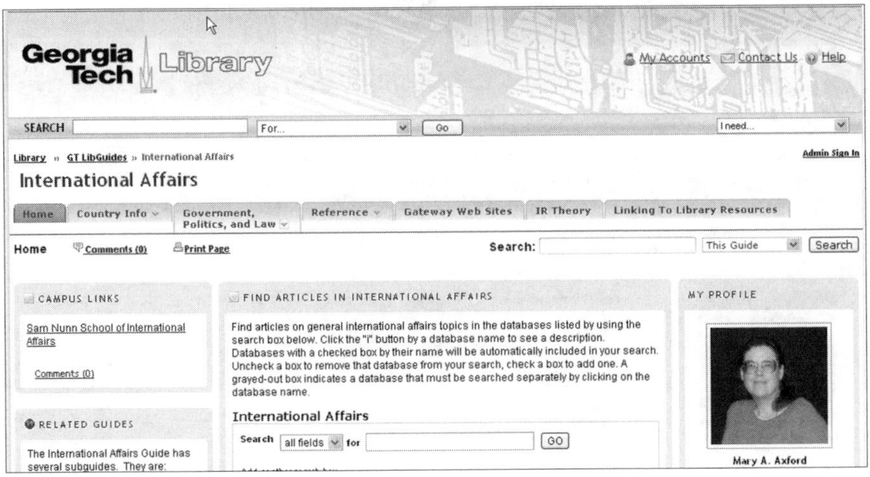

Image courtesy of Georgia Tech Library

Highlighting Library Collections

Librarians also might desire a simple way to highlight their various collections that may otherwise be hidden to the end user. (See figure 1.3 for an example, which highlights an e-book collection.) These types of guides can be specific to a broad collection type, such as electronic books, or they could highlight resources for a specific collection area, such as images. Public libraries can use this type of guide as an online readers' advisory service, showing books that are in a particular genre or interest.

Other examples of this type of LibGuide can be found at the following universities:

- George Mason e-books. Tabs explain different subjects in which e-books are available and how to locate them (http://infoguides.gmu.edu/ebooks).
- MysteryGuide at Vernon Area Public Library. Highlights different types of mystery novels (http://guides.vapld.info/content.php?pid=80311).

FIGURE 1.3
Ebooks LibGuide, Shippensburg University, http://library.ship.edu/ebooks

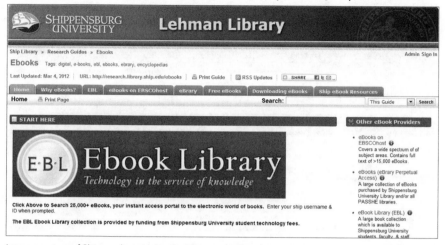

Image courtesy of Shippensburg University Library

How-tos

This category focuses on LibGuides that guide users on how to use library resources to carry out an end goal. For example, The Research Process Step by Step created by Lori Micho is a good how-to guide that condenses what could be a very complicated research process into just five steps, which keeps the number of tabs to a minimum. (See figure 1.4.) How-to guides can run the gamut from how to do research, to how to find audiobooks, or how to use a specific resource. These are very common uses for LibGuides.

Other examples:

- Job Search 101 from the Westerville Public Library. Shows what resources the library has for job seekers, while aiding them through the various elements of the job hunt process. This is a great guide because it condenses the number of steps into a three-tab format (http://explore .westervillelibrary.org/jobs).

FIGURE 1.4

The Research Process: A Step-by-Step Guide, Johnson & Wales University, Denver Campus Library, http://jwudenver.libguides.com/researchprocess

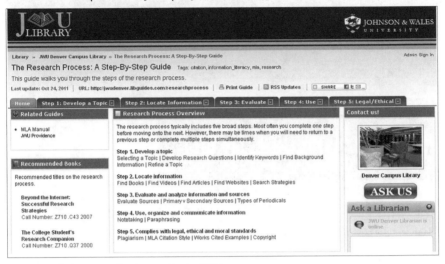

Image provided courtesy of and created by Lori Micho

- How to Bloomberg from Cornell. Narrowly focused guide on just one resource. The tabs indicate individual features of the resources and could be overwhelming to a new user. However, they actually aid in helping the user to easily go to just the area that interests them without having to look through all the guide's content (http://guides.library.cornell.edu/bloomberg_intro).

Highlighting New Technologies

Since technologies change rapidly and there is a constant stream of new information released about them, LibGuides are a good way of passing this information on to library users, or even to library staff. Kimberley Stephenson (see figure 1.5) gives the basics of what RSS is and then applies the technology to the library context with a LibGuide. Since LibGuides can both be created and updated quickly, they are a great medium for new technology information. These guides can take different formats, including a news feed for new information, a tutorial on the various aspects of the technology, or a way of sharing what resources the library has devoted to the new technology. Another example of a LibGuide of this type is

FIGURE 1.5
How to Use RSS Feeds from Library Databases, Azusa Pacific University
Libraries, http://apu.libguides.com/rssfeeds

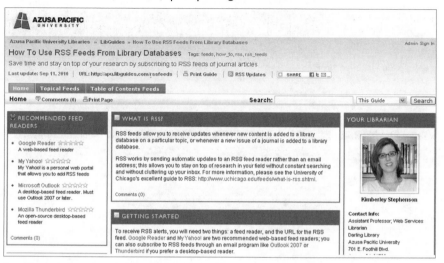

Image provided courtesy of and created by Kimberley Stephenson

Mobile Applications for Law Students and Lawyers by the UCLA School of Law (http://libguides.law.ucla.edu/mobilelegalapps).

Training

Some libraries have utilized LibGuides as a training mechanism for library staff. Figure 1.6, "Collection Management & Technical Services, Shippensburg University," is a good example of a LibGuide used for professional development as well as an informational guide for patrons. Using guides for training can take different formats. Although Shippenburg's Collection Management Department started this guide as an internal document to organize their policies for the staff members in the area, it soon became valuable enough to make it available to the public. Libraries started using LibGuides internally because they are so easy to create and use and the layout is comfortable for staff with all levels of technology expertise. Additionally, the social functions such as commenting can be utilized for training librarians to create a conversation with and solicit feedback from library staff. Other examples of LibGuides for library personnel are

FIGURE 1.6
Collection Management & Technical Services, Shippensburg University, http://library.ship.edu/collectionmanagement

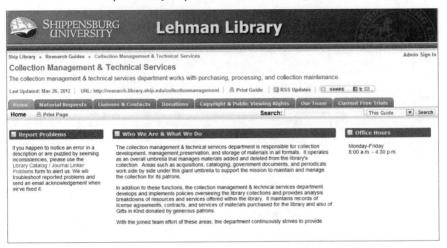

Image provided courtesy of Shippensburg University Library

- LibGuide How To from Ashland University (http://libguides.ashland.edu/libguideshowto)
- University of Illinois's Guide on Customer Service for Library Staff: (http://uiuc-training.libguides.com/customerservices)

Library Home Pages

Library home pages are a controversial use of LibGuides, as many librarians feel that HTML or CMS pages are more robust and better suited to meet the needs of library users. However, for libraries that do not have the technical expertise to set up a web server and create their own pages or are constrained by campus systems that give the library little flexibility in home page content or design, LibGuides can serve as a simple CMS system. Kaiser Permanente Libraries' home page (see figure 1.7) currently uses a LibGuide as a home page. Another similar example is the MIT Libraries Staff Directory (http://libguides.mit.edu/content.php?pid=110460&sid=1057503).

FIGURE 1.7
Kaiser Permanente Libraries home page,
http://kplibraries.libguides.com

Image provided courtesy of Kaiser Permanente Health Sciences Libraries

CONCLUSION

Library guides can take many different names and can be created in a multitude of different formats and content types. Starting as print bibliographical pamphlets in the late nineteenth century before evolving into print pathfinders and finding aids in the twentieth century, and eventually moving online in the 1990s, library guides have always served as a cornerstone of the library mission to connect users to information. Deciding what technology is needed to create them is a decision an individual library or librarians must make on their own, based upon what resources they have available to them, and what comprises the needs of both staff and patrons. Whether an individual library chooses to implement LibGuides, a similar open source product, use a CMS, or create HTML-based web pages, the decision depends on each unique environment. However, the platform is only a part of the implementation of library guides, as the content should be the most important aspect of any system. Additionally, libraries need to take into account other aspects such as marketing, location, information type, and interactivity when implementing library guides, and be sure that all guides accomplish the mission of connecting library users to relevant, timely, and easy-to-understand information at their point of need.

This chapter not only overviewed the history of library guides and different products and methods that can be used to create guides, but also provided examples of the many different types and categories of guides that libraries have implemented for themselves so that librarians can see how others use LibGuides to provide information to library users. There are many different applications of LibGuides and their content types, which will be elaborated upon in subsequent chapters.

The remainder of this book will provide you with information about using LibGuides to its utmost potential. For example, chapters 6, 8, and 9 have a number of strategies you can utilize to ensure that your LibGuides are easily understood by your target audience. As with other software products, LibGuides does have a learning curve. However, with basic training and guidance, librarians can create web guides that appeal to and meet the needs of library patrons. Keep reading for more help on how to use LibGuides at your library.

REFERENCES

Canfield, Marie P. 1972. "Library Pathfinders." *Drexel Library Quarterly* 8 (July): 287–300.

Cipolla, Katherine G. 1980. "M.I.T.'s Point-of-Use Concept: A Five-Year Update." *Journal of Academic Librarianship* 6 (January): 326–28.

Coombs, Karen A. 2007. "Building a Library Website on the Pillars of Web 2.0." *Computers in Libraries* 27, no. 1: 16–19.

Glassman, Nancy R., and Karen Sorensen. 2010. "From Pathfinders to Subject Guides: One Library's Experience with LibGuides." *Journal of Electronic Resources in Medical Libraries* 7, no. 4: 281–91.

Harbeson, Eloise L. 1972. "Teaching Reference and Bibliography: The Pathfinder Approach." *Journal of Education for Librarianship* 13 (Fall): 111–15.

Jackson, Rebecca, and Lorraine J. Pellack. 2004. "Internet Subject Guides in Academic Libraries: An Analysis of Contents, Practices, and Opinions." *Reference & User Services Quarterly* 43, no. 4: 319–27.

Large, J. A. 1996. "Hypertext Instructional Programs and Learner Control: A Research Review." *Education for Information* 14 (June): 95–106.

Overhage, Carl. F. J., and J. F. Reintjes. 1974. "Project INTREX: A General Overview." *Information Storage & Retrieval* 10 (May/June): 157–88.

Reeb, Brenda, and Susan Gibbons. 2004. "Students, Librarians, and Subject Guides: Improving a Poor Rate of Return." *Portal: Libraries and the Academy* 4, no. 1: 123–30.

Shera, Jesse Hauk. 1965. "Librarians' Pugwash, or *Intrex* on the Cape." *Wilson Library Bulletin* 40 (December): 359–62.

Smith, Michael M. 2008. "21st Century Readers' Aids: Past History and Future Directions." *Journal of Web Librarianship* 2, no. 4: 511–23.

PART 2

Administering and Maintaining LibGuides—for System Librarians

## Chapter Two

Making the Case Campus-wide for Purchasing LibGuides

Stephanie DeLano Davis

While LibGuides may be relatively new on the library scene, the need for subject-oriented guides to library resources is not. In their quest to help students and faculty know and use the resources of the library, academic librarians have long had instructional guides as a core mission of the library. As discussed in chapter 1, the emergence of the Internet in the late 1990s brought changes to the academic world by providing online access to previously closed stacks. As Smith (2008: 511) said, "The major objective of an academic library is to connect its users with its available resources." This represents the fundamental selling point of LibGuides: they help librarians fulfill their mission of making resources known to users. While there are clearly other reasons to purchase LibGuides, which will be explored in this chapter, each point harkens back to this primary goal of instruction. At many colleges and universities, libraries were leaders in transitioning to the Internet as a means of serving users (Zumalt and Smith, 2000). During this period of innovation and change, libraries saw the potential of web-based tools and moved in that direction without a significant amount of formal decision making. Librarians embraced the quickly occurring changes of the day. They experimented with a variety of online formats for subject guides, and it did not take long for academic libraries to discover the communication potential of the Web for informing users about library resources.

Moving from a print-based tool, like the pathfinder, to a web-based tool changed the scope of library research guides and expanded the process libraries followed in decision making. What once existed primarily in the realm of the library to help librarians serve students and faculty became visible and more relevant to the wider campus community. The stakeholders involved increased, extending beyond the confines of the library and moving into other campus domains: information technology, web design, and even public relations, among others, depending on the structure of the particular institution. When LibGuides emerged in 2007, librarians were open to a new means of sharing subject-oriented information. As Verbit and Kline note, regarding their process of selecting a web-based subject guide tool, "In short, we needed a CMS [content management system] that was designed specifically for libraries" (2011: 23).

The decision to purchase a software product such as LibGuides should not be made lightly. Beyond the actual cost involved, there are numerous points to consider and many people to consult. This chapter will first outline the campus groups that need to be contacted (or at least considered) before making a purchase. (As each institution is different, please remember that this chapter is provided as a general guide and your independent needs may be somewhat different.) The various viewpoints of each stakeholder will be examined, making clear some of the marketing which must be done campus-wide before expending money for the project. Finally, the chapter explores case studies of several actual university purchases of LibGuides, and will expand on points made regarding stakeholders.

STAKEHOLDERS INVOLVED

Like any change, purchasing and then implementing LibGuides require convincing stakeholders of the value and superiority of this product in providing subject-oriented library content to students and faculty as compared to traditional web-based research guides or print guides.

A diversity of stakeholders is common with information technology projects (Littau, Jujagiri, and Adlbrecht, 2010). Stakeholders connected with LibGuides may differ from institution to institution, but, as defined, "stakeholders are individuals, groups or institutions with an interest in the project, and who can affect the outcome" (Boddy and Paton, 2004: 231). When employing a web-based product like LibGuides, libraries move beyond the library and intersect with other campus units. Engaging in a stakeholders' analysis is an important first step for libraries considering LibGuides and "consists mostly of identifying the different stakeholders, their influence and their needs" (Thiry, 2010: 68). This process allows the library to pinpoint the key players and determine how best to secure their support for the project. Stakeholders want to know both what the project requires of them and, ultimately, how the project impacts them. For some the up-front involvement is significant, while for others, it is the end result that matters.

Library administrators, information systems managers, and other campus stakeholders will all have different questions that need to be answered. Likewise, each group in the decision-making process will be looking at different factors. Library administrator questions may include: "Why spend financial resources for another web-based online system?" "Why not simply continue designing subject research guides using web-design tools or the institution's web management software?" In a world of constrained budgets, it must be asked, "What is it about LibGuides that makes purchasing another web-based system worthwhile?" For subject liaison librarians, the questions may include, "Another change? Why can't we stick with something?" Campus-wide public relations staff may ask, "Can this tool be branded? Will it fit in with the design and brand of the rest of our university website?" Information technology staff may note, "We can't support this software. If

Librarians Need to Listen to a Number of Campus Stakeholders in Order to Have a Smooth Transition to LibGuides

Students as Stakeholders—"We need online access 24/7 to library resources."

Faculty as Stakeholders—"Can I easily insert a LibGuide into Blackboard?"

Librarians as Stakeholders—"How quickly can I learn LibGuides in order to create a guide?"

Library Administrators as Stakeholders—"How much does it cost?"

Information Technology as Stakeholders—"How much of our server space will it use?"

Web Designers as Stakeholders—"What support will librarians need to get LibGuides up and running on the Web?"

Institutional Marketing as Stakeholders—"LibGuides must be able to be branded with the university's logo and colors."

you use this system, you are on your own." For busy web designers, the questions may focus on workload: "How much work will it take to customize this system?" "Can librarians do the work or will I have to get involved?" Each stakeholder has their own valid questions and concerns. Making the case for LibGuides requires considering the needs and interests of the main stakeholder groups: end-users, creators, and supporters. After these are identified, then a tailored response for each group becomes possible. As noted earlier, the process really begins with focusing on the core mission of the library and then defining the benefits of LibGuides for the main users: students.

Students as Stakeholders

What are the advantages of LibGuides for students? Why would they prefer this interface for accessing library information? Student users and advantages for them must be kept in mind when making the case for LibGuides to all stakeholders. This will enhance the prospect of gaining support and buy-in. Here is a sampling of the advantages of LibGuides for students:

- LibGuides provides students, including virtual students, with 24/7 online access to library resources and information.
- LibGuides offers resource customization for students. A student researching anthropology, for example, can easily discover the tools available for research in that discipline via a LibGuide.
- LibGuides includes a printer-friendly option for students who prefer print materials.
- LibGuides offers students one-stop access to research information. Through a LibGuide students can locate resources, learn about library help resources, and find out which librarian to contact for additional information.
- LibGuides incorporates multiple Web 2.0 tools of interest to students: videos, RSS feeds, chat boxes, and so on that can be embedded into LibGuides.

As the core users of LibGuides, understanding the needs of students is vital when making a decision regarding the purchase of LibGuides. Linking LibGuides with student achievement reminds stakeholders that LibGuides are not only about meeting the needs of the library, but ultimately about helping students learn.

Faculty as Stakeholders

Most librarians and library administrators see the advantages of LibGuides for students, but outlining these benefits helps prepare library staff for discussion as they move across campus and present the idea of LibGuides. Students may represent the central user group for LibGuides, but it is also important to get faculty on board with the project. The need to obtain faculty buy-in stems from their connection with the student end users. In addition to librarians, faculty can help spread the word about LibGuides, get students using them as a tool for research, and even use LibGuides themselves. Reaching to the faculty stakeholder group involves the following:

- Informing them about LibGuides and showing the advantages of the system for providing information to students.
- Seeking their support in promoting LibGuides use among students. This might include listing the LibGuide address in the course syllabus and linking to LibGuides from a course management system, such as Blackboard or Moodle.
- Eliciting their ideas for what to include in LibGuides. This can really enhance LibGuide usage, helping the guide to more clearly represent the information resources needed for success in a course, including information directed toward specific assignments.

Students and faculty are the end users of LibGuides. Considering their needs for access to research information is a first step in the process of making a decision to purchase and implement LibGuides.

Librarians as Stakeholders

Is LibGuides the right research guide tool for our library? In addition to considering the benefits to students and uses for faculty, librarians must assess LibGuides from their own perspective as there are several considerations regarding adoption and implementation of this technology. The popularity of LibGuides makes it tempting to consider adoption without much analysis. A library acts prudently however, when it takes the time to carefully review LibGuides and understand the implications of purchasing this software. Some of the considerations are straightforward and simple. Others are more complicated. Initially, a library needs to outline the advantage of LibGuides over other print or digital systems for creating and maintain subject-oriented research guides. What are the selling points of LibGuides for academic librarians?

- LibGuides is easy to use. This represents one of its greatest assets. Librarians without high levels of technical ability can use it. Conversely, librarians with high levels of technical savvy will find ways to enhance their use of LibGuides.
- LibGuides' parent company, Springshare, provides excellent help and documentation on the LibGuides help website (http://help.springshare .com). There are multiple avenues available for obtaining assistance in creating, updating, and maintaining LibGuides. Librarians can receive help by e-mail, through chats, at specific training sessions, and via an online lounge for discussion and interaction among users.
- LibGuides offers multiple avenues for presenting library information. From links to videos to book covers to chat options, the software is designed so that librarians can highlight all elements of a collection.
- LibGuides hosts library guides on its server, not the institution's server. This is a key advantage at many institutions, for it means librarians can update and change LibGuides as frequently as needed without having to maintain their own server or seeking outside assistance.
- LibGuides can be updated, changed, and altered easily. When a change is made on a LibGuide by a librarian, the change shows up immediately in the guide available to users.

As a web-based, library-specific web management platform/content management system, LibGuides shines. This CMS was built to meet the needs of librarians as they seek to make research information easily accessible. This functionality may strengthen librarian support for LibGuides.

Library Administrators as Stakeholders

Librarians often work in tandem with their administrators as they deliberate on the purchase of a software product like LibGuides. For library directors or deans, considering the purchase of a LibGuides subscription involves mulling over various factors and weighing the benefits against the costs. These considerations are essential in that process:

- What is the yearly price for a LibGuides subscription at our institution? What is included in the cost? Are there limits on the number of users? Are there limits on the number of guides a library can create? Are there add-on packages? What yearly price increases can be expected?
- What kinds of training will be needed for librarians? How long will it take for librarians to learn LibGuides and start creating guides?
- Is our library staff open and willing to move from the existing system to a new tool like LibGuides? This is a question that can only be answered by each individual library. However, by understanding the advantages to students and library staff, undertaking the change process becomes more manageable.

As Drucker states, "A decision is a judgment. It is a choice between alternatives" (1967: 143). Library administrators must judge the merits of LibGuides, not just for their own library and staff, but also for the larger institution. Once a library has considered the benefits to students, faculty, and librarians—and believes adoption of LibGuides is the right choice for all involved parties—it is then equipped to engage the other stakeholders around campus and elicit their support for LibGuides. At this point, the decision-making process moves beyond the library.

Information Technology as Stakeholders

Instead of deciding for themselves how to create and manage online research guides, most academic libraries have to consider the interests of other institutional stakeholders, including information technology departments, web designers and, in some cases, public relations officers. The online availability of LibGuides means they reach beyond the library. And stakeholders within the institution connected with web services and outreach will have an interest in the LibGuides decision-making process. Understanding the needs and concerns of each group is a vital part of making the case for LibGuides. LibGuides are structured to make creating a guide straightforward and simple, especially in the early stages. However, any web presence by an academic library needs to fit within the larger institutional web presence. Most libraries seeking to purchase and use LibGuides need, first, to connect with information technology (IT). Considerations for this stakeholder group include:

- What institutional server requirements are needed for LibGuides?
- What web address fits most closely with the institutional domain?
- What expectations does the library have for IT? Are they looking to IT for support in managing and maintaining LibGuides?

The good news in regard to LibGuides and their connection to campus information technology is that the relationship is minimal. One of the great selling points of LibGuides is that it is a self-contained system and is maintained by Springshare. It does not require much, if any, institutional tech support. LibGuides resides on Springshare's web server, not on institutional web space. In fact, LibGuides was created as a tool for libraries that does not require campus information technology involvement. Slaven Zivkovic, the creator of LibGuides, points out, "My goal with Springshare is to create easy-to-use tools for librarians to publish information online, directly, without having to go through intermediary steps of IT" (e-mail interview by Stephanie DeLano Davis, August 22, 2011). As a software tool, LibGuides are uniquely designed to meet the needs of librarians and allow them to create and maintain a web presence of subject research guides without needing to burden campus information technology. Presenting these advantages to information technology units helps enlist their support for the library's decision to purchase LibGuides.

Web Designers as Stakeholders

Web designers' concerns parallel those of information technology personnel, but deal more readily with the question of web design assistance:

- What support will librarians need to get LibGuides up and running on the Web?
- Will web design staff time be needed?
- Will librarians need training on basic web management?
- Will librarians require special assistance in initially designing LibGuides banners and matching LibGuides' style to the institutional CSS (cascading style sheets)

The web skill level of librarians plays a key role in answering these questions. If librarians are not web savvy then it may be necessary for the campus webmaster to take an active role in developing the LibGuides' public appearance and ensuring it conforms to the institutional website. However, if librarians possess knowledge of cascading style sheets, and the like, then successfully branding LibGuides with the campus look and feel is not a significant problem. Coupled with the support available from Springshare, most librarians with basic web skills can create and maintain LibGuides. For the web design and information technology stakeholders, making the case for LibGuides involves convincing them of the ease of LibGuides from the technological perspective, assuring them of the library's commitment to the tool, and acquainting them with the support available through Springshare to help librarians navigate technical and design issues. While assistance and support may be needed from this stakeholder group from time to time, the LibGuides system provides most of the technological support services libraries need—an important selling point for LibGuides.

Institutional Marketing as Stakeholder

Reaching out to another important campus stakeholder, institutional marketing, requires another approach. The concerns of this group are not as technical, but revolve around marketing issues. Branding and institutional consistency are important marketing considerations for higher education, and the presence of LibGuides on the Web makes consulting with this stakeholder group vital. Just as library use of the Web has evolved and strengthened, so has institutional use of the Web. The websites of colleges and universities are vital parts of a broader marketing mix. Marketing professionals need assurance that LibGuides offers the design capacity to help the LibGuide interface connect with the larger institution. When a student clicks on a LibGuide link from the library website and moves away from the institutional website, the process should be seamless. Branding may necessitate the need to make the color scheme and other aspects of LibGuides match with the institutional web presence. Developing a banner to match the college or university website is one way to maintain design consistency. While the campus webmaster may be responsible for helping in this process, institutional marketing must be convinced this is possible. LibGuides is structured to allow for such customization, and making this known to public relations and marketing departments is important for making the case for LibGuides. When discussing the purchase of LibGuides with the marketing or public relations department, considering the following can help make the case for LibGuides:

- Can LibGuides be customized to match the institutional website?
- Will the transition from the institutional library web page to the LibGuide web page appear seamless to the user?
- Can the user return easily from LibGuides to the institutional website?
- Will librarians exercise good judgment and high-quality design standards in the development of LibGuides?

Working with institutional marketing requires commitments from the library staff to maintain the same level of institutional excellence in LibGuides as is applied to the greater institutional website. Building trust helps libraries garner the support of public relations staff as they make the case for the purchase of LibGuides, emphasizing the diverse functionalities of the software and the loyalty of the library to maintaining a web presence designed to mirror what is done institutionally.

■ CASE STUDIES ■

Three Libraries' Adoptions of LibGuides

There are myriad perspectives to consider when making the case for LibGuides, including those of students, faculty, web designers, and marketing staff. Each stakeholder views the tool differently and different factors impact each stakeholder's support for the software. Making the case for LibGuides not only leads to the purchase of the tool, but it also offers academic libraries a chance to promote their relevance to a broader audience—audiences often not familiar with the resources available through the library. Every library's process of making the case for LibGuides will be different, and the issues and concerns vary by institution as well. A look at three different libraries and their process of LibGuides adoption gives insights into the process of making the case for LibGuides.

MICHIGAN STATE UNIVERSITY

A Move from an Existing Web-Based System

For many institutions, the adoption of LibGuides means moving from an existing web-based system for creating research guides. At Michigan State University

(MSU) in East Lansing, Michigan, the decision to switch from LibData, an open source tool for creating research guides, to LibGuides was prompted by LibData's announcement in 2008 that maintenance for the software would no longer be supported. LibData had served as MSU's subject guide software since 2005, but MSU librarians knew they eventually would not be able to adequately maintain their collection of over 1,500 pages on the LibData system by themselves. As MSU began exploring other options, LibGuides rose to the top, discovered by a library staff member at a conference. Several factors led MSU to settle on LibGuides as their replacement, including maintenance and technical support, cost, and the ability to customize the LibGuides interface to match the interface of the MSU website. According to Christine Tobias, reference and technology librarian, and original member of the MSU LibGuides team,

> We knew from the start we could cut costs with LibGuides. The freedom to manipulate the guides was a huge benefit, too. We wanted the guides to have the same look and feel of our website. The ability to customize LibGuides to match the MSU website was an important factor in choosing LibGuides. (e-mail interview by Stephanie DeLano Davis, August 12, 2011)

After LibGuides was purchased by MSU, the process of training librarians and migrating guides began, guided by a three-member LibGuides team, consisting of Tobias, Emily Alford, former reference librarian, and Terrie Wilson, fine arts librarian. During this period, the MSU LibGuides team provided assistance and support to MSU librarians as they moved to LibGuides. As the transition occurred, Jennifer Brandon, reference librarian and web designer, began to notice the advanced functionality of LibGuides with regard to customization. Successfully customizing LibGuides pages does require some advanced skill, so together with Brandon and Kelly Sattler, head of web services, the MSU LibGuides team developed a four-hour workshop to train librarians to use LibGuides and effectively integrate the customization process. The successes of these sessions led the team to offer training at national librarian conferences, including the Library Technology Conference in Minnesota, the 2010 ALA Annual LITA Pre-Conference Workshop, and the 2010 Internet Librarian Conference. A review of the MSU collection of LibGuides shows they have achieved a high level of customization, making the transition from the MSU Library website to LibGuides seamless from a design perspective, as figures 2.1 and 2.2 demonstrate. MSU also selected a LibGuides

FIGURE 2.1
Michigan State University Libraries home page,
www.lib.msu.edu

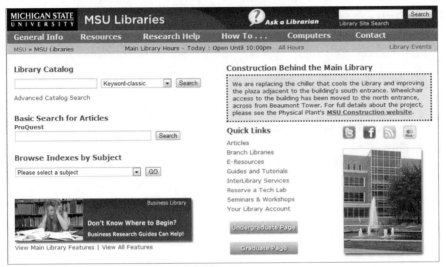

Used by permission of Michigan State University Libraries

FIGURE 2.2
Michigan State University LibGuide, Career Resources,
http://libguides.lib.msu.edu/careers

Used by permission of Michigan State University Libraries

web address, http://libguides.lib.msu.edu, which closely matched their library web address, www.lib.msu.edu, adding to the seamlessness between the two systems.

As their experience shows, selling LibGuides to staff involves not just convincing people the guides are the right choice for their institution, but also includes offering training and support to help librarians find success in using LibGuides. At a university like MSU, classified as a Carnegie Doctoral/Research institution with a fall 2011 full-time equivalent of 43,796, library staff with the skills and abilities to offer technical support exists. For MSU, switching to a new tool for creating and maintaining subject research guides was a necessity. MSU had to make a switch and LibGuides met their needs. Making the case for LibGuides at MSU was primarily an internal library decision, driven by the need for a new online system for creating and maintaining subject research and course guides. The key stakeholders in this situation were librarians and the library administration. Currently, MSU students have access to 675 LibGuides. The MSU LibGuides team now consists of two members, Tobias and Wilson, who provide one-on-one support to librarians new to LibGuides and also help those already familiar with the tool continue to expand their information and offerings.

NORTHWESTERN MICHIGAN COLLEGE

A Move from a Campus-wide CMS

Not all institutions considering LibGuides, however, must make a switch; rather, they find themselves interested in LibGuides for other reasons, as was the case at my institution, Northwestern Michigan College (NMC) in Traverse City, Michigan. In early 2008, NMC purchased a new CMS to create, maintain, and manage the institutional website. For the NMC's Osterlin Library staff this meant moving online pathfinders, and some remaining print pathfinders, to the new CMS along with migrating all the other library information on the library website. The nature of the new CMS changed the design ability of the subject guides as the CMS template governed the spacing and organization of the page. For library staff, making the switch required significant work. When I was hired in early 2010, I immediately saw the potential of LibGuides for NMC and quickly urged the adoption of LibGuides. Library staff at NMC were understandably hesitant about making a switch. "We had just completed a major migration to the new CMS," Mary Beeker, digital resources librarian, notes. "The idea of undertaking a new project was a bit overwhelming" (e-mail interview by Stephanie DeLano Davis, August 13, 2011).

Ann Swaney, government document librarian and archivist, offered additional concerns, "I initially thought LibGuides were just another fad and I did not realize the extent of customization available. I did not want our library page looking like the pages of other libraries using LibGuides" (e-mail interview by Stephanie DeLano Davis, August 20, 2011).

Convincing NMC library staff to adopt LibGuides required some significant persuasion, starting with an initial staff meeting presentation where librarians tabled the idea and asked for more time to consider the tool. The response of my colleagues fits with the common experience of organizational change. Library staff needed time to let go of one system and discover the possibility of a new system (Bridges, 1991). Armed with my past positive experience with LibGuides, yet cognizant of the need of library staff to ponder the switch, I kept the issue on the table and an agreement to obtain a LibGuides demonstration account was reached. The demo account proved to be a key factor in helping librarians see for themselves the advantages of LibGuides. It served as what Bridges (1991, 35) calls the "neutral zone," giving the library staff mental transition time. During the demo period, librarians were especially impressed by the potential of LibGuides for the library information literacy program.

The course-integrated information literacy program at Northwestern Michigan puts librarians into the two core English classes twice a semester. The ability of LibGuides to serve as an extension to instruction acted as a major selling point, as did the ease of uploading changes and updates. LibGuides allowed librarians to make changes themselves, quickly and easily. This strongly influenced the librarians toward adoption. Another factor of concern was cost. "We hesitated to add another expense to our already growing electronic resources budget," notes the director of library services, Tina Ulrich (personal interview by Stephanie DeLano Davis, August 29, 2011). NMC is a Carnegie-classified Associate's Public College, with a full-time equivalent of 3,281, and there was a need to show that the return on investment for LibGuides was worth the cost. After spending a month working with the LibGuides demo, at the next staff meeting, librarians approved the purchase of LibGuides, determining the benefits of LibGuides outweighed the relatively low cost. Even though the workload would be significant, especially considering the recent CMS migration, library staff, recognizing the strength of LibGuides for providing students with important information, undertook the task with excitement.

After internal agreement among library staff was reached, it was necessary to consult with the campus web design staff and the campus public relations director since they governed the campus CMS. Their approval was needed for the library to adopt a product that would move users away from the NMC website. A meeting between librarians and the public relations staff resulted in the required approval to purchase the product and begin the process of moving information from the CMS-based subject guides to LibGuides. Two factors helped convince public relations staff of the viability of LibGuides. First, librarians helped college public relations staff recognize the need of librarians for a tool specific to libraries. As software designed specifically for libraries, LibGuides provides avenues for featuring the myriad of resources available through libraries. Lists of titles from the library catalog, accompanied by pictures, links to subject specific websites, and direct contact information for librarians embedded within the LibGuides were all possible with LibGuides.

The campus CMS system could not match the ease and flexibility of LibGuides for disseminating information about library resources. Second, librarians helped public relations staff see the advantages of LibGuides for public relations staff. No longer would changes to the library subject pages, a frequent occurrence, require review and upload of files by the public relations team. The ability to customize

FIGURE 2.3
Northwestern Michigan College course-specific LibGuide, ENG 111,
http://nmc.libguides.com/ENG111

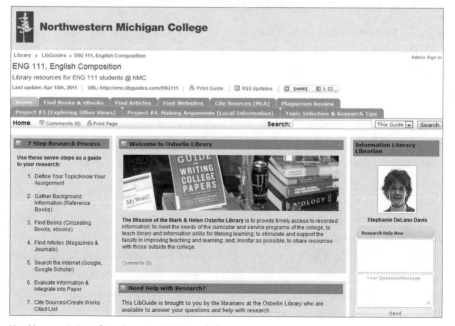

Used by permission of Northwestern Michigan College

LibGuides to match institutional colors and design was also a critical factor in gaining support. With all stakeholders now in agreement with LibGuides, the next step was purchasing and implementing the guides. At NMC, where there is no systems librarian, I briefly trained librarians, but most discovered for themselves how to create pages. This serves as a testament to the usability of LibGuides. They truly do not require advanced web ability. Today LibGuides at NMC are a crucial component in the library's information literacy instruction. Course-specific guides provide students with tailored help for their assignments. Instructors appreciate the LibGuides as they allow for easy customization, "The local resources on LibGuides are especially useful for my students. I require that they have a personal or local connection for all their essays, so these links are a huge help," comments Janet Lively, English instructor and writing codirector at NMC (e-mail interview by Stephanie DeLano Davis, August 29, 2011). (See figure 2.3.)

Transitioning from one system to another, as was the case with both MSU and NMC, includes making the case not only for the LibGuides software, but also for the work required to make the change happen. At both institutions, the process has been a success.

KELLOGG COMMUNITY COLLEGE

Starting with No Subject Guides

When a library has no web subject guides in place, making the case for LibGuides involves a different set of issues. There are academic libraries with no online subject-oriented research guides. Print pathfinders may remain popular, or there may be no library staff member with sufficient time or the web skills needed to design and develop online research guides. This was the situation at Kellogg Community College (KCC) in Battle Creek, Michigan, a Carnegie-classified Associate's Public institution with a fall 2011 full-time equivalent of 3,472. KCC did not have a pathfinder repository, and while the library did have a web presence, its resource guide section consisted of links to general websites, not lists of books, journals, and other resources available in the library customized by subject. With only two professional librarians employed, including myself and the library director, there was really no one available in the library to develop web-based subject guides. Springshare launched LibGuides in 2007 and as references to LibGuides began appearing in the library blogosphere and publications, Marty Stilwell, director of library services at KCC, took note, sharing this information with me and with other library employees.

At the 2008 Library Information Technology Association (LITA) National Forum in Cincinnati, Ohio, the poster presentation, "LibGuides: More Than Just Another Pretty Interface" (Green and Melian, 2008), garnered my attention. The timing was right. KCC was looking for ways to connect more directly with users about library resources and services through a web-based tool. In later discussions, the presenters emphasized LibGuides' ease of use, as well as the great customer service provided by the LibGuides staff at Springshare. Upon returning from LITA, I suggested to Marty we obtain a LibGuides trial. During this initial period we found the LibGuides system met our needs perfectly. It was not long before the library purchased LibGuides and I created the first subject guide, one for Dental Hygiene.

Making a decision to adopt LibGuides was fairly simple for us at KCC. It was relatively inexpensive, and the interface was attractive and user-friendly, meaning librarians could develop and create their own guides without any assistance from the college's information technology department. Furthermore, it meant students would, for the first time, have online access to information about library resources. At KCC the move to LibGuides involved change (adopting a new technology tool), but did not entail transition (moving from one product to another), allowing librarians to focus energies on implementing the LibGuides (Bridges, 1991). The main hurdle was connecting with stakeholders and getting their support, a process that began during the trial phase. We consulted with campus stakeholders, receiving positive feedback and support for the endeavor. In particular, Kassie Dunham, manager of digital resources, and I knew it would need strong backing from the web design team as their skills would be needed to design a customized banner and select the correct colors and fonts so the LibGuide would mirror the campus website. Library staff had an idea and graphic for the banner, but the graphic design skills of a web designer were needed to make the banner a reality. (See figure 2.4).

Collaboration with the webmaster strengthened library ties to the web design team. And along with resulting in an improved visual look for LibGuides, this collaboration helped pave the way for a future redesign of the library website. Today, under the leadership of the user education/experience librarian, Kelly Frost, KCC sports over thirty guides and is moving beyond the traditional static guide, incorporating new content into its guides, including slide shows, video tutorials, and RSS feeds. As KCC discovered, reaching beyond the library helped confirm the library decision to purchase LibGuides and helped enhance the library's connection with other campus departments. Faculty are now very involved as coauthors and are essential in promoting use of the LibGuides with their students (e-mail interview by

39

FIGURE 2.4
Kellogg Community College LibGuides home page,
http://guides.kellogg.edu

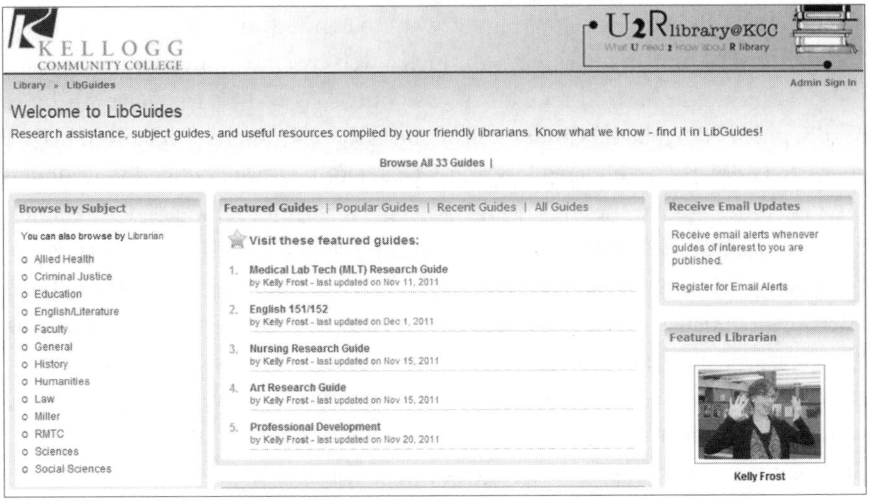

Used by permission of Kellogg Community College

Stephanie DeLano Davis, November 30, 2011). As these considerations point out, using a software tool like LibGuides for creating library research guides involves a level of institutional collaboration. Keeping all parties involved strengthens the library because it models a process of thoughtful deliberation.

■ ■ ■

CONCLUSION

Each institution considering purchasing and implementing LibGuides will encounter different issues and concerns during the decision-making process. Making the case to adopt LibGuides is fairly straightforward when starting from scratch. However, choosing LibGuides involves a different set of considerations when a library already has subject-oriented research guides, as this transition involves managing and changing from one system to another. There are common themes, regardless of whether or not you have an existing system, and by addressing them, libraries will find the process of making the case for LibGuides efficient and manageable. The core mission of academic libraries is to connect users with resources, and this gives libraries needed focus as this is exactly what LibGuides achieve.

Reaching out to all stakeholders, including faculty, information technology staff, web designers, and public relations staff, is critical. Connecting with these groups and addressing their specific concerns related to LibGuides is necessary for successful implementation. Gaining their support allows libraries to show the value of LibGuides to any educational institution's key constituencies—students—and achieve buy-in for the product. By working with these stakeholders beforehand, libraries promote goodwill and demonstrate their willingness to support institutional goals while at the same time meeting the information needs of library users.

REFERENCES

Boddy, David, and Robert Paton. 2004. "Responding to Competing Narratives: Lessons for Project Managers." *International Journal of Project Management* 22: 225–33.

Bridges, William. 1991. *Managing Transitions: Making the Most of Change*. Cambridge, MA: Perseus Books.

Drucker, Peter F. 1967. *The Effective Executive*. New York: Harper & Row.

Green, Dave, and Carlos Melian. 2008. "LibGuides: More Than Just Another Pretty Interface." Paper presented at the Library Information Technology Association (LITA) National Forum, Cincinnati, OH, October 16–19.

Littau, Paul, Nirmala Jyothi Jujagiri, and Gerald Adlbrecht. 2010. "25 Years of Stakeholder Theory in Project Management Literature (1984–2009)." *Project Management Journal* 41, no. 4: 17–29.

Smith, Michael M. 2008. "21st Century Readers' Aids: Past History and Future Directions." *Journal of Web Librarianship* 2, no. 4: 511–23.

Thiry, Michel. 2010. *Project Management*. Burlington, VT: Gower.

Verbit, Daniel, and Vickie L. Kline. 2011. "LibGuides: A CMS for Busy Librarians." *Computers in Libraries* 31, no. 6: 21–25.

Zumalt, Joseph R., and Rebecca A. Smith. 2000. "Internet Reference Services: General Sources and Trends." *Journal of Library Administration* 30, no. 3/4: 335–50.

## Chapter Three

Administering LibGuides
Planning, Implementation, and Beyond

Beth Larkee Kumar and Tabatha Farney

Once your library has decided to purchase LibGuides, there is still a great amount of planning and development to be undertaken before the system is ready for your users. We will guide you through the administrative options Lib-Guides provides and will share advice for planning and implementing the system based on our experience of launching it at the Kraemer Family Library (KFL) at the University of Colorado, Colorado Springs (UCCS). As administrators for our library's LibGuides, we devised the implementation strategy which we recently launched; and we continue to manage the system. This chapter is designed for LibGuides administrators, so if you cannot view the options we describe in this chapter, you may not be set up as an administrator in the system; you should notify your LibGuides' primary contact or any known administrator in the system and have them check your permission settings.

Since LibGuides is a completely hosted service that is ready to use out of the box, administrators do not need to have HTML or web programming expertise to maintain it. However, in our experience it is useful for at least one administrator to have web programming skills, especially if your library decides to customize LibGuides' appearance and functionality. We will focus primarily on the decisions you, as the administrator, need to make in the planning process. So if you are interested in the more technical customizations that require these skills, please refer to later chapters in this book, chapter 4 in particular.

This chapter begins by describing the options for setting up and administering LibGuides for your library. We will share a variety of administrative styles and workflows to assist the implementation process and help you to maintain the system. Next, we will discuss some basic admin settings you should consider during the setup phase and how to decide what content and type of guides your library can create. After the planning phase, we provide suggestions for successfully launching and marketing LibGuides. We also include a checklist of steps/decisions that need to be made through the planning and implementation process. (See table 3.1.) After launching LibGuides, your work as an administrator is truly just getting started, so we conclude this chapter with continuing administrative issues you may face.

DEFINING YOUR ADMINISTRATIVE STYLE

LibGuides offers two roles in the system: librarian and administrator. Springshare defines the librarian role as one who can create and edit guides. In essence, this person is an author as he or she develops the content for the guides. An administrator has full system privileges, such as creating, modifying, and deleting user accounts, customizing system settings, and accessing all other administrative tools. The administrator also can create and edit any guide. Since most LibGuides administrators are librarians, we will refer to the non-administrative role as "author." At your library, the authors may be subject librarians, academic staff, or student assistants.

Administrative Structure

As an administrator, it is up to you to set up the organization of the guides and the roles of the authors. Depending on the size of your staff, your structure may vary from those suggested below; and your administrative style will ultimately depend on your library's culture. Nevertheless, you will need to make decisions about who can do what before any LibGuides are created.

The following are some potential scenarios that may reflect the culture of your library. It is best to think about this before you implement LibGuides, as well as how these workflows will fit in with your existing structure.

> **Single Lead:** Have one LibGuides administrator, and allow all authors to create, edit, and publish guides independently. The workflow would allow for authors to work in their own time frame without having to wait for others to approve new guides. The LibGuides administrator would

TABLE 3.1

A checklist of steps/decisions that need to be made through the planning and implementation process

STEP 1—Management and Organization	
Completion	**Task**
	Select LibGuides administrators and give them access to the system.
	Decide your LibGuides organization style (Single Lead, Task-Specific…).
	Determine your workflow, which may or may not include a review process.
	Design naming conventions for titles, URLs, and subject categories.
	Create best practices documentation (preferably as a LibGuide) and assign an administrator to continue to maintain the information.
	Consider options for LibGuides launch.

STEP 2—Technical Initial Steps	
Completion	**Task**
	Add web analytics tracking code.
	Customize LibGuides appearance.
	Review and modify settings on the System Settings page.

STEP 3—Content Strategy	
Completion	**Task**
	Create author accounts and train staff.
	Work with website manager to identify potential content on library's website.
	Consult with key authors to develop a content development strategy that outlines what type of guides will be prioritized for launch.
	Assign authors to update and migrate content into LibGuides.
	Develop reusable content you want authors to use (grab page).

STEP 4—Preparing for Launch	
Completion	**Task**
	Customize LibGuides home page if using it.
	Determine how to best integrate LibGuides into library's website.
	Work with library website manager to integrate LibGuides into library's website.
	Design and implement a marketing strategy.

STEP 5—Continuing Maintenance	
Completion	**Task**
	Routinely check for broken links using Link Checker.
	Devise a schedule to make backups of the content if you have the Add-on Module.
	Develop a schedule to identify out-of-date guides.

still have overall control of the look and feel of the guides, but limited control over content.

Task-Specific: Divide the technical duties among an administrative team with each person managing a particular aspect, for example "link manager," "analytics manager," or "accounts manager." This system might be best for libraries that have authors with little technical experience, as your administrators could monitor broken links and user accounts. This workflow could allow for the LibGuides to be overseen by technical editors, with the authors concentrating on content. The administrators could work independently with the authors, or disseminate the LibGuides reports at regular intervals.

Large-Team Solution: Have two administrative teams, one for technical and one for content. The technical team would manage links, interface, and analytics while the content team would approve all content for accuracy and consistency before each guide is published. The content team would also work with the authors to ensure the guides are kept up-to-date, while the technical team would focus on functionality. This workflow could begin with an approved template from the content team for new guides, or post-creation, prepublication approval. Alternately, the content team could periodically review older guides to either update content or change the guides to "unpublished" as individual authors revise inaccurate guides.

Divided Leadership: Create administrative teams for the natural divisions of your content creators' subjects. For example, you could have administrators for the social sciences librarians, humanities librarians, science librarians, or one at each branch library. This workflow would allow authors and administrators to work closely within each area. Functionally, this setup could allow large libraries to segment the guides, almost as if they have separate installations. Each team could choose a similar layout; for example, the science librarians might choose to use a two-column layout, with similarly named tabs. Or a branch library could use a standardized box on the home tab of each guide listing their location, hours, and unique collections. Ultimately, there will still need to be a lead administrator who serves as the contact for Springshare, but the day-to-day management would be distributed.

Buddy System: Pair authors with administrators to provide individual technical help, rather than having a single administrator help each content creator. However, you would maintain a lead administrator for system-wide changes. This workflow allows for flexibility in a small library, as there are not approval processes in place before guide publication but rather hands-on involvement in the creation process between each administrator and each author.

Remember, these restrictions are put in place by you, the administrator, not the LibGuides software. The number of individuals you will have working on your LibGuides may help to determine your structure. At KFL, we have a small staff consisting of eight librarians using LibGuides; four are administrators and four are authors. We use the buddy system structure, which works for our library. Larger libraries may find this structure impractical. You may want to blend several styles to come up with an organizational style that will work for you.

Regardless of workflow and administrative structure, you may need to incorporate individuals other than your librarians into your process. As an administrator you only have the option to create librarian (author) accounts and administrator accounts. However, your authors may want to allow student assistants or teaching faculty to contribute to a guide. Authors can add external people to their individual guides, without giving them access to the full LibGuides system by using a collaborator account (http://help.springshare.com/introlg).

Review Process

The LibGuides system is designed so that administrators provide the technical administration while authors create and publish the guides. This is the default LibGuides workflow, but libraries can implement their own workflow if they develop a structure to review content before it is published. If you choose, you can set up a review process for guides, no matter which organizational structure you implement. There are four options for review: prepublication review, a self-check against a list, using a template, or not using a review process before publication. The first option is to set up a committee or have another librarian review each guide, formally, before the author publishes and advertises the guide. Option two is to create a checklist of best practices that authors are asked to check before they publish their guides. If you are interested in developing a best practices checklist, we recommend using basic styling advice such as standardizing the

47

title and "Friendly URL." (LibGuides allows the author to create a "Friendly URL" for a guide that can easily be remembered.) For example, the authors could verify that particular information is included, or that column size and colors are consistent. Your checklist may require content such as: Ask a Librarian chat widget, liaison contact information, library account log-in, in addition to subject-specific boxes. The third option is to have the administrator or administration team create templates, allowing the authors to create the content without having to decide the layout of the guide. For examples of documentation, the Springshare "LibGuides Best Of" has a section on "getting started" guides (http://bestof.libguides.com/bestpractices). And some of these have a workflow requiring that each guide be reviewed before publication. Finally, you could empower your authors to check their own guides and publish independently.

Since we are using the buddy system and our administrators are working closely with our authors during the creation of their LibGuides, we do not check each guide before publication, nor do we use a template. As many of our recent guides are copies of older guides, the result is a consistent look and feel. This works for us because we are small, and we can easily keep track of the guides we have without having an official review process or checklist. A decision to set up a prepublication workflow could have a large effect on time, should you decide to review every guide before it is published. If a review process is right for your library, set it up early, have clearly defined roles regarding who will act as reviewers, and document the steps to publication for authors.

INITIAL SETUP PHASE

As mentioned earlier, the technical setup for LibGuides is minimal because LibGuides is a completely hosted service; there is no option to install the system on a local server. This is a great boon for libraries that do not have the web server space or technical support to install and maintain the software. Administrators do not need to be concerned about upgrading the system since automatic updates are part of the LibGuides package. The downside is that the content you create will not be accessible should you cancel your LibGuides subscription. Additionally, this also means your role as an administrator is limited to whatever functionality Springshare provides, and if the LibGuides website crashes, you would need to contact Springshare technical support.

After purchasing LibGuides, your system is turned on and functional. Before training your authors, there are preliminary decisions and settings that you will need to implement. LibGuides provides many options, some that you as administrator have full control over, such as the main subject categories, while other options, such as column width, can be changed by the authors. We recommend creating a "private" LibGuide for your authors and including your preferences, setup instructions, and your checklist for publication—should you decide to use one. (A "private" guide cannot be viewed by the general public.) However, you do not need to create one from scratch; many "Getting Started" guides can be found on both the LibGuides Community (http://libguides.com/community.php) and LibGuides Best Of (http://bestof.libguides.com). We used one of these as our template, and then modified it to fit our needs and our workflow. Moreover, a Getting Started guide serves as an excellent place to document decisions and best practices for your staff. Consistency and documentation from the start allow your authors to work independently, but more important, requires less maintenance for you over the life of the system.

Developing your LibGuide Brand

Administrators should agree upon naming consistency that will be included in the content creator's training; this should include the Friendly URL and the title of the guide. A Friendly URL is shorter and easier to remember. For example, authors can rename the URL to http://libguides.uccs.edu/CURR5090 rather than use the default URL generated by LibGuides which was, in this case, http://libguides.uccs .edu/content.php?pid=177918&sid=1497161. While both addresses go to the same place, the Friendly URL is far easier for your users to remember.

Creating a standard naming convention for your library's LibGuides titles and URLs is recommended at the initial setup stage. At KFL we decided to use the four-character department code followed by the course number for both URL and title for all class guides. In courses where there are multiple sections taught by multiple instructors, such as our English Writing classes, we followed the course number by an underscore and the name of the instructor (ENGL1410_Smith). These conventions make it easy for the students and faculty to find and remember the guides, and also make it easy for authors to reuse the course content over multiple semesters, without re-creating an entirely new guide. For example, at UCCS, the Master's Project course for Curriculum and Instruction is taught every semester, and we do not need to update the LibGuide very much, other than adding new resources or changing links. The basic resources remain the same.

Subject categories are another way to increase consistency in your brand. These categories are displayed on the main page of your LibGuides website. Administrators can create these using the admin options and authors can tag each guide with a subject association. This allows library users to view all guides on that subject. By using subject categories, anyone accessing your institution's LibGuides can browse the guides by subject or contact the department liaison. By using subject categories, you are creating your library's controlled vocabulary for affiliating the guides with a specific subject area. Since we are creating primarily class guides, we created subject categories based on campus departments (Sociology, Political Science, etc.). We could have used the name of majors offered at our university, which are similar to the department names, but some departments offer several degree programs and so it was not a feasible option. Our method of naming matches how each course is listed in the course catalog.

We have a few guides that are listed by topic, rather than by department, but these guides are intended to be interdisciplinary, covering library basics, such as the difference between a scholarly journal and a popular magazine. In addition to subject categories, administrators and authors can assign custom tags to individual guides, once the guide is published. Tags could help unify a topic across the disciplines or connect a workshop series. While this worked for our library, it is up to your library to decide how to standardize the subject categories and the tags in order to assist your users in browsing your guides.

LibGuides offers many options to customize the system's appearance, making it possible to brand LibGuides to match your institution's colors, logos, or theme. Administrators have the option to change styling choices, such as uploading a new banner image, or implementing advanced style customizations using HTML and CSS. Chapter 4 will discuss best practices in modifying the LibGuides interface; however, administrators need to decide if all guides will have a consistent style or if authors will be allowed to implement their own. While much of the style is locked down, there is an option to allow or block authors' ability to modify guide characteristics. This decision will determine if authors have permission to add JavaScript and CSS, or modify the colors used for boxes and tabs in their guides. We elected to block the ability to customize the style of the guides because most of KFL's authors are uncomfortable with web programming. To determine if authors need this functionality, administrators need to ask:

- Do authors have the technical knowledge (JavaScript, CSS, etc.) to use the advanced styling options?
- Does the library want a consistent brand that includes the same colors and design on each of the guides?
- Does the parent institution require all departments to have a consistent brand?
- Do administrators want to be responsible for the long-term maintenance of highly individualized guides that can require additional time for upkeep?

As an administrator, it is important to understand which features can be controlled and which functions the author can modify. Administrators control LibGuides' appearance, functions of tabs, and box colors. LibGuides allows administrators to add custom HTML code to stylize the system's interface. They also can modify the institution's name, system name, and proxy settings as well as additional settings that will impact every guide, such as the ability to enable or disable user comments or instantly produce RSS feeds. The administrator can control the default label of the first tab in every guide and the default column width for each page in a guide. If having a consistent layout is important to you, make sure you communicate this information to your authors, because there are not system-wide settings to prevent authors from making changes in the column width.

LibGuides has the ability to detect mobile devices accessing the site and automatically directs those users to the mobile version of your LibGuides, but this feature can be turned off. Administrators can improve mobile users' experience with LibGuides by customizing the mobile settings for the site on the Mobile Settings page. You can modify the header and background colors if your library wants to differentiate the mobile version from the web version, and create customized text to welcome users to the mobile version's home page. Additionally, you may add custom HTML or scripts designed for the mobile version, as well as hiding or displaying a search option to mobile users. Chapter 13 will discuss this in greater detail.

Adding a Web Analytics Tool

LibGuides includes a statistics report that shows basic usage data for individual guides in addition to system-level reports. (See figure 3.1.) As a LibGuides administrator you have the privilege to access the statistics reports for all guides in the system whether they are public, private, or unpublished. The individual guide statistics report provides the total number of visits to a page within a guide

FIGURE 3.1
LibGuides' guide-level statistics report, University of Colorado at Colorado Springs

DASHBOARD	GUIDES▾	STATISTICS	TOOLS▾	MODULES▾	ADMIN STUFF▾	JUMP TO▾	HELP	tfarney@u... Edit My Account	S

"ENGL 1410 News Media" Page Hits 2011 *(generated 2011-11-30)*

Page	Jan	Feb	Mar	Apr	May	Jun	Jul	Aug	Sep	Oct	Nov	Dec	Total
Boolean Operators	-	29	5	-	-	-	-	-	1	22	1	-	58
Finding articles	-	32	132	16	1	-	-	-	-	144	68	-	393
Finding Books	-	47	3	-	-	-	-	-	-	25	-	-	75
Home	-	144	250	17	1	2	-	-	7	242	74	-	737
Ideas from other students	-	7	5	-	-	-	-	-	-	11	1	-	24
Reference sources	-	71	31	1	-	-	-	-	5	104	11	-	223
Scholarly Journals vs. Popular Magazines	-	4	29	-	1	2	2	-	1	43	3	-	85
Useful web sites	-	14	27	1	-	-	-	1	-	37	8	-	88
What a Book Looks Like in the Catalog	-	13	-	-	-	-	-	-	-	8	-	-	21
Totals	-	361	482	35	3	4	2	1	14	636	166	-	1704

Widget & API Hits 2011

No results were found

Link Hits 2011

Link	Jan	Feb	Mar	Apr	May	Jun	Jul	Aug	Sep	Oct	Nov	Dec	Total
Academic Search Premier	-	4	74	10	2	-	-	-	-	61	37	-	188
CQ Researcher	-	25	8	-	-	-	-	-	2	57	5	-	97
Gale Virtual Reference Library	-	26	9	-	-	-	-	-	-	37	-	-	72
Academic OneFile	-	-	89	6	-	-	-	-	-	84	51	-	230

Used by permission of UCCS Kraemer Library

and usage statistics for certain content box types, such as the Links & Lists content box that reports the total number of times a user clicked on a link within that box. The system-level reports include a summary of total guides and content box types in use within the system, a summary of usage statistics for the system's home page, and a report that compares all the guides' total page hits per month.

While this information is useful, it is highly recommended that LibGuides administrators add some type of web analytics tool, such as Google Analytics, because it will provide more comprehensive data about your LibGuides' users and how they are accessing the guides. For example, a Google Analytics report can reveal how long users are spending on a web page, if users are interacting with that web page by clicking on any of the links, and much more. These data can be used to improve the layout or content of a guide or for the entire LibGuides system because they can give you a more precise picture of your users and how they are utilizing your guides. Chapter 11 will go into assessment tools in more detail.

Many libraries are already using some type of web analytics tool to track usage on the library's main website. If you are unfamiliar with web analytics or the tool in use at your library, contact your library's web manager to learn more about the options available. After a web analytics tool is identified, LibGuides administrators can add the tracking code to the Custom Analytics Code box on the System Settings page.

DEVELOPING A CONTENT STRATEGY

LibGuides makes it possible to create all types of guides. The most common guides are class guides that are designed for a specific course and subject guides that provide resources in a discipline. There are guides that complement library workshops or events and help guides that explain how to use specific library resources. Before inviting your authors into LibGuides, we recommend designing a content strategy that outlines which types of guides will receive priority and clearly defines what type of content belongs in LibGuides. Administrators should consult the library's website managers and key authors to devise a LibGuides content strategy.

53

If you are not the manager of your library's website, you should meet with that person early in the planning phase in order to identify the content, such as online class guides or subject guides, already available on the library's website that could be migrated into LibGuides. The website manager will be able to report when those guides were last updated. This helps identify the guides that need to be updated before being added to LibGuides. Another benefit to meeting with the website manager is that you can avoid repetition of website content on LibGuides; you and your website manager should differentiate the content that belongs in LibGuides versus the library's website. Copying entire web pages or sections of content from a library's website directly into LibGuides is not a good plan because it requires additional effort to keep the content updated in both areas. (In some situations, however, it is possible to replace the entire library website with LibGuides.) Important questions to ask your library's website manager include:

Is there a list of all the course-related web pages? Is there a list of all subject guides found on the library's website? If so, it will be easy to identify the content that should be moved from the website and converted into a LibGuide.

When was the last date the course- or subject-related web pages were updated? Who created or maintains these web pages? This information will identify old web pages that may need considerable updating before they are useful enough to migrate. Additionally, you may be able to pinpoint who created or maintains the content, and they could be excellent candidates to become authors in LibGuides. This could entice them to update the old content as part of learning the LibGuides system.

What content is appropriate to include in LibGuides? LibGuides administrators can create a content development strategy (think collection development policy) that outlines the type of content to be developed as guides in LibGuides so authors clearly understand what type of guides to create and so the guides do no compete with the library's main website for content and purpose. Even as your LibGuides grow, administrators will always have a content development strategy to guide and manage that growth.

Key authors are individuals who express strong interest in being involved with LibGuides development or have instructional web design experience, such as developing online library-related tutorials. Key authors will have essential knowledge of what content is needed or desired by your library users. The number of authors you wish to involve will vary depending on your library, but you should keep the team manageable. This team's tasks can include recommending the primary content to prioritize in LibGuides for its launch and suggesting new content to develop for inclusion into LibGuides in the future. Depending on the level of commitment of this team, they may also be instrumental in reviewing available content for currency and usefulness to be included at the launch of the system. This team may also create or motivate other authors to create new guides as needed. In our library, our key authors suggested a schedule that prioritized the launch of class guides and a selection of the general help guides already available on the library's website. Several individuals stepped up to help migrate the web pages into guides during our LibGuides implementation. After launch, the same team helped motivate other authors to create guides to accompany library instruction sessions. The next phase is to have this group identify potential areas to expand LibGuides to include other guide types such as subject guides and additional help guides.

Designing Reusable Content

It is good practice to develop reusable content that can be used by your authors. The LibGuides system allows authors to copy or link to boxes of content, which saves time for the authors and provides administrators a method for more easily maintaining and updating the massive amount of content in the guides. Administrators should take the time to create a "grab" guide that contains useful widgets, which we broadly define as reusable applications or text that could be embedded into many different guides. These widgets should not be confused with LibGuides' widget tool which is designed to create widgets, such as a listing of an author's guides, to be embedded into web pages outside of LibGuides in order to increase the visibility of the guides (http://help.springshare.com/guidewidgets). The KFI's grab guide consists of applications such as chat widget, catalog search widget, journal search widget, in addition to text-based widgets like the instructions for remote access or reference desk hours; all are designed to be integrated into any guide in the LibGuides system. This guide is private, so only our authors may access it. We recommend our authors to link to these widgets rather than create their own. It saves them time, but it also allows us to maintain just the widget on the grab guide. Any modifications to a grab guide widget automatically update any guides that link to it so we do not have to visit each guide to fix an issue.

55

Administrators should also consider creating a master guide of the library's database holdings within LibGuides because it saves authors' time in creating the content while administrators can easily maintain all the database links in the system from one guide. This master database guide should include database links and descriptions for your authors to link to in their guides. This can be done manually by either creating a separate guide dedicated to the database holdings or the process can be automated using LibGuides' A-Z Subscription Database List Management tool. This tool imports a library's database holdings if they are a Serials Solutions 360 or Summon subscriber. An administrator initiates the process by entering their Serials Solutions client identifier. The complete list of databases found in the library's Serials Solutions profile will display and the administrator can delete any of the databases so they would not be included in the import. Once that is complete, the tool will generate a guide titled A-Z Resource List and create a tab for each letter of the alphabet as needed. Each tab will automatically be populated with the database links, and these links can be modified individually to include more information about the databases.

IMPLEMENTING YOUR LIBGUIDES

By the time LibGuides is ready to implement, your authors should already have LibGuides accounts, have gone through training on how to use the system, and be busy creating and publishing guides of their own. The next step is to make your LibGuides available to your library users, and we recommend deciding how users will access your LibGuides before you launch. Devising an implementation plan will vary by library, but there are common decisions administrators must consider as part of this process.

Integrating LibGuides into the Library's Website

Your library will invest a lot of time in LibGuides. To ensure its continued success, the contents of your LibGuides need to be promoted properly on the library's website or main online presence. One study found "in order for online help to be effective, it must be fully integrated into the functioning of a library's website and available at the user's point of need" (Arnold, Csir, Sias, and Zhang, 2005: 132). If you are not the library's website manager, you may have little control over how LibGuides are displayed on your library's website. Thus, it is essential for you to work with your website manager during the planning phase. Together you and the website manager should decide if the library's website will link directly to the LibGuides' home page, if each guide will have its own link, or if you will implement a combination of the two.

If you decide to use the LibGuides' home page as a gateway from your library's website, the Customize Homepage option controls the content for that page. Administrators can create custom content boxes and text, include a welcome message, set preferences for displaying a featured author profile, and decide the placement of the content boxes on the home page. LibGuides includes some basic content boxes for the home page such as the Guides Box that displays the top ten most used or recently published guides. These boxes may be disabled if administrators do not want them displayed. Additionally, libraries can opt out of using the LibGuides home page and instead set up a redirect to a preferred web page on the library's site or any other web location desired. Some libraries have also used this main LibGuides page to replace their main web page.

Our library chose to list all the guides on the library's tutorials and guides web page (see figure 3.2), which is prominently linked on the library's home page, because we wanted to only list the class guides for the current semester, while

FIGURE 3.2

Guides & Tutorials web page, University of Colorado at Colorado Springs

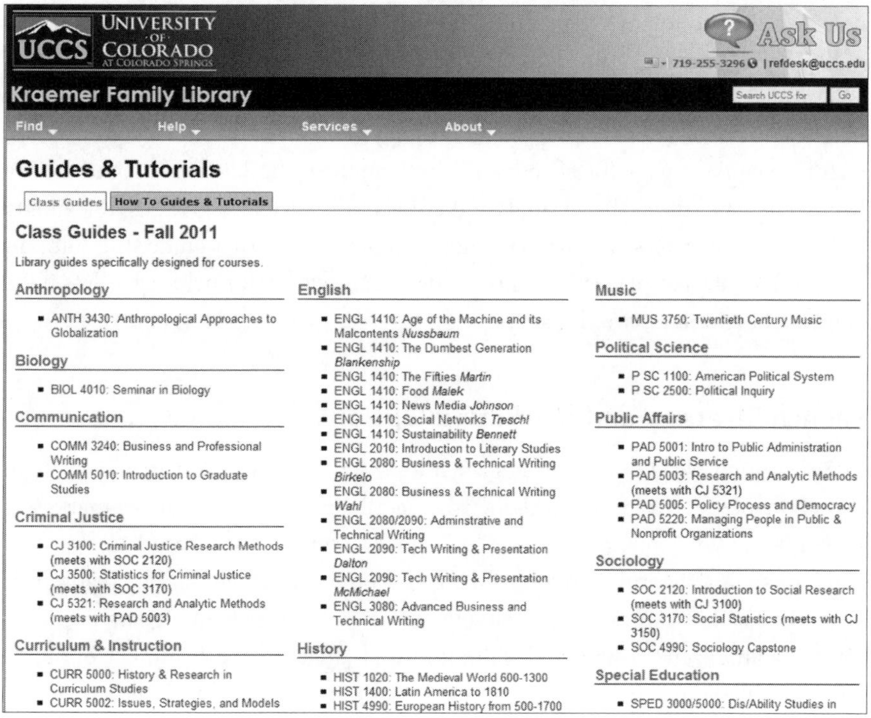

Used by permission of UCCS Kraemer Library

keeping all other guides published. This reduces the amount of guides our students need to scroll through to find their class. Additionally, when a class is taught again, it is simple for us to re-add the link to that guide. The tutorials and guides web page displays the current class guides with a link to all past guides. Additional how-to guides are accessible on another tab on this page, but not all of these have been moved into LibGuides yet. The web services librarian maintains the tutorials and guides page and authors must contact her when they have a link for a new guide to add to the page. Since the web services librarian is one of the LibGuides administrators, this model works well for KFL, as she ensures that all published guides use the naming conventions we suggest for the guide's title and URL as well as apply the appropriate subject categories if the author forgot them.

For libraries that do not want to manually create a list of guides, LibGuides also has a helpful API utility that can automatically generate a list of all published guides and their links. This list can be embedded into the library's website via a link or JavaScript. The list will automatically update every six hours to include new guides or to remove the guides marked as private or unpublished. Examples of this may be viewed at http://help.springshare.com/subjectmenu.

However you decide to integrate LibGuides into your library's website, your links to LibGuides must be prominently displayed either on the library's home page or top secondary page for effective dissemination of the LibGuide contents. We have found that using the tutorials and guides web page also gives us a flexibility to link to other pages that we have not yet converted into a guide; the tutorials and guides page is a place where library users can refer to for help regardless if the help is a LibGuide or a web page.

Launch Strategy and Marketing Options

There are two basic release strategies: a hard launch and a soft launch. A hard launch involves creating a comprehensive set of guides and intensively marketing LibGuides to your intended users. The major advantage of the hard launch is that you can set a date and start publicizing LibGuides as a new service before it is released. The hard work is up-front, creating many guides before going live. This might be an excellent strategy for libraries that already have a number of online guides available on their website that can be easily migrated into the LibGuides system. This method allows administrators to focus more on an effective marketing campaign.

A soft launch option uses limited marketing to targeted audiences and allows authors to build new guides after the system is open to the users. This is a good option for administrators to first learn how certain users interact with the guides and then fix any potential flaws. Our library decided to use the soft launch option. With our small staff, we felt it would not be feasible to create comprehensive guides for all classes by our LibGuides launch day. Since all of our authors also provide library instruction to their assigned liaison departments, each of the authors contacted their faculty and informed them about LibGuides. A guide was created for each class requesting library instruction. The links to the class-specific guides can also be placed in the course content management site, in our case, Blackboard. While we started with a soft launch, we plan to expand our LibGuides marketing to include the entire campus as we develop subject guides and other guide types in the future.

As with any web-related project, marketing is an important aspect because it informs your community of the new service. Your library should not have just one marketing strategy, but should instead develop a marketing plan that incorporates a variety of modes to reach your target audience. One strategy is to inform faculty about requesting a guide for their class. This process could be as informal as an e-mail or word of mouth or as structured as a presentation at a planned meeting. KFL targeted our English Writing Program because it requires a library instruction component. We decided to present LibGuides to the instructors to demonstrate how it could be implemented in their classes. Prior to our presentation there were only a handful of online guides for the English Writing Program. After implementing LibGuides it is now the norm to have a customized guide for each of the classes because the instructors saw the usefulness of LibGuides. Using LibGuides in instruction sessions introduces students and faculty to the service and encourages them to use LibGuides for their research classes. If students and faculty have a positive experience with the guide, they are more likely to ask for another class guide for future classes.

Beyond classroom instruction, using LibGuides in workshops, presentations, and for campus events will increase the visibility of your resources. For example, we created an exhibit and a LibGuide for our All-Campus Read Program and we used Quick Response (QR) codes on the display case to link to the guide. A QR code is a special bar code that can be read by the camera of a smartphone using a free app. The QR software would redirect the user to the mobile version of the LibGuide. An additional approach to advertise your guides is to train your reference desk staff, who may not be your authors, about LibGuides so when they receive course-related reference questions, they can refer to the guides for assistance. Another marketing strategy is to promote LibGuides in a library blog, newsletter, news feed, or social media website.

CONTINUING ADMINISTRATIVE ISSUES

Even after LibGuides is launched, your role as an administrator is ongoing. Depending on your chosen administrative style, you may have certain responsibilities to perform that this chapter does not specifically cover. This section contains general administrative issues that you will experience when managing the LibGuides system.

Guide Maintenance

As a LibGuides administrator you have the ability to edit any guide in the system, but it is not always possible to ensure all guides are current and contain correct data. At KFL we perceive that the role of administrators is to manage the system and the role of authors is to maintain and update the guides they publish. However, there are some system admin features that allow administrators to assist authors in keeping their content current. One tool available to both administrators and authors is the Link Checker which is available under the Tools option. (See figure 3.3.) Link Checker runs a report of broken links on either an individual's guides or on all guides in the system. This makes it easy to see what links need to be updated on what guide. Link Checker reports broken links, or links that display a 404 error status (page not found); it does not include links that take users to an incorrect or a redirect web page. This tool can only search with selected content box types, so any links included in a rich text box cannot be checked with this option. It also cannot check broken links behind a proxy, making it necessary for authors to verify their links regularly.

FIGURE 3.3

LibGuides' Link Checker report, University of Colorado at Colorado Springs

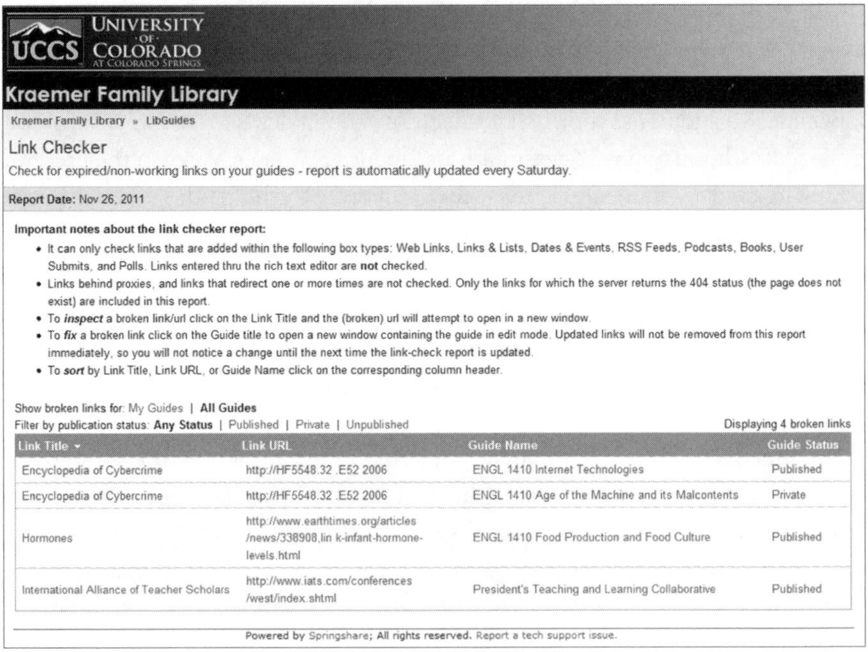

UCCS University of Colorado at Colorado Springs

Kraemer Family Library

Kraemer Family Library » LibGuides

Link Checker

Check for expired/non-working links on your guides - report is automatically updated every Saturday.

Report Date: Nov 26, 2011

Important notes about the link checker report:

- It can only check links that are added within the following box types: Web Links, Links & Lists, Dates & Events, RSS Feeds, Podcasts, Books, User Submits, and Polls. Links entered thru the rich text editor are **not** checked.
- Links behind proxies, and links that redirect one or more times are not checked. Only the links for which the server returns the 404 status (the page does not exist) are included in this report.
- To ***inspect*** a broken link/url click on the Link Title and the (broken) url will attempt to open in a new window.
- To ***fix*** a broken link click on the Guide title to open a new window containing the guide in edit mode. Updated links will not be removed from this report immediately, so you will not notice a change until the next time the link-check report is updated.
- To ***sort*** by Link Title, Link URL, or Guide Name click on the corresponding column header.

Show broken links for: My Guides | **All Guides**

Filter by publication status: **Any Status** | Published | Private | Unpublished

Displaying 4 broken links

Link Title	Link URL	Guide Name	Guide Status
Encyclopedia of Cybercrime	http://HF5548.32 .E52 2006	ENGL 1410 Internet Technologies	Published
Encyclopedia of Cybercrime	http://HF5548.32 .E52 2006	ENGL 1410 Age of the Machine and its Malcontents	Private
Hormones	http://www.earthtimes.org/articles /news/338908,lin k-infant-hormone-levels.html	ENGL 1410 Food Production and Food Culture	Published
International Alliance of Teacher Scholars	http://www.iats.com/conferences /west/index.shtml	President's Teaching and Learning Collaborative	Published

Powered by Springshare; All rights reserved. Report a tech support issue.

Used by permission of UCCS Kraemer Library

Another solution is checking to see when guides were last updated by going to the Guide Index and sorting all guides by the update category. (See figure 3.4.) Again, both administrators and authors have the ability to do this, but it is particularly important for administrators to review this information on a regular schedule to identify guides that could potentially be out-of-date. Once identified, administrators can contact the authors of those guides and suggest they may want to review their content and links for currency.

Administrators also have access to the Manage Assets feature that lists all objects such as links used in the Simple Web Links or Links & Lists content boxes or embedded videos in the Streaming Video/Audio content box found in your institution's LibGuides. Note that the rich text content box cannot track assets, so any images, links, or other objects included in the rich text content box will not appear here. Most other content box types do track assets, and administrators can use the Manage Assets feature to see what assets are used and on which guides they are found. This tool is particularly useful for finding old links or content that should be removed. For example, we recently cancelled a subscription to a

FIGURE 3.4

LibGuides' Guide Index, University of Colorado at Colorado Springs

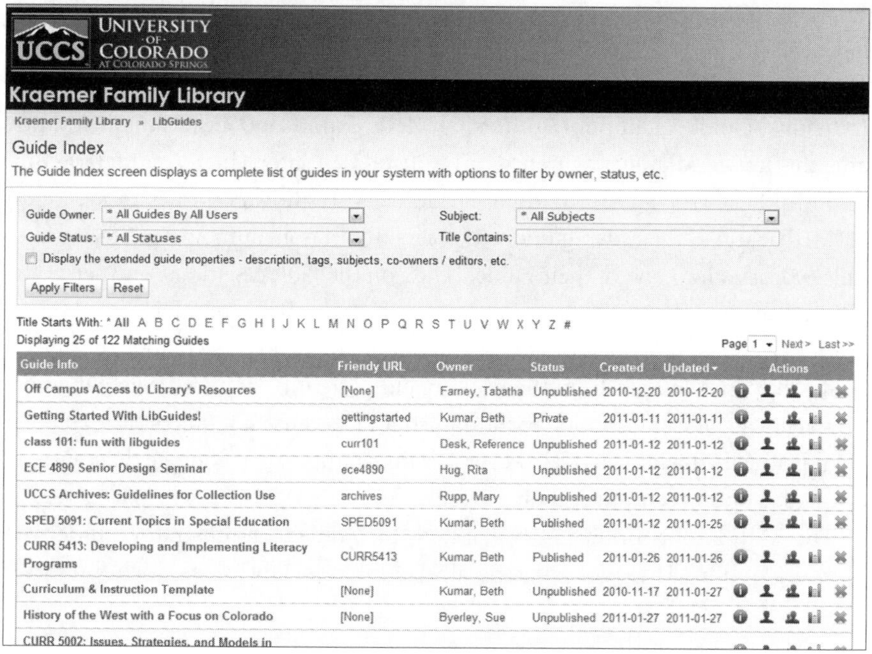

Used by permission of UCCS Kraemer Library

database. Instead of searching all of LibGuides for those links, we were able to see which guides listed that database from the Manage Assets tool. The tool is designed to help administrators find assets; if any editing is required, admins will need to go directly to the individual guide to do so. For example, if our authors used a link from the A-Z Database list as we recommend, we can easily delete that link if needed by deleting it once in the A-Z Database guide, which automatically deletes it from all guides. However, if an author created their own link and did not copy it from the A-Z Database guide, then we use this tool to see where that link is and directly access the guide to manually remove the obsolete database link.

While administrators have several tools to help them manage the currency of the guides, we find it is more practical to stress during training that guides are a work in progress and each semester, authors should revisit and test their guides' content and links. As an administrator you may want to develop guidelines or policies for handling old guides or nonresponsive authors. Creating a culture of continuing maintenance of content will help administrators focus on other aspects of managing the system and provide a better user experience for the intended audiences.

Creating Backups

There are two possible ways to create backups using the LibGuides system; however, neither option offers a simple way of restoring lost data. Both methods require libraries to purchase LibGuides' Add-On Module, which offers access to an Individual Guide Backup for authors, an XML Export option for administrators, and the Image Manager which will be discussed later (http://guidefaq.com/a.php?qid=1927). The Individual Guide Backup allows authors to create an HTML backup of their own guides. To access this option, authors need to log in to LibGuides, go into one of their guides, click on the Guide Settings, and select the Create Backup option. This feature downloads the content to a local hard drive, but it does not save the tab or column layout. If any content were lost, the author could copy that content from the backup and paste it back into the actual guide. This is not an efficient solution for administrators because it requires each guide to be individually downloaded. However, administrators can encourage their authors to use this option to protect their content.

The XML Export option is available to LibGuides administrators under the Modules option. This tool converts all data held in LibGuides, including user information and guide content, into an XML format which can be exported to a local hard drive. Again this is not a true backup whereby you can easily upload the data back into the system if needed, but administrators can use the data for archival purposes. Although there is no "restore" functionality, regularly exporting your content to a local server is a good backup strategy. If something disastrous ever happened to your LibGuides, for example, one of your authors accidently deleted several important guides and did not create any type of backup, your best solution is to contact LibGuides' technical support for help. LibGuides does make daily backups of content, but that does not guarantee they will be able to recover all lost content (http://guidefaq.com/a.php?qid=4485).

Archiving Users

For various reasons, authors will leave your institution from time to time. When that happens, your natural inclination may be to delete their accounts, but this is not so simple. Any guide that an author developed is associated with that creator. LibGuides does not allow you to delete any creators that have guides associated with them until you reassign their guides to another creator. Rather than letting those guides go unmaintained, administrators can assign them to a different author. Another solution is to create a generic LibGuides author account that can store and manage the guides until a new author can be assigned. Depending upon the usage of the guides, administrators may want to mark the guides private or unpublished. This process will help administrators identify guides that need owners and to keep them updated if necessary.

Another caution: if your library has access to LibGuides' Image Library (part of the Add-on Module), your authors can upload and store images directly in LibGuides for use in their guides. This is not a shared Image Library. Instead each LibGuides author has an Image Library that is accessible only to that individual. When an author is deleted, their associated Image Library is no longer accessible even to the LibGuides administrator. If pictures are deleted along with the user's account, that could impact the content of the guides that person created in addition to other guides that copied content from those guides. In this instance, administrators should contact Springshare to have them move the image libraries to alternative authors' accounts to avoid the issue of accidentally deleting important images.

CONCLUSION

LibGuides contains tremendous functionality right out of the box. Although this chapter mainly discussed planning and launching your LibGuides, your role as an administrator is just beginning. By taking the time to plan and implement the system, administrators will smooth the launch process for their authors and themselves. You will continue to maintain your library's LibGuides by monitoring broken links or identifying old content. Although LibGuides has defined roles, libraries can create an internal administrative style and workflow process to fit their needs and the culture of the institution. Our final suggestion to new LibGuides administrators is to be flexible as the system will change. Springshare may add new features that affect the administrative features. Your LibGuides' intended purpose may evolve as you maintain the collection of guides. We consider our LibGuides to be in perpetual beta, as it grows and adapts to fit our users' expectations. As a LibGuides administrator, prepare to develop with your system and change your administrative style and duties based on your library's need.

REFERENCE

Arnold, Judith M., Floyd Csir, Jennifer Sias, and Jingping Zhang. 2005. "Does Anyone Need Help Out There? Lessons from Designing Online Help." *Internet Reference Services Quarterly* 9, no. 3/4: 115–34.

## Chapter Four

Strategies and Techniques for Administrators

Aaron W. Dobbs and Rich Gause

Because LibGuides is almost infinitely customizable, it is quite possible for you, as a site administrator, to completely individualize the formatting displayed in your installation. Chapter 3 dealt with the overall planning and decisions that need to occur before LibGuides is launched at an institution. However, after initial decisions are made either to match your institution's web or to create a completely individualized look and feel, it is the job of whomever has been given administrator rights at your institution to access the LibGuides Admin Stuff menu to make these changes.

Once the initial implementation of your institution's LibGuides site is completed, local administration of the site should not require much day-to-day attention. Since LibGuides is hosted on Springshare's servers, the local administrator does not have to install updates or otherwise maintain the general functionality of the site. Nevertheless, there are maintenance tasks which ought to occur regularly in order to keep the software functioning smoothly.

At some institutions the responsibility of site administrator might be assigned to a systems person or to someone who coordinates the library's contact with multiple vendors. If the principal site administrator does not routinely create and edit guides, assist guide authors with troubleshooting, or conduct guide author training, it is a good idea to have additional individuals with administrator rights who are engaged in those activities. Those who are regularly working with the guides are best positioned to recognize when some of the features available only to administrators can be used to provide greater flexibility and creative opportunities.

Additional information which might be of particular interest to site administrators can be found in chapters 3, 10, 11, 12, and 13 of this book.

This very practical chapter will step through the Admin Stuff menu which allows LibGuides customization. The following menu choices will be discussed:

1. Customize
   - System Settings
   - Look & Feel
   - Subject Categories
   - Mobile Settings
   - Groups

2. Manage
   - Accounts
   - Admin Alert Boxes
   - Link Management
   - Assets

LibGuides Terminology and Functions

Like many software programs, LibGuides has a number of functions that may be unfamiliar to the new site administrator. Some of the terms to which this chapter and others refer are:

A-Z List of Resources—this page provides an alphabetized list of all databases and electronic resources available to your patrons.

API Utility—a Dashboard tool used to create an application programming interface (API), a section of code, to be inserted into a page to perform specific routines or display certain information.

Box—a box is the basic content holder and building block of the LibGuides system.

Box ID Number—a unique identification (ID) number assigned to each box in the LibGuides system.

E-mail Signup Box—a home page content box which displays the e-mail alert subscription box for patrons.

Featured Profile Box—a home page content box which displays the profile of a featured (or randomly chosen) author/librarian.

Guides Box—a home page content box which can display a list of featured, popular, or recent guides.

USING THE ADMIN STUFF MENU TO SET UP AND MAINTAIN YOUR LIBGUIDE SYSTEM

The Admin Stuff menu is found on the Dashboard at the top of the screen when a user who has been assigned administrative rights signs into the system. The Admin Stuff menu has two main categories—Customize and Manage.

Customize

This section describes options for modifying the formatting of the site, with particular attention paid to options impacting the LibGuides home page. A decision to brand LibGuides in a similar fashion to the institutional website can make the initial setup of LibGuides very complex. Such customization typically makes use of

Homepage—the LibGuides administrator menus use "home page" to refer to the main page within the site which is the initial landing page for users and serves as a directory to the other content within the site. Within this chapter any references to the main web page of the institution as something distinct from the LibGuides home page will refer to the "institutional home page."

Info/Alert Box—a home page content box which displays the customized content defined using the Look & Feel section of an administrator's Dashboard.

LibGuide—a guide created by an author on a specific topic. A LibGuide consists of at least one (usually more) page of content boxes. Each page usually represents a subtopic of the LibGuide.

Page—a page is made up of a number of content boxes. A page is a single screen view of a LibGuide. A page is designated on a Guide menu bar by a tab. It is common to refer to a page as a tab.

Rich Text Box—the default box which can be completely customized using HTML or JavaScript.

Subjects Box—the home page content box which displays the list of subjects you use to organize your LibGuides.

Tag Cloud Box—the home page content box which displays the Tag Cloud.

Cascading Style Sheets (CSS), and so on, set up by the institution. CSS code from the institution's website must be included in each LibGuide. This can be planned to automatically occur in the Admin Stuff menu. Although it is not the scope of this chapter to discuss CSS, reference will be made to Springshare resources which will explain CSS, and so on, in more detail. Primarily, this section will deal with the changes that can be made to LibGuides via the toolbar Admin Stuff menus.

System Settings

The System Settings menu choice includes four tabs or pages which provide access to various options—General, Search Options, Link Options, and Access Rules.

General Tab

The Institution Information section allows the customization of the names that will be used to refer to your institution, your library, and so on. This section essentially builds the bread crumb trail displayed at the top left of the LibGuides pages. The General Tab allows one person to be designated as the troubleshooting contact with Springshare by including that person's e-mail address in all support queries coming from the system.

LibGuides provides the potential of allowing users to comment or provide feedback on each LibGuide. The Comments section provides three options: (a) patron comments can be disabled for all content items, (b) patron comments can be automatically displayed on all content items, or (c) patron comments can be held in a moderated queue where a librarian or administrator can approve of relevant comments and decline inappropriate comments before they are displayed on the guide. If comments are enabled, guide creators can disable comment options for individual boxes on guides they create. If comments are disabled here it is also possible for each author to add a feedback box to a LibGuide. Some institutions feel that they are legally responsible for all patron comments, particularly negative ones, which are posted on the website. You should check your institution's guidelines to determine how to set this default.

The RSS section offers another way to make your content more interactive, by syndicating your content with RSS feeds. If you choose to enable your LibGuides RSS feeds, this decision will allows others to pull your LibGuides' content into their pages.

The New Guide Defaults section allows customization of newly created LibGuides. The default name of the first tab in a brand-new guide is "Home." The LibGuides administrator can change this default name if desired. Depending on the overall library website layout design, the LibGuides administrator can also change the default column widths for new guides. The out-of-the-box default consists of three columns—a wide column in the middle (520 pixels) and a thinner left column (230 pixels) and a thinner right column (209 pixels). For example, if the library's website is generally a two-column design with a narrow left column and a wide right-side content space, the default three-column layout can be changed to a two-column default with the correct pixel width defined for each column. Guide authors can still be allowed the freedom to adjust the column widths when needed, but the majority of guides will share a common look and feel.

The system administrator may want to provide a template guide demonstrating what various column widths look like so that guide authors have examples to follow, for example:

- 209 pixels, 541 pixels, 209 pixels—slightly wider center column with side columns of equal width
- 209 pixels, 758 pixels, 0 pixels—much wider center column— useful for embedded videos
- 300 pixels, 667 pixels, 0 pixels—less narrow left column
- 322 pixels, 645 pixels, 0 pixels—column widths of 1/3 and 2/3

The Custom Analytics section offers expanded options beyond the use statistics provided for overall LibGuides use as well as use of specific guides, sortable by user. If desired, LibGuides also offers a place to insert custom analytics tracking code, such as Google Analytics, and so on. This allows site administrators a way to compare the use and performance of LibGuides to the library website or other managed websites. See chapter 11 for more information about Google Analytics and tracking codes.

Search Options Tab

Each LibGuide has a search box which allows the user to search for a topic on the LibGuide displayed or on every LibGuide in the system. This menu choice allows the administrator to control how this search performs. The administrator may limit the number of pages returned from a specific guide or enable the highlighting of the search terms on resulting guide pages.

The administrator can also add a drop-down menu to this search box which will allow the patron to search outside the LibGuide system; for example, the catalog, a federated search, or a Google search can be included. In the Search Box

Options section, give each search category a short name, enter the search URL, and create a new search option. Multiple Search Box Options can be created. See the LibGuides Help & Documentation website (http://help.springshare.com/searchboxes) for more information about constructing search URLs. Shippensburg University, for example, has designed our search box to initially search the guide displayed. A drop-down menu allows the patron to then choose to search all guides in the system, or the library catalog, or the Web. See http://library.ship.edu/faculty for an example.

Link Options Tab

The Proxy Server & Link Target section allows the administrator to configure one of the most important back-end services of the LibGuides system. Most libraries have a configurable proxy server which allows the library to authenticate their users for seamless access to subscription resources. This configuration will only change if the URL for the proxy server changes.

Another part of designing the user's experience is deciding whether external links will default to opening in a new window or in the same window. Most libraries prefer to allow a link to open in the same window, so that a multitude of windows are not open by the end of a search session. However, opening a link in a new window is preferable if the user needs to return to the previous page regularly. For example, in an instructional session based on a LibGuide, opening a new link in the same window (a database, for example) makes it very difficult for students to return to the instructional LibGuide. The LibGuide page is replaced by the database when its link is chosen. Students may search for a number of minutes and then be unable to find their way back to the instructional guide.

In the Resource Icons section, you can create a small graphic indicator of the type of resources to be expected when a user clicks on a link. Symbols can be displayed next to items listed in Links Boxes to help users identify features of the resources, such as databases with particular types of content, for example, audio, data, e-books, full text, government resources, images, journals, and so on. The images selected to use as resource icons should already be very small because they will display as 16 × 16 pixel images. Near the bottom of the Link Options page is the section for Resource Icons. Browse to retrieve the image to be used and give it a short name in the Description box. The Link Options menu allows the icons to be created. When a new resource is added to the system, the author or administrator can then associate an existing icon with that link.

Access Rules Tab

It is worth noting at this point that Springshare has created an add-on to LibGuides, called Campus Guides/Community Guides. The primary difference pertaining to the initial setup and customization of this add-on is that it is possible to create a number of subgroups within LibGuides in which each can be provided with a different look and feel. CampusGuides/Community Guides options, such as Access Rules, show up in the LibGuides menu but are not functional unless the system is upgraded to CampusGuides/Community Guides. Since our focus is LibGuides, CampusGuides/Community Guides functionality will be mentioned only in passing. For more information regarding the CampusGuides/Community Guides upgrade see www.springshare.com/campusguides.

Look & Feel

LibGuides provides a number of ways to change the formatting of guides to match your library's or your parent institution's branding and color scheme so your users experience a seamless transition between the websites. The Look & Feel menu option has three tabs—System-Wide, Homepage, and Language Options.

System-Wide Tab

The Background and Title Colors section does just what it implies: allows the administrator to set the default background and title colors for your LibGuides. The Box and Tab Color Options section provides configuration for the various tabs and boxes. You can make the default tabs and boxes have rounded or square corners. You can change the outline of boxes or remove outlines completely. You can also make the choice to lock down these defaults or to allow authors to change them.

As discussed in chapter 3, it is a good idea to set up standards or guidelines for the colors and shapes used by authors for the pages and boxes to provide a cohesive look and feel for the system. It is possible to lock the look and feel settings system-wide, but many institutions just create default settings to be used on most pages, while allowing authors some flexibility in customizing. If the default design is later changed, but not locked, then only the new guides created after the change will use the new color and shape settings. To apply the new default design to previously existing guides, contact Springshare for assistance and provide them with a list of any guides to be excluded from the global reset.

The System Banners section is where Springshare provides a basic header; or you can build and use your own header image to appear at the top of each LibGuides page. The image to be used for a customized banner must be exactly 985 pixels wide to match the default LibGuides layout.

It is also possible to match the formatting of the parent institution's website by adding custom entries to the Custom <head> Code box and the Custom Header Code and Custom Footer Code boxes. For example, the administrator can reference external CSS and JavaScript code, or enter custom style code which will override the LibGuides default displays. In addition to these, the administrator can copy the HTML code which wraps the content areas of the library's or parent institution's web pages to exactly match the layout and design of those pages. See Springshare's help documentation for more detailed information about these options (http://help .springshare.com/settinguplg).

At Shippensburg University we have decided to lock down colors and shape settings and have wrapped our guides with the university's custom style codes. (Guide authors can still change column widths.) Our Office of Communications and Marketing requires that our LibGuides be as similar as possible to the university's main website. Compare Shippenburg's official main web page (www .ship.edu) with our LibGuides home page (http://library.ship.edu) to see the results.

Pages designed for display in web browsers occasionally do not display as well on paper as they do in a web browser. Using the "Code Customizations – Printer Friendly Pages" section, the LibGuides administrator can customize the "<head>" section of the web page as well as the header and footer code of the web page to improve the layout for printed versions of the web page. These code customizations can become extremely complex, particularly if the LibGuides administrator is not familiar with CSS, HTML, or JavaScript. It may be possible to obtain customization help by talking to your institution's web manager. As these codes can be cut and pasted into boxes on this tab, it may be possible to ask an administrator of another LibGuides library to share their codes with you as a basis for your own customized guides. Fortunately, though, Springshare does provide a simple default banner which is very usable. For more assistance refer to Springshare's Help Guide— Customizing LibGuides—at http://help.springshare.com/customizelg.

Homepage Tab

Your LibGuides installation has a main home page which acts as a portal for the rest of your LibGuides content. Similar, in concept, to your institution's home page or your library's home page on your institution's server, this page can be customized to provide easy and organized access to your guides.

LibGuides home page content boxes can be put in any order in any of the three columns on the default LibGuides home page; however, it is not necessary to include all of them. The default home page boxes include the Subjects Box (S), Tag Cloud Box (T), Guides Box (G), Info/Alert Box (I), E-mail Signup Box (E), and the Featured Profile Box (P). The letter of each box type is used to indicate the location and order of these special boxes on the default LibGuides home page.

The Welcome Message and Introductory Text section allows you to customize a heading and description at the top of the page under the bread crumbs and banner image on the LibGuides home page. Neither option is required; if these fields are left blank the white space at the top of the page is reduced between the bread crumbs and the home page content.

The Featured Guides section controls which guides are highlighted, in what order, in the Featured Guides box. Featured Guides tend to be more heavily used. It is a good idea to include guides that are useful to all your patrons, such as the Database List, general Subject Guides, and so on.

The Default Guide List section is where the administrator configures which list of LibGuides displays in the Guides Box (G). When choosing between displaying the list of Featured Guides, Popular Guides, and Recent Guides first consider whether there are often-requested but difficult-to-find guides that you wish to provide easy access to. You can also let the system show the most used or most recent guides.

The Featured Profile section allows you to select a particular author's profile to highlight on the home page if you choose to display the Profile Box (P). Only profiles of LibGuides authors who have created at least one LibGuide will show by default. If you have created a general "Reference Librarian" profile, this can be set as the Featured Profile so that information about your reference service is always on display. (See http://library.ship.edu/profile.php?uid=25668 for an example.)

In addition to the LibGuides' Homepage Boxes already discussed above, there are several other boxes which are populated by the LibGuides system. The Subjects Box (S) displays a list of the subject classifications; clicking on a link in this box brings up the page displaying all the guides assigned to that subject; this box generally looks better on one of the two side columns. The Tag Cloud Box (T) displays either an alphabetical or frequency sort of tags assigned to LibGuides; this box generally looks better in the wider center column instead of being squeezed into the left or right column, but many libraries leave it off entirely. The Info/Alert Box (I) displays any custom message, including JavaScript, set by the administrator.

The E-mail Signup Box (E) allows patrons to sign up for e-mail alerts when new content is posted to your LibGuides pages.

The Ordering of Content Boxes on the home page section is where the placement and layout of the LibGuides home page boxes are controlled. Near the bottom of this section are fields to enter the single-letter designation for each type of content box as given in the Admin Stuff menus and in this chapter (for example, S designates a Subjects Box). There is a Left, a Center, and a Right Column Box field. The designated box listed first displays at the top of the page, and so on.

Custom boxes can be added to these fields by including the numerical box ID number. (Every box on every page of your LibGuides system has a unique box ID number which can be discovered in the administrator or author editing mode by hovering over the right edge of the boxes' title bar.) The original box can even reside on a private guide specifically created to hold reusable content. Boxes you might want to consider creating and adding to the home page include boxes for a catalog search, frequently asked questions (FAQs), ask a librarian, LibAnswers queries, RSS feed of library events, links to other library resources, and so on. (LibAnswers is a Springshare module which can be purchased to field e-mail questions, create an FAQ database, and track reference statistics. See chapter 10 for more information.)

The default LibGuides home page can be replaced with a customized home page by using the Redirect feature. The replacement home page can be a published guide within the library's LibGuides site or an HTML page hosted externally to the Springshare servers, such as a page from the library's main website.

One difficulty with using a redirected home page is that the standard content types of home page boxes cannot be replicated exactly, but most of the functions can be closely approximated. The only function that is not currently available on a redirected guide is the E-mail Signup Box. It is possible to use the API Utility Tool or the various box types to provide most of the functions available on the default home page content boxes.

Replacing the default home page with another page from within the LibGuides site provides several benefits not available on the default home page: the number and width of columns can be adjusted and tabs and subtabs can be used to organize the home page. Using a page external to the LibGuides site provides complete access to whatever features are available at that hosting site.

The Info/Alert Homepage Content Box can be used to call attention to specific news that has a short life span, such as special library hours or network problems. The box must have a location identified in the Ordering of Content Boxes section so that it will appear on the home page, but the location only needs to be identified once and thereafter can be left alone; the Info/Alert Box will only appear on the home page if it is also defined. Since the primary purpose of this box is to alert users to special information, it should be positioned at the top of one of the columns. If there is nothing special to announce then the box does not get defined/created and does not appear. After the box is created options appear to Edit Title, Edit Content, and Delete. The rich text editor makes it possible to add an image or modify the text with color so that it calls attention to the message.

Language Options Tab

The last tab on the Look & Feel page is the Language Options tab. This tab offers options to customize the terminology displayed in the LibGuides users' interface. Most of the terminology is standard; however, if your institution has a terminology preference which is different from the LibGuides' default, this extensive menu allows you to substitute terminology. For example, one of the many system responses is the error response, "Uh oh, it didn't work! Please try again." This can be changed to any phraseology you desire. As well, you can also default to display system terminology in another language, such as French.

Subject Categories

One of the most useful components of the LibGuides home page is the list of subjects under which guides have been created. This Subject list acts as a table of contents to your LibGuides. Patrons who prefer to browse can easily skim through the list of subjects to find a desired guide. This menu choice populates the default home page Subjects (S) box. After a basic list of subjects is created, a LibGuide author can associate their guide to a subject, allowing it to display when that Subject is chosen on the home page. The individual Subject Category page can also be used to display an author or subject expert's profile on the page listing a particular subject category. Doing so increases patron awareness that help is available.

The Subject Categories page under Admin Stuff is completely customizable. For example, at Shippensburg University we started with a list of our academic majors, after a focus group informed us that the idea of a "major" was more meaningful than the concept of "subject." (See http://library.ship.edu/content .php?pid=353835&sid=2894581.) Pragmatically, we also needed to add some subjects that were not related to majors, such as "Library Exhibits."

The Subject Category page is used to create this initial list of subjects. Subject categories automatically display in alphanumeric order in various system boxes, including the Subject (S) box on the home page. If certain subject categories should be grouped in the list, use colons or hyphens in the subject name to create subcategories (for example, "performing arts: dance," "performing arts: music," "performing arts: theater"). To adjust where a subject appears in a list consider using synonyms (for example, "drama" vs. "theater"). Rearranging phrases will also move a subject up or down in the alphanumeric list. For example, the label "dissertations & theses" puts this topic much closer to the front of the list than would "theses & dissertations."

If a subject category were subsequently divided into two or more new subject categories, it would be a tedious process to open each existing guide one at a time and edit the guide information to associate it with the new subject and disassociate it from the old subject. The Subject Categories page can be used to perform this function. Create the new subject categories and then open up a second window to the same location so that the list of guides associated with the old subject category is visible side-by-side with the new categories. Associate each guide with the appropriate new category, then remove it from its old association.

The system administrator can use the "Subject Categories" page to control the order in which guides display under each subject category. Each subject can display differently. One subject category can be set to order the guides alphabetically and each new guide associated with that subject category will automatically appear in its appropriate alphabet position. The order of the guides in another subject category can be customized, but each new guide will be listed at the bottom of the list until it is manually repositioned.

Suppose one of the subject categories is "Course Guides" and there is one overview guide that needs to stay at the top of the subject list. The rest of the guides in that category are listed in course number order and new guides are being created frequently enough that manually reordering the guides every time is inconvenient. One option is to change the name of the overview guide to move it to the front alphanumerically by using a non-breaking space at the front of the guide title. Note that a non-breaking space is created within text by holding down the Ctrl key while hitting the Space Bar, but to enter it into the box for the guide title the six characters " " must be used. That entire subject category can then be set to order alphabetically. Another option for forcing a guide to appear near the top of an alphabetically ordered list is to rename the guide so that it begins with "a" or "an." See http://library.ship.edu/content.php?pid=353835&sid=2894581 for an example. We forced "Ezra Lehman Library" to the top of the Subject list by placing a non-breaking space in front of "Ezra." We use this subject to gather helpful LibGuides we have created which don't fit under any topical subject.

While discussing subjects it is important to also consider the tags authors use to label LibGuides. An advantage in using tags is that they allow the library to keep the subject list short enough to avoid scrolling off the bottom of the screen. (This is why we at Shippensburg decided not to use the default Subjects [S] box.) If the library is not using tags then the subject categories might need to be more specific, resulting in a very long list. If the library is using both subject categories and tags, then the same terms should not be used in both places. Keep the list of subject terms relatively short, covering broad categories. Use the tags to provide greater specificity in the Tag Cloud. Imagine if there were fifty guides in the subject category of Business tagged with "accounting," "advertising," "finance," "management," "marketing," "swot analysis," and so on. If each of those guides were also tagged with the term "business" then the frequency of that tag would completely override all other tags in setting relative font sizes in the Tag Cloud. Everything other than that one term would appear in a uniformly small font. Visitors would lose the visual clues distinguishing tags that are used four or five times from those used only once.

77

Mobile Settings

The last Look & Feel topic we will discuss is Mobile Settings. Mobile Settings provides a default interface for any smartphone or tablet device which a patron uses to access your LibGuides pages. This function attempts to interpret your LibGuides into a format that will display on a small smartphone screen. This is a default function which can be enabled and customized here. Colors can be customized, as well as the Mobile Site Introductory text. It is also possible to customize codes specifically for the mobile alternative. The Mobile Settings function is discussed in more detail in chapter 13.

Groups

The final choice on the Look & Feel menu list is Groups, which is only available to organizations that have purchased the CampusGuides/Community Guides add-on.

Manage

Although customizing and setting up your LibGuides is a time-consuming task, it will not be the last time that you, as a LibGuides administrator, will need to use the Admin Stuff menu. Functionalities we will be discussing under Manage are Accounts, Admin Alert Boxes, Link Management, and Assets.

Accounts

Choosing accounts allows you to perform a number of tasks related to the persons who have been given access to the LibGuides creation system. The Accounts menu choice has five tabs: Manage Accounts, Create New Accounts, Profile Options, E-mail List, and Collaborators.

Manage Accounts Tab

The Manage Accounts Tab displays a list of all users currently included in the system. This alphabetical listing provides the user's name, e-mail/log-in, activity indicators, and status—librarian (author) or administrator. Several actions can be performed— view the account profile, reset the account password, or delete the account.

The system administrator can use the account management section to delete a specific account. If the account has no guides associated with it then the process just requires a confirmation in the pop-up window. If there are guides associated with the account then all of the guides must first be reassigned to another account. If one author is assuming ownership of all the guides, then it can be done in a single step during the deletion process. If ownership of the guides is being divided between two or more people, then each guide needs to be done one at a time.

Create New Accounts Tab

As you would expect from the name, the Create New Accounts tab allows the administrator to add new users to the LibGuides system. Hopefully this is self-explanatory.

Profile Options Tab

The system administrator can establish up to five additional fields for guide authors to fill out in their user profiles. For example, the standard profile includes a field for Subject Specialty, but individuals in higher education might also want to indicate the specific academic departments for which they serve as collection liaisons. Other options for the fields could be research interests, personal interests, favorite books, languages spoken, skills, academic degrees, job title, department, and so on. If authorship rights have been extended to nonlibrary individuals, then one or two of the additional fields might be used to provide relevant descriptive categories about them.

Once the additional fields are set up in the system each author will need to fill in the appropriate information. The system administrator might need to call authors' attention to the options because the Additional Fields section has to be separately selected to display after the tab for Customize Profile Box is opened. If authors leave some fields blank, then the labels for those empty fields will not display in their profiles.

E-mail List Tab

This tab displays the e-mail addresses of all registered guide authors. The semicolon-delimited list of e-mails can be copied and pasted into an e-mail application if the entire list needs to be e-mailed.

Collaborators Tab

Occasionally a LibGuides creator may find it worthwhile to collaborate with a non-LibGuides user on creating and maintaining content in a particular LibGuide. In academic libraries, classroom faculty members are one group of frequent collaborators. This tab displays a list of all collaborators in the system, including guides with which they have been associated. Although collaborators can be displayed and deleted from this tab, collaborators cannot be created here. In order to create a collaborator, a LibGuide author must do so with the guide settings of an individual LibGuide. The collaborator has access only to that page.

79

Admin Alert Boxes

This menu choice allows an administrator to create alerts to all accounts registered as users of the system. One alert appears on the users' Dashboard page when they log in. The other appears on the Create Guide page. These boxes can be used to provide basic information to authors or reminders of guidelines that have been set down by the library. They could also be used to provide a temporary reminder to users.

Link Management

The Link Management menu choice provides a method to create and maintain links to all electronic resources to which your library subscribes. This choice includes a tab to manage the List of Links and a Global Replace function to change link URLs in the system.

A-Z List Management Tab

The A-Z Resources List is a list of all databases and electronic resources to which the library has subscribed. This master list provides one location to add or change URLs or descriptions for each of these resources. When first created the system automatically alphabetizes the resources and places them on a page that is named with the first letter of each resource's name. When the patron views the A-Z List they see twenty-six tabs across the top of the screen, allowing them to browse or search for a resource alphabetically. The list is also important to the LibGuide author as it acts as a stable location for a resource to be added to a content box. The resource link and description are freshly pulled from the A-Z List each time the LibGuide displays.

To assist in creating an initial list, Springshare provides an import tool for creating and updating an A-Z list of subscription databases for institutions with a Serials Solutions account. Springshare may develop similar import functions in the future for other systems, but libraries should not wait until such tools exist. Creating an A-Z List should be a high priority for the library soon after setting up a LibGuides subscription. For those institutions that are not Serials Solutions clients, Springshare can import links into a new A-Z List if the library submits an Excel spreadsheet with specific information about the library's database subscriptions. See the LibGuides Help & Documentation website (http://help.springshare.com/azlist) for help in setting up a database A-Z List.

Having a single guide with all of the library's subscription databases makes it much easier for guide authors to incorporate those links into new guides rather than each author reinventing the wheel. The URLs for the links can be kept up-to-date in one place. Guide authors have the option of changing the description when they reuse a link, so there is no reason to create a new version of a database link unless the link is going deeper into the database, such as to a special search form. For example, see http://library.ship.edu/azlist to view Shippensburg University's A-Z List. Notice that we added a "Home" tab and titled it with a period to place it at the beginning of the alphanumeric list. This tab provides an opening page which includes information about the resources plus help information.

Global Search & Replace Tab

Database URLs can be updated using the Global Search and Replace feature of Admin Stuff, but caution is advised. Even if only a short portion of the URL needs to be replaced it is best to include a complete replacement URL to avoid accidentally breaking unrelated links where the short portion also happens to appear. This function can also be used to replace wording, other than URLs. These changes cannot be undone, so tread lightly.

Assets

The final menu under Manage is Assets. This function can be used to review assets in the system for problems. Opening this choice provides you with a number of tabs each representing a different resource format—Books from the Catalog, Documents & Files, Embedded Media and Widgets, Links, Podcasts, RSS Feeds, and User Submitted Links. Each of these tabs represents assets that have been included in a LibGuide by an author. Assets represent much of the content inside boxes added to pages by authors. Assets cannot be added to a specific LibGuide with this menu choice. Assets are added to the system by authors when they add a particular box type to a LibGuide. Specific box types are discussed in more detail in chapters 8 and 9 of this book.

Occasionally, the Asset Lists should be browsed to identify where multiple versions of an asset exist which might be consolidated into a single version which is reused in each of the locations. This audit can allow you to eliminate confusion for authors by ensuring that only one version of a link to an asset is in use. Instances where guide authors are creating new versions unnecessarily can reveal where additional training is needed to help guide authors work more efficiently.

Another maintenance task that should be undertaken periodically is a check for broken links. Rather than using the Admin Stuff menu, the Link Checker is on the Dashboard Tools menu and is available to authors as well as administrators. Since the Link Checker cannot check for broken links in rich text boxes, it is important to train guide authors to enter links using link boxes.

CONCLUSION

This chapter reviewed the administrative menu choices in their two broad categories—Customize and Manage. The Customize menu choices primarily allow the administrator to change the formatting of all LibGuides in the system to match the standards decided upon by the library.

The System Settings menu choice includes tabs that provide access to various system-wide options—General, Search Options, and Link Options. With these three tabs the administrator can control institutional information displayed, configurations for new LibGuides, the main system search box, and the inclusion of a proxy service address for electronic resources.

The Look & Feel menu choice provides a number of ways to change the formatting of LibGuides to match your library's or your parent institution's branding and color scheme. The Look & Feel menu option has three tabs—System-Wide, Homepage, and Language Options—which allow control of default colors, allow complete customization of the system home page, and allow the administrator to change terminology within the system.

One of the most useful components of the LibGuides home page is the list of subjects that acts as a table of contents to your LibGuides. The Subject Categories menu choice allows a subject hierarchy to be created, customized, and maintained.

Mobile Settings provides a simple default LibGuides interface which, if enabled, will display for any patron using a smartphone or tablet device. This function allows basic control of this display, allowing basic institutional information and colors to be customized.

The Admin Stuff Manage menu choice functions we discussed were Accounts, Admin Alert Boxes, Link Management, and Assets. Much of the maintenance of the system occurs from these menus.

The Accounts menu allows the administrator to create an initial list of users of the LibGuide system. The list of users can be viewed and maintained here.

Adding an Admin Alert box to the author's Dashboard page or the author's Create Guide page allows the administrator to communicate special notices to all users or to provide point-of-need information when authors log in.

Link Management allows the administrator to initially set up and then maintain the LibGuide systems' A-Z List of databases and electronic resources. This list allows patrons to easily find electronic databases and also acts as a stable master list of resources for authors to add to individual guides.

The Assets menu allows the administrator to track the documents, files, images, podcasts, and so on which authors have added to individual LibGuides. This function provides a method of maintaining what could potentially be a long list of items.

One of the major benefits of LibGuides as a platform for providing information to patrons using the Web is that it is extremely customizable. Fortunately its out-of-the-box defaults are quite useable; however, if your institution desires, the system can be tailored in many ways. In fact, most libraries attempt to make their LibGuide system match their university's web pages as closely as possible.

After the initial installation of LibGuides, the administrator should keep in touch with users of the system to ensure that LibGuides' functionality remains as effective as it can be. If you, as the administrator of the system, are not a LibGuide author you may want to keep in regular touch with the authors in the system. Also, there are so many possibilities of different methods to provide content that do not show up in the author's interface, that you may want to create a list of these enhancements to share with authors.

Although this is the most technical chapter in the book for administrators, you may also want to become familiar with other chapters of note. Chapter 3 will provide you with an overview of the administrative decisions which need to be made for the initial launch of LibGuides. Chapters 8 and 9 describe functions available to LibGuides authors. These chapters explain the various content box types used to add assets to the system. Chapter 10 discusses the LibAnswers add-on to LibGuides. Chapter 11 discusses the use of LibGuides' resident statistical analysis tools as well as the use of Google Analytics. Chapter 12 discusses the use of LibGuides with a campus-wide course management system, such as Blackboard. And finally chapter 13 discusses settings which will enhance the use of LibGuides for smartphone and tablet users.

## Chapter Five

Developing LibGuides Training
A Blended-Learning Approach

Laura Westmoreland Gariepy, Emily S. Mazure,
Jennifer A. McDaniel, and Erin R. White

A successful institutional implementation of LibGuides often includes training the staff who will be using the technology. Using examples drawn from experiences at Virginia Commonwealth University (VCU) Libraries and other academic institutions, this chapter describes how libraries can use a variety of online and face-to-face staff training methods to facilitate a smooth LibGuides implementation. Specifically, a blended-learning approach is applied to development of LibGuides training methods and materials. Blended learning promotes the use of multiple instructional formats such as face-to-face and online activities. This learning approach is well-suited to libraries where staff often work varied schedules in multiple locations, possess different levels of technical skills, and have an array of learning preferences.

This chapter covers a variety of issues pertaining to staff training for LibGuides, but could also be applicable to the development of other software training programs. The chapter begins with a discussion of factors to consider when determining whether training is necessary for software implementation. Next, it focuses on the application of blended-learning strategies in the development of training materials and activities. Finally, building on experiences at VCU and examples from other institutions, the chapter suggests what content might be covered in LibGuides staff training and explores using documentation, in-person training sessions, and personalized support for training.

The authors of this chapter were appointed by the VCU Libraries administration as the LibGuides implementation team (henceforth, the team) in February 2010 to manage the LibGuides project from inception to launch. This group was responsible for ensuring that authors were aware of design guidelines and also had the technical skills needed to create LibGuides. In addition to relying on experiences at VCU, the authors obtained examples from other libraries by sending an e-mail request to the ACRL Library Instruction electronic discussion list, ILI-L (ili-l@ala.org) in June 2011. Respondents were asked to indicate whether or not they had developed and provided LibGuides training for staff and to describe the content and structure of their training, if applicable. The intent of the request was not to make any generalizations about LibGuides training, but to gather examples from other settings. Ten institutions responded, ranging from large research universities to small liberal arts schools to community colleges. These responses, in addition to other LibGuides examples found on the open Web, provided cases for describing the varied methods for providing LibGuides training. Appendixes at the end of this chapter provide examples of training materials available online from other libraries.

WHY BOTHER WITH TRAINING?

Before deciding to offer LibGuides training for library staff, it is important to consider whether specialized training is necessary at all. The decision depends on factors specific to each library's needs and resources. For example, organizations planning a systematic LibGuides implementation with institution-specific design guidelines may find training helpful in encouraging authors to adhere to policies and guidelines. Training can also be useful at large institutions with many LibGuides authors, where it may be more efficient for designated administrators to develop a formal training program for groups of LibGuides authors instead of attempting to reach authors individually.

Conversely, there may be instances where specialized training is deemed unnecessary. For example, a small library with limited staff may opt not to provide training. Similarly, libraries that will not require their LibGuides authors to adhere to institution-specific design guidelines may not see the need to develop training materials. In cases like this, it may be more beneficial for the library to rely on Springshare's large and constantly growing collection of support materials including help documentation, online tutorials, webinars, and community sharing (see Appendix B).

At VCU, the LibGuides implementation team elected to train LibGuides authors for a number of reasons. With more than thirty LibGuides accounts for librarians and staff at two libraries on two separate campuses, the team determined it would be more efficient to deliver information about LibGuides in an organized fashion instead of fielding questions from many authors. The team also decided that it would be beneficial to develop a consistent look and feel for LibGuides and define a clear, specific scope for the type of content to be included in each guide. Given these factors, the team decided that a variety of training materials and components would ensure that authors understood the goals for the use of LibGuides at VCU Libraries. Training would also ensure that authors would understand the desired style and scope of LibGuides and be equipped with the technical knowledge to develop them. The team felt that the time spent to develop training materials and programming would ultimately reduce time spent correcting problems that might arise out of later misunderstandings.

DEVELOPING LIBGUIDES TRAINING: A BLENDED-LEARNING APPROACH

Blended learning has been defined by Bliuc, Goodyear, and Ellis (2007: 234) as "learning activities that involve a systematic combination of co-present (face-to-face) interactions and technologically-mediated interactions between students, teachers and learning resources." Blended-learning techniques can and should include combinations of instructional methods, such as face-to-face workshops and consultations, communication through e-mail and electronic discussion lists, online tutorials and learning modules, and/or documentation (some form of written instructions). One of the benefits of blended learning is that it offers a flexible learning environment well-suited to staff members with varied schedules, and to staff members who are physically located in different places (Harris, Connolly, and Feeney, 2009), as is often the case at institutions with multiple libraries. Components of a blended-learning approach can be formal or informal. See figure 5.1 for a list of possible components.

Ideally, a library could implement LibGuides training using all these formats and instructional strategies. Realistically, there are limiting factors that must be considered and often require selection of only a few of these strategies. Important considerations when developing a training program include the stability of the

FIGURE 5.1
Components of blended-learning approaches
(adapted from Rossett, Douglis, and Frazee, 2003)

Live face-to-face (formal)	Live face-to-face (informal)
• Instructor-led classroom • Workshops • Coaching/mentoring • On-the-job training	• Collegial connections • Work teams • Role modeling
Virtual collaboration/synchronous	**Virtual collaboration/asynchronous**
• Live e-learning classes • E-mentoring	• E-mail • Online bulletin boards • Electronic discussion lists • Online communities
Self-paced learning	**Performance support**
• Web learning modules • Online resource links • Simulations • Scenarios • Video and audio CD/DVDs • Online self-assessments • Workbooks	• Help systems • Print job aids • Knowledge databases • Documentation • Performance/decision support tools

content that will be taught, implementation time line, cost of development, need for access to learning resources over time, and preferred learning styles and environment for each author (Rossett, Douglis, and Frazee, 2003). All of these concerns are relevant to the development of training programs for implementation of LibGuides in libraries.

According to responses from our query to the ILI-L discussion list calling for examples of LibGuides training strategies, blended-learning approaches have commonly been used at other institutions. The following sections of this chapter explore the most popular training methods, focusing specifically on documentation, in-person training sessions, and one-on-one consultations as components of training. Discussion for each component incorporates experiences at VCU, examples gathered from the ILI discussion list e-mail responses, and the tenets of blended learning.

DOCUMENTATION

Documentation is a useful training tool because it can be accessed conveniently at staff members' point of need and allows staff to learn at their own pace. It can also be a useful tool as follow-up to other types of training, such as in-person sessions or one-on-one consultations. Examples of instructional documentation for LibGuides staff training emerged following the call for examples on ILI-L. Additional examples are available on many libraries' websites (see Appendix A). Although documentation is a popular choice, whether or not an institution should create documentation for training and to what extent will depend on factors such as the time available for implementation, the stability of the software for which training is being created, and the length of time people will need to access training resources (Rossett, Douglis, and Frazee, 2003).

Creating documentation can be time consuming. If implementation is occurring in a short time period, developing documentation may be an unattainable goal or may result in insufficient detail. Furthermore, the length of time that staff will need to access the materials will play a role in whether documentation should be created and how detailed it should be. Consider the time required for development of documentation and compare it to how long the information will be needed by authors. One of the advantages of documentation as a learning tool is that learners can access it at their convenience. Rossett, Douglis, and Frazee (2003: "Learning Resources and Experience" section, para. 2) suggest that

Should You Create Your Own Documentation or Rely on Springshare?

89

1. How quickly do you need to bring up LibGuides? If quickly, you may not have time to create documentation.

2. How often does Springshare make changes to LibGuides? Springshare regularly changes the software so local documentation would need to be updated often.

3. How long will staff need to access documentation? If you have high staff turnover, documentation may be necessary.

> the value of most job aids, documentation, performance support tools, and online knowledge bases is that they're available over time and

provide assistance on an as-needed basis. Extended access to such resources is desirable when people are overloaded with information, content changes frequently, topics are complicated, or material is infrequently used.

LibGuides certainly fits this description in some ways: it is constantly evolving, and its numerous features can be overwhelming. By creating documentation and keeping it updated, libraries can provide staff members access to current LibGuides information as they need it. On the other hand, since LibGuides is constantly evolving software, it is advisable to limit the amount of time spent on creating very detailed, task-specific documentation, particularly if you plan to use it over a long period of time. While the documentation needs to be detailed enough to be useful, it is important to remember that the more detailed the content is, the more effort it will take to make changes as the software evolves.

An additional factor to consider is that Springshare already makes some documentation available. If time for implementation is short, this could be used in place of institution-specific documentation. The disadvantage to using Springshare's documentation is the inability to personalize the instructions for any formatting or design guidelines your institution may have made.

With those considerations in mind, VCU's implementation team chose to develop institution-specific online documentation prior to rolling out LibGuides for author use. The instructions were designed to address technical skills (details about the content are addressed in a later section of this chapter), and were arranged so that authors could work through them linearly, or jump to certain sections via hyperlinks in order to find answers to particular questions they might have. The documentation also incorporated VCU's predetermined design guidelines and content scope throughout. Other institutions that provided examples of LibGuides training also indicated that one of the reasons they created their own documentation was to include institution-specific information.

The format and storage of documentation are two big decisions. Institutions must decide between numerous formats: print versus electronic, online versus electronic file, and placing the documentation within LibGuides versus on a site restricted from the public. It is worth considering the formats typically used in a particular library for training documentation, and where training materials are usually located. Other libraries have created documentation in a number of formats and hosted them in various locations, including in a LibGuide. One of the advantages of placing instructional documentation in LibGuides is that it is an easy way to organize information and expose authors to a LibGuide so they can experience some of the software's features. VCU elected to post the online documentation on the library staff intranet rather than in print or within LibGuides itself. This decision was influenced by the common practice of using the intranet for posting and accessing other library training documentation.

IN-PERSON TRAINING SESSIONS

VCU and many other libraries offered in-person LibGuides training sessions and workshops for their staff. One of the most beneficial aspects of in-person workshops is the opportunity for human interaction:

> If the program is controversial, abstract, or complex, it makes sense to invest in human interactions . . . Through interactions with other people, you can solidify attitudes and murky concepts. (Rossett, Douglis, Frazee, 2003: "Touches and Cost section," para. 1)

Introducing any new software can sometimes generate reluctance and misunderstanding among staff members. Some libraries may find it difficult to convince all staff members of the benefits and ease of using LibGuides, or may also need to clarify misconceptions about the software. In-person training sessions provide a face-to-face opportunity to address issues and concerns staff may have, as well as ensure understanding of concepts. This was an important factor in VCU's decision to offer in-person training sessions for staff members.

At VCU, the implementation team offered three in-person LibGuides training sessions for staff: one at the health sciences library and two at the general academic library, where the majority of LibGuides authors are located. The sessions complemented the online documentation that was highlighted as a resource for authors to consult later. The implementation team taught the sessions as a combination of lecture, task demonstration, and open discussion between trainers and authors. Authors had already received log-in information for their LibGuides accounts at the time of the in-person sessions, so they were invited to experiment with the software during the training sessions.

Other institutions that responded to the request for examples employed active-learning components of training. For example, one large research institution offered basic and advanced workshops, both of which included hands-on opportunities for authors to try out features in LibGuides. The basic workshops covered the bare-bones aspects of LibGuides, such as creating a profile, while the advanced sessions addressed features such as embedding video and audio and customizing the look and feel of a particular LibGuide. The advanced sessions were tailored to the needs of authors as requests were made. Other institutions offered LibGuides drop-in sessions, when LibGuides trainers were available to provide assistance to individuals or small groups who wished to stop in. At VCU, authors sometimes arrived with specific questions and sometimes came to work without specific questions. The implementation team sought to create an environment where authors could easily ask questions as they came up.

All types of in-person training sessions are likely to work best in environments with a reasonably large number of LibGuides authors, simply because the chances are higher that multiple authors will attend, thus making best use of LibGuides trainers' time. Other issues, such as the scale and complexity of the institution's LibGuides implementation, need to be considered in determining whether to institute some type of in-person training sessions. They are traditionally more appropriate to use in situations with longer implementation time lines and in which the content of the software is more stable (Rossett, Douglis, and Frazee, 2003). The effort to coordinate and plan in-person training sessions may be too great if implementation needs to be done quickly. Additionally, although the major features of LibGuides tend to remain stable, the software interface is constantly evolving. As with documentation, each library must weigh the cost of developing in-person training and either adjust the level of detail in the training or decide to forgo this method of training.

PERSONALIZED SUPPORT

In addition to documentation and in-person training sessions, personalized support is an option often incorporated into training, and will likely happen whether LibGuides administrators plan for it or not. From e-mail communication to informal discussions to one-on-one consultations, it is a good idea for all libraries, regardless of size or type of LibGuides implementation, to be prepared to offer personalized support that meets the unique needs of individual LibGuides authors. Although providing personalized support can be very informal, it fits well into the array of blended-learning techniques that meet the needs of a variety of learners.

Depending on the size of the institution, it may be helpful to designate more than one individual as a contact for personalized support, as was done at VCU. Offering personalized support for more than thirty LibGuides authors was time-intensive. Having the three-person implementation team available to offer LibGuides support made it possible to share the burden of personalized support, thus decreasing the workload for any one member of the team. Since, in many cases, questions from authors highlighted problems or issues that had not been considered yet, it was helpful for members of the team to continue to share with each other questions and concerns that came up. Sharing and reflecting on authors' questions and problems provided an excellent opportunity for the implementation team to learn from authors and then make changes to training and documentation that provided solutions for everyone.

As with in-person training sessions, offering support via e-mail and personal consultations provides the opportunity for staff to become more comfortable with the software and to learn how others are using it. Interaction with other users and administrators can ease staff into the process of collaborating and sharing material. In fact, smaller institutions may find that personalized support can entirely take the place of organized in-person training sessions for groups. One institution explained that since they were a small library and because most librarians were already familiar with LibGuides from use at other institutions, documentation shared online along with personalized support proved to be sufficient.

At VCU, one-on-one assistance was available for everyone who needed help with particular tasks, and was recommended for any authors who were unable to attend a training session. Only a few authors were unable to attend a training session and required a comprehensive, one-on-one meeting to learn how to use LibGuides. However, many authors obtained one-on-one help from the implementation team to meet their unique needs.

CONTENT COVERED IN TRAINING

The format in which training is delivered is important, but the content delivered in training is even more critical to a successful LibGuides implementation. Ideally, the content covered should address best practices and equip new LibGuides authors with the knowledge and skills needed to create guides meeting the scope and design criteria set out by the institution. VCU, and other institutions that responded to the e-mail request for examples, structured training content around two main areas: (1) information on institution-specific design guidelines, scope, and best practices, and (2) basic technical skills needed to develop LibGuides.

The goal of training at VCU was to introduce authors to the process of creating a guide from start to finish within the context of the institution's design guidelines and scope. The online documentation, which was created first, served as a skeleton for in-person training sessions. Both the documentation and in-person training sessions began with a heavy emphasis on the goals and scope of LibGuides at VCU:

- LibGuides should provide a relatively uniform introduction to discipline- or course-specific resources.
- LibGuides should be created with the information needs of users in mind.
- LibGuides should be easy for patrons to use and for library staff to maintain.
- LibGuides should be clear and concise; they should not duplicate the library's website.

It was important to emphasize this information since many of the technical skills covered in training were directly influenced by the goals and scope of the project.

The in-person sessions and documentation were designed to demonstrate step-by-step what authors would need to do to begin creating guides, the various options available when creating a guide, and finally how to publish a guide. As much as possible, training was designed to mimic the real-life use of LibGuides. The online documentation, in-person sessions, and one-on-one consultations covered both big-picture issues and technical skills. Each type of training introduced authors to the goals, scope, and guidelines for the project, as well as the more technical skills needed to create guides.

Another big-picture issue training covered at VCU was the importance of reducing duplication of effort, and trainers stressed the features of LibGuides that supported efficiency. The team taught and encouraged authors to use features such as "linking," "copying," and "reusing" (as defined in LibGuides), and VCU-specific widgets and boxes that were created for authors to share and reuse. Additionally, a glossary of terms and definitions (such as "copy," "link," "page," and so on) was provided.

In addition to large-scale concepts, training at VCU covered the basic technical aspects of working in LibGuides. Processes covered included:

- Signing in and changing passwords
- Customizing a profile

- Creating a guide from a template; copying other guides
- Adding editors and co-owners to guides
- Adding or changing boxes and overview of box types
- Adding or deleting pages
- Publishing: developing Friendly URLs, public versus private publishing.

Respondents to the ILI-L e-mail indicated that they covered similar information, and preferred not to focus on LibGuides' more advanced or less used features for the initial stages of training.

Some of the responding institutions opted to create institution-specific LibGuides templates. These templates served as a starting point for all guides to follow and provided structure for authors to develop their LibGuides. The template created at VCU (see figure 5.2) standardized color schemes and provided a blueprint for the way each guide should look. Having this standard in place allowed the implementation team to concretely illustrate the consistent look and feel described in the institutional design guidelines. Instructions, suggestions, and

FIGURE 5.2

LibGuide template created at Virginia Commonwealth University

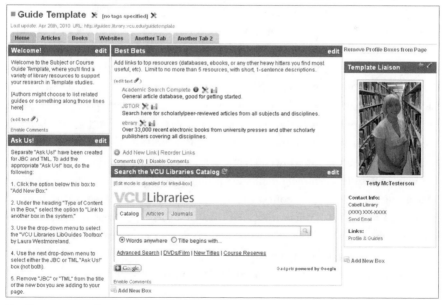

Used by permission of Vrginia Commonwealth University

examples were included in the template to help authors learn how to use LibGuides and to understand the many available features. Additionally, the template reinforced the guidelines authors were asked to follow.

VCU's implementation team adopted the "less is more" philosophy of training, and sought not to cover everything authors might want to know, but just what they needed to know to get started. With the wide and ever-expanding variety of features available in LibGuides, it can be tempting to cover more than what is necessary to begin working with the software. Other institutions that responded to the ILI-L e-mail query also indicated they chose to stick to the basic features of LibGuides to get authors started. Those who elected formalized training or support for more advanced features of LibGuides chose to do so after the initial implementation, presumably after LibGuides authors had mastered the basic technical skills of creating LibGuides.

CONTINUING SUPPORT

Trainers should anticipate spending time not only developing and administering training, but also following up with trainees, answering questions, and keeping any documentation up-to-date during and after implementation. After the initial rollout of the LibGuides software at VCU, members of the implementation team made themselves available as on-call technical support to all LibGuides authors and continued to modify documentation as necessary. The team was committed to keeping the lines of communication with authors open and used blog posts that were automatically sent to all LibGuides authors to announce changes. Updates included information about large-scale interface changes that were likely to affect authors' work, progress during the software implementation, and any changes to the scope or design of LibGuides at VCU. As new authors joined VCU Libraries, training was offered on an as-needed, one-on-one basis or the users were referred to the VCU LibGuides documentation and Springshare's support and training options, depending on the author's comfort level with LibGuides. Other institutions that responded to the ILI-L query indicated that they, too, continued to offer support for their LibGuides authors after the initial implementation was completed.

Both during and after implementation, effective communication with LibGuides authors should be a priority. As previously mentioned, communication from authors to LibGuides administrators can be instrumental in developing and updating LibGuides guidelines that best serve authors and users at a particular institution.

CHALLENGES

Training staff to use LibGuides can present a number of challenges. Trainers must define the scope of the content to be covered in staff training to help mitigate the amount of time invested in developing a training program. Designing training materials and the training itself can become time consuming if the scope of the training has not been clearly defined. It is easy to get carried away. The features, widgets, and possibilities in LibGuides are extensive, and the options grow regularly as the interface evolves. At VCU, particularly with the online documentation and in-person training sessions, the amount of content to teach was strategically restricted. Since the level of detail that could be provided was virtually endless, and Springshare also offers many thorough and up-to-date support options for free, training was not exhaustive. Instead it concentrated on delivering only the information that authors needed to know. Some training time was allotted to address the nuts and bolts of the interface, but greater emphasis was placed on higher-level concepts like content reuse, design consistency, and writing for the Web, with concrete examples to reinforce those concepts. The team also made note of Springshare's documentation and the community site, where other institutions' guides could provide inspiration. Given LibGuides' rapidly evolving capabilities and interfaces, it is helpful not only to narrow the focus of training to essential concepts, but to triangulate training with vendor-supplied support documents and keep an open line of communication with LibGuides authors.

Institutions might also face a challenge in cases where authors attend training sessions but do not begin work immediately in LibGuides. This presents not only the possibility of some of the information being forgotten, but also the opportunity for changes to occur with LibGuides before some authors even begin their work. Thus, keeping documentation current and offering readily available personalized support is important. This problem can also be remedied by ensuring that LibGuides training sessions occur at times when authors have incentives to begin work immediately. Keeping up with the changes in LibGuides and ensuring that these are adequately communicated to your authors are time consuming and therefore a challenge, which requires a conscious commitment. Over time, as authors became more comfortable with the LibGuides platform and concepts, the necessity of ensuring they are aware of updates lessens. However, it remains important that authors are notified of changes affecting scope and design guidelines.

CONCLUSION

Staff training is an optional but beneficial component of a successful LibGuides implementation. The size of the institution, number of authors, existing in-house expertise with LibGuides, and the number and types of institutional customizations are all considerations for deciding whether training should be offered. Training also serves the organizational benefit of clarifying goals and expectations for software implementations and can facilitate buy-in from stakeholders within the library.

If training is deemed necessary, a blended-learning approach that combines in-person and remote training methods will solidify learning of both concepts and technologies and will support learners of all types and technical skill levels. Training materials must also be developed with knowledge that LibGuides' interface features change regularly. Documentation, for example, offers the benefit of constant availability and can reinforce in-person training methods, but care must be taken to keep documentation informative without being overly detailed. As Springshare expands its training and documentation offerings, institutions may do well to pare down their own training materials to focus on big-picture concepts (i.e., linking versus copying) and institution-specific design and style guidelines, while referencing vendor documentation and tutorials for interface-specific concepts. The ever-changing nature of the Web means that interface-specific documentation can easily become outdated, so LibGuides administrators can benefit from leaving these tasks to the vendor while serving as a point of contact for authors at their institutions in order to make best use of staff time.

Regardless of the length of the implementation time line, training scope should be defined clearly and early, and should be monitored closely. It can be easy to lose focus, so defining the key learning objectives of training and building curricula around them is vital. Communication is also an imperative component of training, both before and after an implementation. LibGuides administrators should anticipate ongoing communication with authors about changes to the platform and how those changes affect the institution's guides. Listening is also an important component of communication; attentive administrators can resolve common issues and field ideas that could benefit other authors and the institution as a whole.

This training model may also be useful for other web-based applications beyond LibGuides. As more libraries begin to leverage cloud technologies, for example, institutions will need to develop training plans that both introduce staff to the software and position the software in the institutional context. As with LibGuides, in-house training if necessary, should clarify the scope and purpose of the software, focus on high-level concepts, and introduce any institution-specific guidelines for the software, while not completely reinventing vendor-supplied training materials.

REFERENCES

Bliuc, Ana-Maria, Peter Goodyear, and Robert A. Ellis. 2007. "Research Focus and Methodological Choices in Studies into Students' Experiences of Blended Learning in Higher Education." *The Internet and Higher Education* 10: 231–44.

Harris, Paul, John Connolly, and Luke Feeney. 2009. "Blended Learning: Overview and Recommendations for Successful Implementation." *Industrial and Commercial Training* 41: 155–63.

Rossett, Allison, Felicia Douglis, and Rebecca V. Frazee. 2003. "Strategies for Building Blended Learning." *Learning Circuits*. www.astd.org/LC/2003/0703_rossett.htm.

APPENDIX A

Selected LibGuides Style Guides

University of Louisville

http://louisville.libguides.com/content.php?pid=32203&sid=235603

James Cook University

http://libguides.jcu.edu.au/content.php?pid=53399&sid=391474

Cornell University

https://confluence.cornell.edu/display/libguides/Creating+a+LibGuide
https://confluence.cornell.edu/pages/viewpage.action?pageId=111224814

Pima Community College

http://libguides.pima.edu/content.php?pid=93139&sid=694485

University of Toronto

http://guides.library.utoronto.ca/content.php?pid=125952&sid=1081615

APPENDIX B

Selected Training Manuals

Southern Illinois University at Carbondale

Word Doc training manual linked from a LibGuide,
http://libguides.lib.siu.edu/content.php?pid=51274&sid=376456

University of Toronto

http://guides.library.utoronto.ca/guideforauthors

Springshare Support

http://help.springshare.com/index.php?gid=179

3

PART 3

Creating LibGuides—
For Guide Creators

## Chapter Six

Design
Why It Is Important and
How to Get It Right

Nedda H. Ahmed

L ibGuides' popularity largely stems from the fact that the interface frees the librarian from having to know HTML in order to make guides that are attractive and useful. Although articles extolling LibGuides' virtues abound, relatively little has been said about how librarians create guides. There has also been no discussion in the library literature about the established conventions of web usability and design principles as they relate to LibGuides. The combined effect of relying less on web programming professionals and a lack of education about design and usability issues has the library community asking questions about design and how it can support user learning.

This chapter will answer some of these design questions and explain how certain design principles work. I will also recommend easy ways you can capitalize on this new design knowledge in your LibGuides. After reading this chapter, you will take away a toolkit of usability guidelines and design principles that you can use to make your guides more user-friendly.

WHY DESIGN MATTERS

Some in the library profession may question why librarians need to know about design; after all, is content not more important than how things look? To answer this question, you need to understand why aesthetics matter. What can good design do for us? How does it support comprehension? Donald Norman's book *Emotional*

Design (2004) deals with these issues in detail. What Norman and his cognitive science colleagues have come to understand is that objects offering a good balance of aesthetics, practicality, and usability are more effective—essentially, he says, attractive things work better—their attractiveness produces positive emotions, which causes mental processes to be more creative and more capable of working through obstacles. "Designers can get away with more if the product is fun and enjoyable. Things intended to be used under stressful situations require a lot more care, with much more attention to detail" (Norman, 2004: 26).

As librarians, we often assist people faced with deadlines, grades, due dates, and tenure reviews. If we accept Norman's assertion about attractive things working better in stressful situations, do we not owe it to our patrons to make our services and resources as usable, practical, and attractive as possible? Moreover, most of our library users have grown up using computers and the Internet and are accustomed to the daily bombardment of media and images. Oblinger and Oblinger (2005) describe these users as visual learners: they absorb information through their eyes (Toksöz, 2011). Whether or not you believe there is substance to this theory of learning styles, visually disharmonious and disorganized information is a major turn-off, given the media-saturated environment in which we live, and as it is more abstract it is also more difficult to utilize. To ignore the design issue, to cast it as a less important element than content, is doing our patrons—and our valuable resources—a great disservice.

COMPOSITION

> Badly arranged space is a bit like mis-timed pauses in speech; they can
> disrupt meaning and emphasis. (Dabner, 2005: 10)

In the art world, "composition" is the term used to describe how objects are arranged within a two-dimensional space. The composition (also sometimes referred to as "layout")—and how the objects in the space relate to one another—greatly affects how viewers perceive an image. Is the image dynamic or static? Orderly or chaotic? Is there an embedded message? Look at the computer sketch of a painting by Raphael, one of the best-known painters of the Renaissance (see figure 6.1). (To see *Madonna and Child Enthroned with Saints* online, go to the Metropolitan Museum of Art's Collection Database at www.metmuseum.org/Collections/search -the-collections/110001822.) Now imagine another painting, this time by Jackson

FIGURE 6.1
A computerized rendition of *Madonna and Child
Enthroned with Saints,* by Raphael

Pollock, a twentieth-century American painter best known for his "drip paintings."
(Not familiar with Pollock's work? Check out the National Gallery of Art's Pollock
website at www.nga.gov/feature/pollock.)

In a Pollock painting, the patterns of the artist's drips and splatters combine to
create a visually dynamic—almost chaotic—composition. His paintings are not
pedagogical in nature: they are about movement, color, and rhythm. The Raphael
painting, on the other hand, contains a visually communicted religious subtext.
First, all the figures are together near the center of the picture plane, arranged in
a roughly triangular mass. This is a very stable composition. We also get a sense
of the subjects' relationships and biblical importance due to the way the artist

has arranged his subjects—the Virgin Mary and Jesus in the middle and saints in supporting roles, standing close by. Everything in this painting's composition combines to give the viewer positive associations about the church and its stability.

Just like Raphael, we can use composition to create visual hierarchies that guide users to prioritized information, thereby reinforcing our content and making it more comprehensible. There are four simple design techniques for building visual hierarchy into your guides: entry points, focal areas, rest areas, and uniformity. (See table 6.1.)

TABLE 6.1
Checklist for building visual hierarchy

Technique	Definition
Entry points	The page element that catches the viewer's eye first and draws them into the page.
Focal areas	Page elements that attract the eye; usually are high contrast or visually active.
Rest areas	Uncluttered or quiet areas on a page.
Uniformity	A coherent layout and aesthetic strategy, deployed across pages; helps cut the user's learning curve.

Entry Points

The entry point is the element that catches the viewer's eye first and draws them into the 2-D space. Eye-catching elements are frequently high contrast, include human faces, or are anything with a lot of visual vibration or movement. In the Raphael painting, the entry point would be the area in the top center, where we see Mary's pale face sharply contrasted against her dark head covering and the highly patterned fabric backdrop.

Visual dynamics work slightly differently in a web environment. Jakob Nielsen, a leading web usability expert, has conducted web page eye-tracking studies (2006) and has found that most users scan a screen in an F-shaped pattern, "entering" a page in the upper left-hand corner. I will call this the "hot corner." You can maximize the hot corner by placing an interesting graphic element somewhere in the top left quadrant of your page. This will visually orient the user and draw them into the content, so it's a good idea to place your highest-priority information adjacent to the hot corner. Look at figure 6.2. Where does your eye go first? For most viewers, the portion in the upper left quadrant, with its highly contrasting black-on-white shapes and dynamic diagonal lines, is visually irresistible.

FIGURE 6.2
Behold the power
of the hot corner!

FIGURE 6.3
A new focal area quietly draws
attention away from the hot corner.

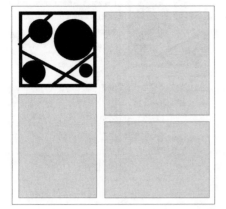

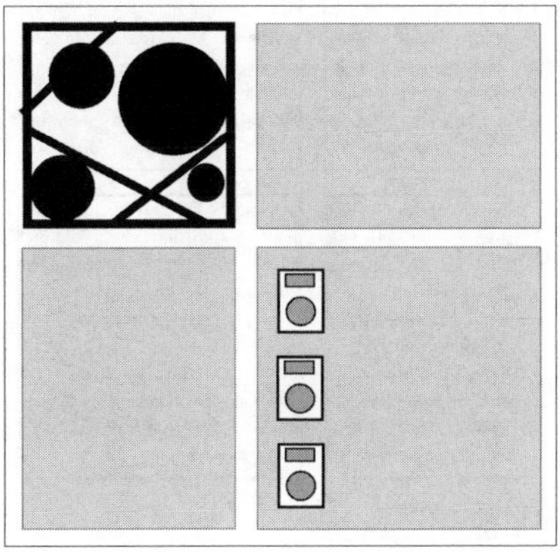

Focal Areas

Focal areas are usually areas of high contrast or visual activity which draw the eye of the viewer. Entry points are one kind of focal point, but there can (and should) be multiple focal areas on a page. Since our eyes are not naturally engaged by large blocks of screen text, you will want to strategically build in multiple focal areas to help guide a user's eye through your content. Additional focal areas should not compete with one another or the entry point, as this can confuse the user as to which is the highest-priority information. You can minimize visual conflicts by making lower-order focal areas smaller or visually quieter and less contrasty. Figure 6.3 builds upon figure 6.2 by adding a smaller, less dynamic visual element into the lower right quadrant of the composition. This new element helps to peel our eyes away from the entry point. It directs our attention to the other areas of the composition without visually competing or clashing with the entry point.

Focal areas can sometimes occur unintentionally on a page. Multiple rows of tabs at the top of your guides, for example, create a visually heavy band of color from which it is difficult to draw away the user's eye. Large blocks of bold text can also create unwanted focal areas. To check a page for focal areas, simply squint. Squinting decreases the amount of light entering the eye and helps reveal the areas of high contrast—focal areas.

FIGURE 6.4
Too crowded!

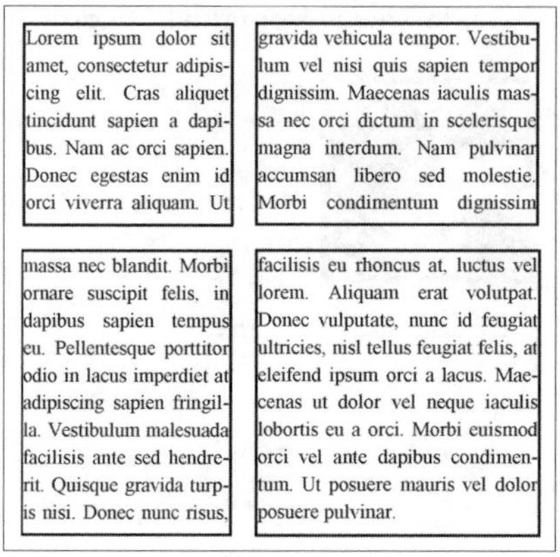

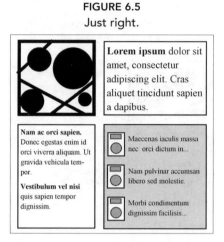

FIGURE 6.5
Just right.

Lorem ipsum dolor sit amet, consectetur adipiscing elit. Cras aliquet tincidunt sapien a dapibus. Nam ac orci sapien. Donec egestas enim id orci viverra aliquam. Ut gravida vehicula tempor. Vestibulum vel nisi quis sapien tempor dignissim. Maecenas iaculis massa nec orci dictum in scelerisque magna interdum. Nam pulvinar accumsan libero sed molestie. Morbi condimentum dignissim massa nec blandit. Morbi ornare suscipit felis, in dapibus sapien tempus eu. Pellentesque porttitor odio in lacus imperdiet at adipiscing sapien fringilla. Vestibulum malesuada facilisis ante sed hendrerit. Quisque gravida turpis nisi. Donec nunc risus, facilisis eu rhoncus at, luctus vel lorem. Aliquam erat volutpat. Donec vulputate, nunc id feugiat ultricies, nisl tellus feugiat felis, at eleifend ipsum orci a lacus. Maecenas ut dolor vel neque iaculis lobortis eu a orci. Morbi euismod orci vel ante dapibus condimentum. Ut posuere mauris vel dolor posuere pulvinar.

Lorem ipsum dolor sit amet, consectetur adipiscing elit. Cras aliquet tincidunt sapien a dapibus.

Nam ac orci sapien. Donec egestas enim id orci viverra aliquam. Ut gravida vehicula tempor.

Vestibulum vel nisi quis sapien tempor dignissim.

Maecenas iaculis massa nec orci dictum in...

Nam pulvinar accumsan libero sed molestie.

Morbi condimentum dignissim facilisis...

Rest Areas

Rest areas can be white space, quiet images, or any uncluttered space that gives the viewer's eye less work to do. It is important to include rest areas in our LibGuides so that users do not feel overwhelmed by the amount of information on any given page. Interestingly, rest areas can also be used to draw a user's eye to a particular area of a page. If a page is full of text, for example, a smaller element surrounded by a large margin of white space appears to stand out because the white space is such a contrast to the busyness of the text all around it. So you can use rest areas as an alternative method for creating focal points throughout your content.

In figure 6.4, the words are crammed into the content boxes with little surrounding white space. It is difficult to figure out where the text begins or where to look first. The text essentially forms a busy pattern which is visually confusing. Our eyes focus instead on the sharply contrasting white spaces between the boxes. In figure 6.5, the text is reduced and broken down into manageable chunks. Sensible margins between the text and the box borders and space between sections of text reduce the text's overwhelming effect. Images also now take up about one-third of the overall composition, which also function as a visual rest area.

Uniformity

Compositional uniformity as it applies to LibGuides means having a cohesive look and structure to pages so that the users' learning curve is lowered. The goal here should be that once a person has used one of your library's guides, they intuitively know how to use all your library's guides because each guide follows a similar structure, even though the content varies widely. To illustrate this point, I like to use the example of the iPhone and the iPad. Apple wisely created the iPad in the wildly successful iPhone's image. They knew users were already well-satisfied with the iPhone's features and controls, so why create something that would disrupt those preexisting (and well-established) user expectations and behaviors?

Uniformity among LibGuides at your library is only going to come through collaborative communication among guide creators. See how far you can go to create a seamless user experience. Can you agree to follow a palette for tab colors, box colors, and fonts? Can you agree to include a core set of tabs? Can you agree to place profile boxes and contact information in a standard location? Some of your colleagues may balk at having restrictions put on their creativity, but standardizing elements like these will help users quickly orient themselves to any guide they visit and will get them to the information they need more quickly (and with less frustration).

For a more detailed discussion of contrast, focal areas, and visual dynamics in general, I highly recommend Shaver's *Moving the Eye through 2-D Design: A Visual Primer* (2010). Capitalizing on these elements of composition—entry points, focal areas, rest areas, and uniformity—will help you create visually dynamic guides that users will find easy to use.

COLOR

> Selecting colors should never be an arbitrary decision. The colors you choose as a designer should enhance the layout and create a visual impact. (Dabner, 2005: 36–37)

Color is another very powerful component to consider when putting together LibGuides. Because we are so keenly attuned to it (psychologists believe our brains comprehend color before shape or other details; Dabner, 2005: 38), color can either be the most useful tool in your design or the most distracting element on a page. Most design and style guides agree: color should always be used sparingly and carefully.

Why is color so powerful? It all has to do with what color theorists call "color attributes." Whether it is the color of your tabs, your content boxes, or the color of a word or two you want to emphasize, here are the color attributes you should think about when you are selecting colors for your LibGuides: aggressiveness and intensity, contrast, vibration, connotation, and proportion. (See table 6.2.)

TABLE 6.2
Checklist of color attributes

Attribute	Definition
Aggressiveness and intensity	How a color sits on the screen—does it shout for attention or merely whisper?
Contrast	How a color relates to the screen background and other colors near it.
Vibration	An unpleasant "hum" which occurs when two high-contrast, highly intense colors are adjacent on a screen.
Connotation	The cultural meanings a particular color may suggest.
Proportion	Amount of a color on a screen (and the easiest way to mitigate the other four attributes).

Aggressiveness and Intensity

Does the color seem to jump off the page (advance) or sit quietly in the background (recede)? Typically, warm colors like reds, oranges, and yellows (though you can have a warm green, for example) seem more intense, and advance toward the viewer, while cool colors like blues, greens, and purples seem lighter, and recede. Obviously, you would not want to use a very aggressive red all over the pages of a guide—the effect would be like shouting at the user. However, a small amount of intense, fire-engine red can be useful if you want to emphasize a word or short phrase. You can also decrease the aggressiveness of a color by playing with its saturation or brightness.

Contrast

How aggressive or passive a color is often depends on what is surrounding it, or what it is contrasting against. A saturated purple placed next to a bright yellow will cause a sharp contrast, since these colors are complementary, or across one another on the color wheel. (Did you graduate from grade school and forget about the color wheel? Get a refresher here: www.worqx.com/color/color_wheel.htm.) Contrast is decreased by using harmonious colors—colors that are adjacent to each other on the color wheel—or by using less saturated (or less bright) colors.

It is important to be sure that text, in particular, has enough contrast to the page background color so that it remains readable. If your guides have a standard white background, users will not pay much attention to text that is formatted with a pale lavender color. And here is a special Americans with Disabilities Act usability tip: roughly 10 percent of men have some degree of color-blindness, so be very wary of using red and green colors for text (Lynch and Norton, 2009d). People with the most common form of color-blindness see red and green as gray, which does not contrast well against a white page background.

Vibration

Complementary colors of equal intensity, when placed near each other, will cause a visual vibration that is powerful yet unpleasant to look at for more than a few seconds. The opposite of vibration (or discord) is harmony—colors adjacent on the color wheel will usually create a harmonious palette. A guide with multiple saturated complementary colors sprinkled throughout will have a Times Square–like effect—a pulsating, sensorial overload which makes it hard for the user to determine where the most important information is on the page. If you want to use multiple colors within a guide, try selecting colors that are adjacent on the color wheel, and therefore harmonious.

Connotation

Like it or not, many colors come with baggage. A guide with red and green together may look Christmasy. Pale blues and yellows together seem beachy. It's important to consider the possible meanings of colors (and color combinations) so that you do not send an unintended visual message. Here is a list of basic colors and their Western cultural meanings:

Red = heat, intensity   Yellow = sunshine, light
Green = springtime, youth   Blue = airiness, water

Proportion

Of all the color attributes, proportion is probably the most important. You can use pretty much any color you want to in your guides, provided you are using an appropriate amount and have a justifiable reason for using the color. Are you just dying to use fluorescent pink somewhere on one of your guides? Be sure it's only one really important fluorescent pink word, and make sure you provide a focal point or rest area elsewhere in the composition to balance the page and draw the viewer's eye to the other content areas.

WRITING FOR THE WEB

> If you cram every page with dense text, readers see a wall of gray and will instinctively reject the lack of visual contrast. (Lynch and Norton, 2009b)

Because text is a major design element of the Web, it's worth discussing in this chapter on design. To most users' eyes, blocks of text on a screen are like chunks of busy grey. These chunks of grey are not very visually enticing, which is probably why, according to Jakob Nielsen's web readability studies, people on average only read about 20 percent of what is on a page (Nielsen, 2008). Text needs to be carefully balanced with the other elements of the design and written in a way that enhances screen readability. Here are three guidelines to consider when writing for your LibGuides (Morkes and Nielsen, 1997): be concise, be objective, and make text scannable. (See table 6.3.)

TABLE 6.3
Techniques for writing for the web

Technique	What it means
Be concise	Cut in half, cut in half again.
Be objective	Take out marketing language and jargon.
Make it scannable	Format the text for screen readability.

Be Concise

People simply are not going to read long paragraphs of text on a web page, so choose words wisely and use them efficiently. A good rule of thumb is to write your text normally, then cut it in half. Then cut it in half again. Because most users will click before they read, write only what the user needs to know before they click into a resource. Any text that explains something that is apparent to the user after they have already started using something is wasted space.

Be Objective

Users can typically sense when they are being marketed to, and they have a low tolerance for this type of writing. Also, if you are following guideline #1 (Be Concise), you probably do not have enough of a word allowance to include much flowery language. Marketing jargon often finds its way onto our pages because we copy and paste database descriptions from the vendors. Look at the vendor-written text critically: does it make the product seem too good to be true? If we pick up on this, our users certainly will too. Overuse of nonobjective language also hinders us when we really do want to emphasize a particular resource. If every resource on the page is the best for that subject area, how can our users really know which one to use? Be direct and keep it simple.

Make Text Scannable

Reading text on a screen makes different demands on our eyes from reading text on a page. Generally our eyes glance, or scan, over the screen, looking for the high-interest information first. Making text scannable means using formatting to make it easier for the reader's eyes to pick up on the most important pieces of information. Here are seven tools you can use to increase scanability: prioritize, list, distill, link, illustrate, key words, and formatting.

Prioritize

Since people only read about 20 percent of what's on a page (Nielsen, 2008), make sure you put the most important 20 percent of your content first. If users are interested or engaged by the first 20 percent, they might even keep reading, Prioritizing also shows users that you respect their time by organizing your thoughts.

List

Bulleted lists and numbered lists are great ways to break up long passages of text. Listing also makes it easier for our eyes to pick up a new line of text on the screen. Use numbered lists for process-oriented information, such as the steps to requesting a book via interlibrary loan. Use bulleted lists for other types of information. Even when list-making, be sure to keep it concise and prioritize list items so that the most important information is presented first.

Distill

Distilling information means thinking about the most essential thing you want the user to know and then stating it in as few words as possible. Remember: this is writing for the Web, not writing for a novel. Sentence fragments are perfectly acceptable. Longer, complete sentences, though grammatically more correct, do not help users glean information quickly, so are unnecessary in the web environment.

Link

Linking to other guides, pages, or external information allows you to include relevant information in a "see also" kind of way. Inquisitive users who want to know more will click the links. Users who are in a hurry, on the other hand, are spared lengthy descriptions of the information contained elsewhere. In yet another usability study, Jakob Nielsen has found that this type of linking actually increases credibility with users, too (Nielsen, 1997).

Illustrate

A picture is worth a thousand words, especially when it comes to increasing readability on the Web. Text on a screen just is not visually engaging to most users, so whenever possible, exchange text for diagrams, short videos, flow charts, graphics, and illustrations. *Note:* Do *not* use animated GIF files. They are distracting and somewhat antiquated, harkening back to the Web's early days when it seemed like every website had a GIF of a hula dancer wiggling her hips back and forth.

Key Words

After you have your text cut down to size, think about emphasizing key words you want the user to remember. Usability studies indicate that users frequently scan a page first, then focus on the portions of a page that seem the most relevant. By emphasizing key words, you can help direct users to the information you want them to see and use. It's important, however, to not overdo the emphasizing. If every sentence on a page has a word or phrase formatted in bold italics, the effect is visually overwhelming and the impact of the emphasis is diminished.

Formatting

You can format text in specific ways to draw the user in or pique their interest. Below are some common text-formatting options (italics, bold, underlining, color, capitals, font, width, and spacing) and guidelines on how to best use them (Lynch and Norton, 2009a).

Italics

Italicized text will attract the user's attention because its shape contrasts with the non-italicized text around it. However, usability studies indicate that italicized text is more difficult to read on a screen, so use this option sparingly, mainly for book or periodical titles, foreign phrases, or key words.

Bold

Bold text also draws the eye because it is visually weightier than the other elements on the page. Bold text is more readable than italicized text, so it's a better choice for emphasizing key words. However, long passages of text set in bold lose contrast (and therefore readability) and look aggressive—like you are shouting at the user.

Underlining

Underlining text should generally be avoided, as users will instinctively assume that underlined text is hyperlinked. Also, underlining can reduce readability, since the line under the letters can interfere with letter shapes.

Color

An earlier section of this chapter discussed choosing colors appropriately for other parts of your guides, but choosing text colors comes with an added set of considerations. Some things to keep in mind: users will assume that any differently colored text is a hyperlink, especially if you choose royal blue or purple to format your text. Blue is the default hyperlink color, purple is the default color for visited links. Next, be sure there is enough contrast between the page background and the text color. Pale, pastel colors, for example, should be avoided if your guides have a white background. Also, be wary of using reds and greens, especially for hyperlink colors, as people with red-green color blindness will not be able to detect these colors. Lastly, show restraint. Using too many colors (e.g., more than two or three) is distracting and does nothing to help the user comprehend your content.

Capitals

Capitalizing the first letter of words in a sentence or phrase helps our eyes notice where a new thought or chunk of information begins. FORMATTING TEXT IN ALL CAPS, however, should be avoided, as it reduces readability and looks like shouting.

Fonts

There are a few considerations when choosing a font for your guides. First of all, do not use too many. A page that has various fonts all over it looks poorly designed and can reduce your credibility with the user. If you want some variety, pick one font for headings and one font for body text, and be consistent. For help in choosing fonts that go well together, I highly recommend "Type Contrasts," chapter 11 in Williams's *The Non-Designer's Design Book* (2008). Keep in mind, too, that different fonts have different levels of web readability. Serif fonts like Times, New Roman, and Georgia are those where letters have a flourish, or serif, at the end points. Sans-serif fonts such as Verdana, Tahoma, and Arial have plain end points. Some usability studies indicate that sans-serif fonts are easier to read on the Web than serif fonts, which are supposedly better for paper documents; other studies say the exact opposite. There is no hard-and-fast rule. The *Web Style Guide* advises, "You can truly judge type legibility only within the context of the situation—on the screen, on paper—as users will see your web page" (Lynch and Norton, 2009c).

The last point to consider is font "personality." If you are creating guides with an elementary school student audience in mind, it may be appropriate to use Comic Sans. Comic Sans, with its playful and informal style, is probably not an appropriate choice, however, for an adult academic audience.

Width and Spacing

Going from left to right, the default LibGuides box widths are 230, 520, and 209 pixels. These widths are actually pretty good for readability, when you consider that our eyes have difficulty tracking lines of text that are greater than 60 to 72 characters in length (Dabner, 2005: 84). Depending on the size font you use, the middle box width (520 pixels) can accommodate lines of text that follow this 60–72 character guideline without going too many characters over. A recent enhancement to LibGuides gives creators the ability to toggle the column widths. Be cautious in expanding your content box widths—the lines of text may increase in width too much and decrease readability, especially when you have a lengthy passage of text on-screen. Readability is also decreased by greatly expanding the space between letters in a word.

Here is an example of text that is not concise, objective, or scannable:

> Database X provides the most robust, quality research solution in areas related to [insert subject area here]. Database X incorporates the content of Database Y (formerly produced by the Major National Association) and Database Z (formerly produced by Big State U) along with numerous other journals in [Subject area 1], [Subject area 2], and other closely-related fields of study to create a research and reference

resource of unprecedented scope and depth encompassing the breadth of the communication discipline. Database X offers cover-to-cover ("core") indexing and abstracts for more than a trillion journals, and selected ("priority") coverage of nearly a billion more, for a combined coverage of more than a kajillion titles. Furthermore, this database includes full text for a million journals.

Now for the cleaned-up version. Notice the superlative language ("robust," "unprecedented," and so on) is gone, as well as the database's history, which is probably not relevant to most researchers. The sentence structure is gone. The most important thing (the hyperlinked database name) is emphasized. The salient facts are reduced to bulleted sound bites. But everything most users need to know is still here:

Database x [hyperlinked]
- [Subject area 1], [Subject area 2] and related fields
- Coverage for 1 trillion journals; Full text for 1 million.

Making text concise, objective, and scannable greatly enhances the likelihood that users will read the text on your pages. These simple techniques will help users to not feel overwhelmed or turned off by the amount of words on the page, but instead will encourage them to engage with the text, to read it thoroughly, and absorb the information embedded within it.

CONCLUSION

This chapter has covered practical techniques for presenting the information in your guides in a way that is appealing to users, such as planning an effective composition, choosing colors wisely, and writing text effectively. Although I have written a lot about creating guides that are visually attractive, the overarching goal is to use aesthetics to engage users and effectively support the pedagogical purpose of a guide. Instead of seeing form and function as two distinct concepts in competition with each other, our efforts can be much more fruitful if we see form and function like a happy partnership where each side supports the other's needs.

When aesthetics, practicality, and usability are all working together harmoniously, then Donald Norman (2004) believes we can attain what he calls "seduction." This is not seduction in the romantic sense: design seduction happens when a user finds an object so easy to use, so comprehensible, so efficient, so attractive, that it becomes integrated into the user's normal routine or workflow. Jennifer Little describes a similar phenomenon in her article "Cognitive Load Theory and Library Research Guides." She states: "Effective research guide design will encourage both the construction and automation of schemas" (2010: 54). Seduction or the automation of schemas—either term effectively describes what good design can do—helps users comprehend your content so that they view your LibGuides as a premier destination for research help online.

REFERENCES

Dabner, David. 2005. *Graphic Design School: A Foundation Course in the Principles and Practices of Graphic Design*. 3rd ed. Hoboken, NJ: Wiley.

Little, Jennifer J. 2010. "Cognitive Load Theory and Library Research Guides." *Internet Reference Services Quarterly* 15, no. 1: 53–63.

Lynch, Patrick J., and Sarah Norton. 2009a. "Emphasis." In *Web Style Guide*. 3rd ed. New Haven, CT: Yale University Press. http://webstyleguide.com/wsg3/8-typography/5-typographic-emphasis.html.

———. 2009b. "Legibility." In *Web Style Guide*. 3rd ed. New Haven, CT: Yale University Press. http://webstyleguide.com/wsg3/8-typography/3-legibility.html.

———. 2009c. "Typefaces." In *Web Style Guide*. 3rd ed. New Haven, CT: Yale University Press. http://webstyleguide.com/wsg3/8-typography/4-web-typefaces.html.

———. 2009d. "Visual Design." In *Web Style Guide*. 3rd ed. New Haven, CT: Yale University Press. http://webstyleguide.com/wsg3/7-page-design/3-visual-design.html.

Morkes, John, and Jakob Nielsen. 1997. "Concise, Scannable and Objective: How to Write for the Web." *Useit.com*. www.useit.com/papers/webwriting/writing.html.

Nielsen, Jakob. 1997. "How Users Read on the Web." *Useit.com*. www.useit.com/alertbox/9710a.html.

———. 2006. "F-Shaped Pattern for Reading Web Content." *Useit.com*. www.useit.com/alertbox/reading_pattern.html.

———. 2008. "How Little Do Users Read?" *Useit.com*. www.useit.com/alertbox/percent-text-read.html.

Norman, Donald A. 2004. *Emotional Design: Why We Love (or Hate) Everyday Things*. NY: Basic Books.

Oblinger, Diane G., and James L. Oblinger, eds. 2005. *Educating the Net Generation*. Boulder, CO: Educause. www.educause.edu/educatingthenetgen.

Shaver, Buy. 2010. *Moving the Eye through 2-D Design: A Visual Primer*. Chicago: Intellect.

Toksöz, Itir. 2011. "Teaching to the New Generation." *University of Venus* (blog). *Inside Higher Ed*. July 10. www.insidehighered.com/blogs/university_of_venus/teaching_to _the_new_generation.

Williams, Robin. 2008. *The Non-Designer's Design Book: Design and Typographic Principles for the Visual Novice*. 3rd ed. Berkeley, CA: Peachpit.

## Chapter Seven

Integrating LibGuides into the Teaching-Learning Process

Veronica Bielat, Rebeca Befus, and Judith Arnold

As librarians, we understand that integrating instruction strategically, aligning instructional content with assignment requirements, and offering point-of-need instruction all increase the effectiveness of library instruction and enhance development and retention of information literacy skills. However, the ability to provide instruction at these strategic points is often out of our control. Class schedules, lab schedules, library schedules, and resource availability are just some of the outside factors that impact our ability to integrate instruction effectively. And many librarians would probably agree that most students do not consult printed handouts once they have left our classroom.

This chapter demonstrates how LibGuides is a good solution for meeting this strategic placement of information literacy instruction. Used in conjunction with face-to-face instruction or as an asynchronous learning experience, a well-designed LibGuide can support learning at point of need and guide students in the use of our resources in the context of their assignments. Also, this chapter takes the reader through some basic learning theory and describes the practical application of these theories in designing LibGuides that support independent student learning.

This chapter is organized into three sections. "LibGuides as a Teaching Tool" discusses the pedagogical principles behind designing focused guides for teaching. "The Course Guide as a Learning Tool" explores the underlying learning theory of the embedded course guide and how it differs from the design of the disciplinary guide. "Collaborative LibGuide Design" analyzes the collaborative design process of a course guide developed for faculty to use as a pedagogical tool. The chapter concludes by drawing together recurring themes of learner-centered design and pedagogical principles that move guides beyond being a repository of resource links to a learning support aligned with well-defined instructional goals.

LIBGUIDES AS A TEACHING TOOL

As chapter 1 has discussed, librarians have historically used a variety of methods to direct users to appropriate resources. LibGuides is the current stop in the evolution of the handcrafted HTML pathfinder, developed in the early days of the Web. For many years, the online pathfinder was mainly a static list of links. LibGuides, however, allows librarians to easily integrate the resources we have been creating since the emergence of Web 2.0 to support our users, such as video, RSS feeds, search widgets, and more.

The flexibility in the LibGuide framework provides an opportunity for librarians to focus on selection and design, and allows for the incorporation of a multitude of content types. After our initial move to LibGuides at Wayne State University, we began to think differently about how we could leverage this flexibility to create a resource that serves as a learning support system and a mechanism for meeting repetitive instructional demands from our large multi-section courses.

We began by discussing LibGuides as an integrated strategy in our instruction program. LibGuides allows for instructional intervention at appropriate points, instead of relying on instructor, lab, and course time availability. We also looked at our instructional demands (and shrinking staff) and understood there were a variety of instructional needs that LibGuides could be leveraged to meet. As an instruction tool, LibGuides could support

- Synchronous use in classroom teaching
- Asynchronous use as an independent learning tool for students to support specific assignments or course outcomes
- Training the trainer—in our case, faculty or graduate teaching assistants teaching multi-section courses that historically integrated assignment-related face-to-face library instruction

We realized that if we were to use LibGuides to bring together and deliver instructional materials and resources for these purposes, we would need to consider pedagogical principles to effectively develop guides to meet those instruction needs. (See table 7.1.)

TABLE 7.1

Incorporate these learning theories to make LibGuides a teaching tool

Theory	Definition	LibGuide Page Example
Metacognition	"Thinking about thinking." The collection of activities and skills demonstrated by the learner as they plan, monitor, evaluate and repair their own performance on a task	Model appropriate steps to help students plan a successful route to task completion, and provide a link to help (reference desk, embedded librarian, chat reference), so students can get feedback to correct performance if their attempt is unsuccessful.
Chunking	Dividing explanations of a process or concept into smaller units in order to facilitate understanding	Create small content boxes, resize columns to create visual support for the chunked units, use color to emphasize important points or steps.
Cognitive load	The theoretical construct that describes information processing in long-term and short-term memory, and how limitations of short-term (or working) memory can impede learning.	Use chunking to present similar information and processes, use consistent language, minimize extraneous text and resources.
Scaffolding	Providing all resources and guidance by an expert to the novice learner to support discovery of new concepts and knowledge	Develop specific resources and demonstration videos that are strategically aligned to the learning outcomes of the corresponding assignment, and place them within the appropriate context in the guide.
Working memory	What a person is able to keep in the forefront of their mind while they are doing tasks such as reading, reasoning, or learning. It is limited in capacity and duration.	Keep content and directions simple, clear, and specific, and implement chunking in design.

Pedagogical and Learner-Centered Design Principles

In all of the situations we identified, we understood that any integrated LibGuides created needed to, within their pages, present an environment that supports individual learning. One way to support the individual learning process is by implementing a method called "scaffolding."

Scaffolding

The term *scaffolding* is generally attributed to Wood, Bruner, and Ross (1976), which was based on their study of Vygotsky's constructivist learning theory. The main tenet underlying the process of scaffolding is that students are provided with all of the resources they need for a learning task plus guidance by an expert to support their discovery of new concepts and knowledge. It is a method of mediating the steps to individual mastery. In the case of LibGuides, the guide itself can act as the expert and mediate this process. Reiser explains that "as applied to software, scaffolding refers to cases in which the tool changes the task in some way so that learners can accomplish tasks that would otherwise be out of their reach" (2004: 275). Scaffolds can be tools, described as memory prompts, or techniques, such as modeling a process (Rosenshine and Meister, 1992: 26). "Effective scaffolding needs to engage students, divide activities into manageable tasks, and direct students' attention to the essential aspects of learning goals" which are set forth by the assignment or through collaborative conversations with the faculty (ERIC Development Team, 2001: 3).

Jamie McKenzie (1999) lays out eight characteristics of successful scaffolding, which supported our design thinking regarding incorporating scaffolding as a teaching and learning strategy into our instructional LibGuides. His steps and our interpretations are set out in table 7.2.

TABLE 7.2

McKenzie's eight characteristics of successful scaffolding
(McKenzie, 1999)

Scaffolding provides clear directions	Explanations are free of acronyms and library lingo, and are written in student-centered language.
Scaffolding clarifies purpose	Guide is strategically aligned to assignment or textbook. Directions and explanations refer back to those documents and assignment outcomes.
Scaffolding keeps students on task	No "nice to know" content—each section sequentially models or provides access to resources aligned with the learning outcome for the assignment or course.
Scaffolding offers assessment to clarify expectations	Provide rubrics, outcome measures, or assignment requirements so students understand how the guide relates to the supporting successful completion of the assignment.
Scaffolding points students to worthy sources	Resources linked are a few selected best. Students will focus on interpretation of information located, not on deciding where to search.
Scaffolding reduces uncertainty, surprise, and disappointment	We commit to checking links and comparing the LibGuide to the assignment regularly, to assure proper functioning and alignment.
Scaffolding delivers efficiency	LibGuide will be aligned with course or assignment goals, incorporate language of assignment and/or course textbook, and meld seamlessly into the course assignment.
Scaffolding creates momentum	LibGuide will model appropriate steps and help students plan a route to successfully complete their assignment.

Metacognition

When scaffolding design creates momentum, propelling students forward in their own learning process, it supports metacognition: a critical thinking skill we so desire to develop in our students. Metacognition is "thinking about thinking." It is associated with a collection of activities and skills demonstrated by the learner as she plans, monitors, evaluates, and repairs her own performance on a task (Kirsh, 2004). This is different than memorizing a strategy. Metacognition includes a self-reflective component whereby the learner examines and improves his own learning strategies using a variety of means available to him. The guides support metacognition by focusing student thinking on the task at hand. The use of prompts (such as exercises in the development of appropriate keywords) and questioning (literally adding a meditative question such as "before moving on, think about. . .") support a reflective process of engaging with the information literacy skills being scaffolded through the LibGuide and the relationship of those skills to successful completion of the assignment.

When designing the actual content of the guide, we understood we needed to be mindful of the design principles aligned with McKenzie's successful scaffolding, and also consider how our learning environment could support a metacognitive learning process. As this chapter continues, we will discuss how these considerations were incorporated in LibGuides designed to align with specific course assignments. Good pedagogical design reduces information overload. Aligning a guide within the context of an assignment requires careful selection and organization of complex resources and processes. These processes and resources need to be isolated and the presentation order needs to be properly sequenced. This can be accomplished through a process called chunking, a term used to describe a method of grouping separate pieces of information together in meaningful ways. When working with complex information, chunking is a strategy that can maintain a learner's focus and reduce distraction from extraneous information (Cooper, 1998: under "2.2 Chunking Information"). Pedagogical strategies such as scaffolding and chunking are supported by the modular design of LibGuides.

THE COURSE GUIDE AS A LEARNING TOOL

LibGuides provide a variety of uses beyond that of the common disciplinary subject guide. As course guides they can be tailored to specific course assignments rather than the entire discipline. These guides can then be used not only by the instructor, but also by the librarian in the classroom who may use the guide as a teaching platform. Either the instructor or the librarian may embed the resource into course management software, such as Blackboard, for students to refer to while working on their assignments. Students, after being introduced to the guide, may then use it as a point of reference as needed.

Cognitive Load

Students, often overwhelmed by the wealth of knowledge presented by librarians during face-to-face instruction, need a way to help reduce the strain on their working memory so that they are able to learn and apply material. Working memory is what a person is able to keep in the forefront of their mind while they are doing tasks such as reading, reasoning, or learning. It is generally thought to be quite limited and not static, meaning chunks of information are being replaced as the person continues the task. Trying to give a person too much information all at once will not give them time to process the information and therefore inhibit the learning process (Cooper, 1998: under "2.6 Working Memory"). Little (2010: 61–62) uses cognitive load theory to make practical suggestions for creating research guides:

1. Tie guides to the course level whenever possible rather than to the broad subject area.
2. Use terminology that is clear and consistent across the library website and provide a guide for basic library and research terms.
3. Provide links to a set of core journal titles or to a relevant subject listing.
4. Include video clips or visual components to provide students with another source for learning skills.
5. Provide clear descriptions of each research guide's purpose and for each resource listed in the guide.
6. Use conversational, not formal, style in the guides: Use "I" and "you" as opposed to the third person.
7. Keep text to a minimum: break up text by using lists or boxes or add images to prompt users' memory as they develop a schema for research and their topic. [Schema is the term used to describe our prior knowledge on a subject and what allows us to build on what we already know.]

8. Increase interactivity using polls, feedback forms, or tutorials.
9. Add a human element by including librarian contact information, pictures, or live chat.
10. Assist students in developing self-regulated learning strategies by breaking down the research process into smaller parts.

These suggestions all work to create a learning experience both in appearance and content that will help balance the information load students will have when using the guide to work on their project. Keeping content and directions simple, clear, and specific reduces the effort it will take to process the information and therefore reduce the load the working memory has to process, allowing the student to reason and learn rather than merely trying to comprehend the page.

Many of these suggestions can be translated to the embedded course guide. However, a specific course guide must also incorporate a few more principles to be effective. Large, disciplinary subject guides may still provide access to more resources than a student would ever need to complete an assignment. This is described by Schwartz (2004) as the "tyranny of choice" which can be paralyzing. Course guides, in contrast to subject guides that provide all resources available, should therefore provide a limited number of resources tailored to the assignment. Furthermore, the course guide should be seen as a scaffold on which students are given the necessary information to complete a particular assignment that may build on previous information rather than giving students all the resources to be used for the entire course all at once.

Wayne State University is a large urban research institution with an undergraduate population exceeding 20,000 students during the fall 2010 semester. A population this large can contain 20 to 30 sections of general education courses a semester, with many of the instructors being adjunct faculty. It can be extremely difficult for one library liaison to provide instruction for all these sections—let alone keep track of the faculty involved each semester. To further complicate the difficulties, a number of the class sections are moving online to Blackboard. Therefore to meet the demand for instruction, a single unified tool was needed to provide support for both types of courses and to provide a framework so that any librarian could come into the classroom and teach the course. The next section will describe how we applied the learning theory discussed thus far to an oral communication requirement.

■ CASE STUDY ■

COM 1010

The Oral Communications Requirement

LibGuides provides an easy-to-use platform for librarians to create and mold research tools for students. While the general subject guide has been a universal tool in libraries, the course-specific guide has become more prevalent as academic librarians work to help students navigate the increasingly complex information world. Using library liaison connections with departments, librarians can help students connect with the right resources for their specific course assignments using LibGuides, inside or outside the classroom.

The oral communications course, COM 1010, at Wayne State University is offered as part of the general education requirement for undergraduate students. Students who take the course can therefore range from a first-year student to a senior. The Communications Department traditionally offers over forty sections of the COM 1010 course each semester, taught by a variety of faculty, adjuncts, and graduate students; however there is one overall coordinator. The "COM 1010 LibGuide" (Befus, 2011) was created in order to provide students with instruction independent of the course and as a supplement to the course pack that was designed by the department faculty. It was also intended to provide librarians who are teaching face-to-face classes with a framework for their instruction. (See table 7.3.)

TABLE 7.3

Make your LibGuide a learning tool by using these strategies: Examples from COM 1010

Strategy	LibGuide Page Example
Make your LibGuide course-specific	COM 1010 page is focused on COM 1010 class assignments only.
Use past experience to generate content	COM 1010 page content is developed directly from face-to-face experience teaching the course.
Keep information assignment-specific	Databases and resources are chosen specifically for the class and not Communication as a discipline.
Include additional resource for students	Provide information for services and resources useful for the particular assignment, such as citation guides or the writing center.

Make Your LibGuide Course-Specific

The course requires students to give four individual speeches throughout the semester, with topics left up to the students' discretion. The first speech is a personal narrative and the only speech that requires no outside research. The next three speeches are an informative speech, a persuasive speech, and finally a ceremonial speech. Each of these last three speeches requires that the students use outside research to support their topic. The research-based speeches specify that students use a variety of references, and at least three of these must be different types of sources. Students may choose any of the following resources: websites, books, blogs, and interviews. Instructors tend to place emphasis, however, on having students work with scholarly articles.

The COM 1010 instructors all use Blackboard as their course management software. Five online-only instructors were provided with the ability to embed the LibGuide material directly into their site. At Wayne State, Blackboard is set up to provide instructors with a stock button for Library Resources which links directly to the subject guide for that particular course. In the case of COM 1010 this link points directly to the LibGuide for the course.

Design Course LibGuide

Applying Little's tenth practical suggestion (2010), the guide is broken down into the three research-based speeches that are required of students in the COM 1010 course. The major portion of the guide, which is 758 pixels wide and aligned to the left, provides the information and resources needed to complete each of the speeches, and boxes are labeled to correspond to the specific speech (see figure 7.1). The language used to describe the requirements of the speech is taken directly from the COM 1010 course pack.

Use Past Experience to Generate Content

The second speech, as mentioned above, is the first assignment that requires students to perform library research (see figure 7.1). The article databases chosen for their research are all multidisciplinary. The description indicates the three types of sources available in them (scholarly journal articles, magazines, and

FIGURE 7.1

COM 1010 LibGuide layout, Wayne State University, created
by Rebeca Befus, but no longer available online

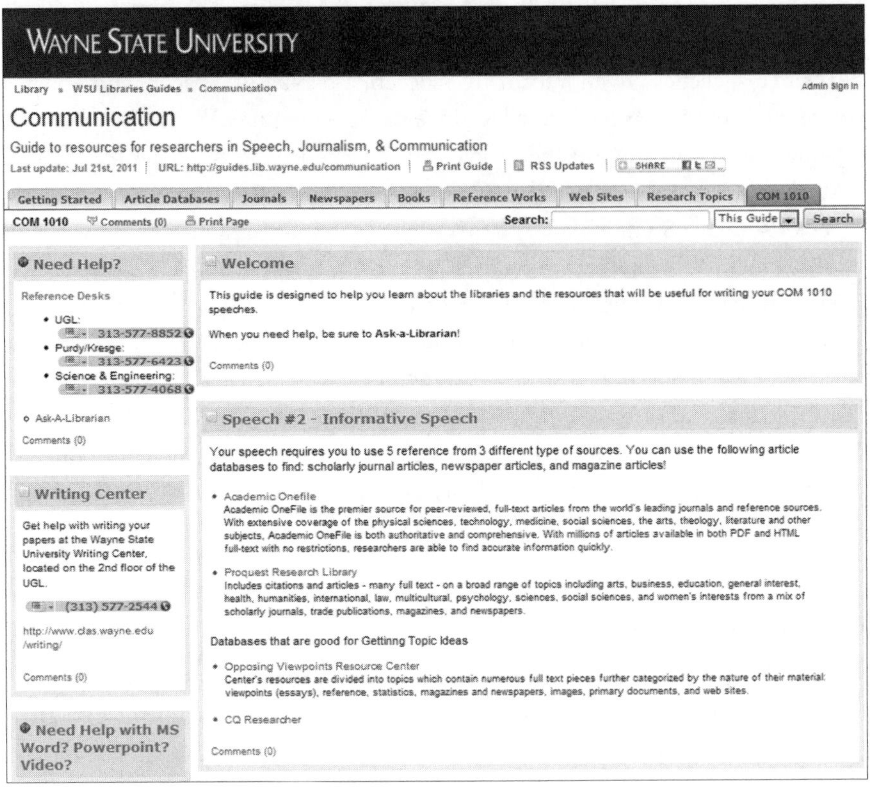

Used by permission of Wayne State University Library System

newspapers), showing students they can fulfill their research requirement just by using a single library database. Past experience working with these students has shown that topic ideas are generally a roadblock for them. Therefore, in order to supplement the topic ideas provided in the course pack, two databases have been included in the list that provides popular topic suggestions for Wayne State students. Because books are not included in the databases but are considered a valid source for their speech, a video is included below the box for Speech #2 followed by a catalog search box for students to use. (See figure 7.2.)

FIGURE 7.2
COM 1010 box for Speech #2, Wayne State University, created
by Rebeca Befus, but no longer available online

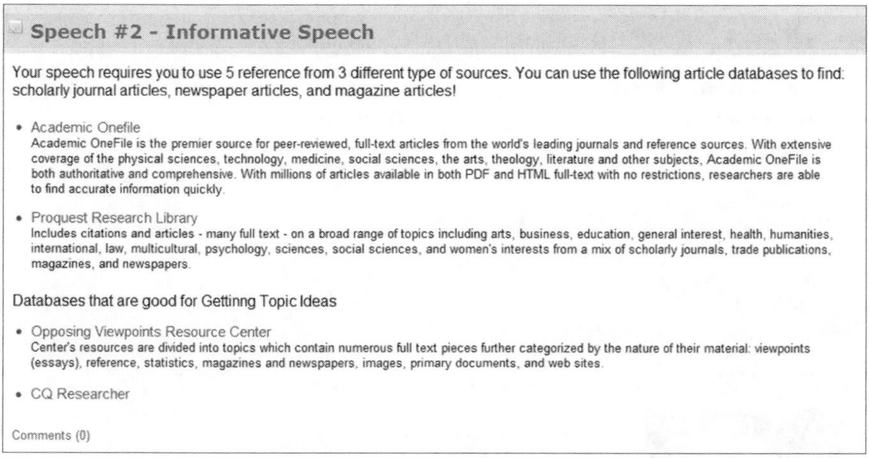

Speech #2 - Informative Speech

Your speech requires you to use 5 reference from 3 different type of sources. You can use the following article databases to find:
scholarly journal articles, newspaper articles, and magazine articles!

- Academic Onefile
  Academic OneFile is the premier source for peer-reviewed, full-text articles from the world's leading journals and reference sources. With extensive
  coverage of the physical sciences, technology, medicine, social sciences, the arts, theology, literature and other subjects, Academic OneFile is
  both authoritative and comprehensive. With millions of articles available in both PDF and HTML full-text with no restrictions, researchers are able
  to find accurate information quickly.

- Proquest Research Library
  Includes citations and articles - many full text - on a broad range of topics including arts, business, education, general interest, health, humanities,
  international, law, multicultural, psychology, sciences, social sciences, and women's interests from a mix of scholarly journals, trade publications,
  magazines, and newspapers.

Databases that are good for Gettinng Topic Ideas

- Opposing Viewpoints Resource Center
  Center's resources are divided into topics which contain numerous full text pieces further categorized by the nature of their material: viewpoints
  (essays), reference, statistics, magazines and newspapers, images, primary documents, and web sites.

- CQ Researcher

Comments (0)

Used by permission of Wayne State University Library System

Keep Information Assignment Specific

The third, or persuasive speech, is often centered on a current event and thus requires students not only to use journal databases to find articles, but to also enhance their speech with newspaper articles (see figure 7.3). Because students have already been exposed to resources for finding articles and books, the information box for speech #3 does not reiterate the article database list; rather, it is assumed students will build on and use their previous knowledge (see figure 7.3). Instead, links to specific newspaper resources are included along with a description reminding students to refer to the information for speech #2.

The final box pertains to speech #4, which asks students to perform a ceremonial speech about a person, place, or thing (see figure 7.3). Therefore the resources provided all have a biographical or historical purpose. The use of vendor widgets, such as the Gale Virtual Reference Library widget, provides students with a simple way to search the resource directly from the guide.

Include Additional Resources for Students

Extra information is provided along the left side of the guide in a column with the width of 209 pixels (see figure 7.1). This information points students to library

FIGURE 7.3

COM 1010 box for Speech #3 and Speech #4, Wayne State University, created by Rebeca Befus, but no longer available online

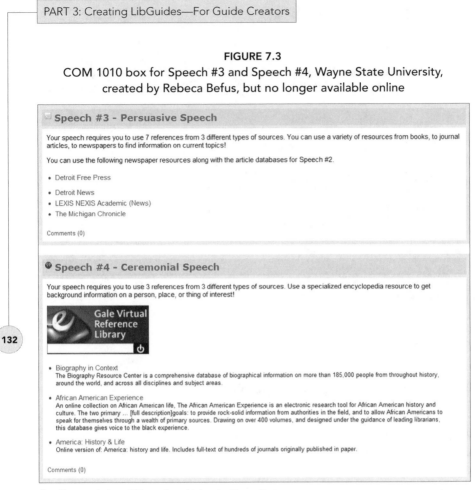

Used by permission of Wayne State University Library System

help resources such as Ask-a-Librarian, video tutorials, and the Student Technology Studio as well as the University Writing Center. This information is described in a way that shows the student how it can be used for their course and is not embedded in the main content area so as not to create distraction from the material.

As part of the general education curriculum, the COM 1010 course is not taken in any particular sequence; therefore some students may have received library instruction in one or more previous courses while others may not have received instruction at all. This common issue was discussed by Quinn and Underwood (2010), who decided that although students may receive library instruction in other courses, the Speech 101 course would be a good course to embed instruction in as it was the general education course with a university-required information literacy component. At Wayne State we have no universal information literacy education built into the curriculum, so we needed to not only teach students how to research for their speech topics but also provide students with a simple foundation in research skills in order for them to understand how to use the resources incorporated into the guide.

In order to improve students' ability to use the resources provided in the LibGuide, instructors are encouraged by their library liaison and the COM 1010 coordinator to assign re:Search (www.lib.wayne.edu/services/instruction/research), our online information literacy tutorial, which provides students with the basics of using the catalog and article databases as well as developing keywords and evaluating sources. This approach to tiered learning can be successfully accomplished whether librarians are working directly in the classroom with students, or if instructors are using the guide independently from in-person instruction. Professors are also given access to a Respondus version of the quizzes that are imbedded in the re:Search tutorial—which they can then embed in Blackboard and use to assess students. Using this tool in conjunction with face-to-face instruction or simply providing access to the guide creates the necessary scaffolding to help students retain and learn the desired skills.

In this COM 1010 example, the liaison librarian took the initiative to create a set of LibGuides based on course materials collected and from previous instructional experience with the course. This approach requires that the librarian obtain buy-in from the faculty after the guide is made. Updates can be made as faculty become more comfortable with using the guide as a learning tool for their students. Another approach would be to involve faculty in the entire creation process in a collaborative effort, giving librarian and faculty members a chance to specifically target student and instructor needs.

■ ■ ■

COLLABORATIVE LIBGUIDE DESIGN

The LibGuides platform encourages a collaborative process through its ease of initial guide development and instant implementation of subsequent changes. Starting with a strong faculty-librarian connection, the decision to create a guide collaboratively involves defining a clear purpose and relevant content, followed by good planning and an iterative process to bring the guide to life. (See table 7.4.) Once created, the guide must be actively integrated into the course through promotion and training.

TABLE 7.4

Make your LibGuide a collaborative tool by using these strategies: Examples from ENG 3010

Strategy	LibGuide Page Example
Seek opportunities in liaison relationships	Existing liaison relationship with composition faculty leads to inclusion in meetings of composition committee undertaking a syllabus revision for ENG 3010.
Collaborate on a page plan	English department liaison and composition committee meet and discuss goals and content for the proposed page.
Draft page and seek feedback	Librarian drafts a page based on mutual goals and content and presents it to committee for feedback.
Integrate page into course	Librarian provides training for ENG 3010 instructors on use of the ENG 3010 page.

The types of customization described with the COM 1010 guide and the resulting benefits for learning and teaching invite collaboration with faculty to design this teaching and learning tool. A recent article (Little et al., 2010) discusses the collaborative development of a research method LibGuide by a faculty learning community. LibGuides offered the advantages of accommodating multiple authors as well as Web 2.0 technologies (Little et al.: 435). As the preceding section discussed, course-focused guides can be designed to effectively support specific courses and assignments. Flexibility in design opens the door to creating assignment or research topic areas and chunking information. Columns can be resized and boxes can use color to highlight key concepts or assignments. Most of all, control over the creation and updating of the guide places a powerful pedagogical tool in the hands of the librarian, one benefit being that it "provides an easy template for editing that does not require extensive programming skills" (Little et al., 2010: 435).

Writing-intensive general education courses such as English Composition provide a natural context for library instruction and are often the site for collaboration between librarians and faculty. In the early 1980s Ford (1982) identified the potential for an integrated approach to teaching information literacy. More recently, discussions by Kautzman (1996) and Elmborg (2003) have touted the composition classroom as a suitable context for teaching research skills and critical thinking. The natural alignment of the writing and research process presents an opportunity to provide meaningful information literacy instruction at a natural point of need. Writing across the curriculum courses provides a common ground where information literacy can take root (Elmborg, 2003: 79).

■ CASE STUDY ■

ENG 3010
The Intermediate Composition Requirement

ENG 3010, Intermediate Writing (see figure 7.4), is a writing-intensive course on writing in the disciplines and as such is the type of environment identified by Elmborg (2003) as fertile ground for information literacy instruction. It is described in the Wayne State University Undergraduate Bulletin as a "course in reading, research and writing for upper-level students" focusing on "conducting research by drawing from the sciences, social sciences, humanities, and professions in preparation for Writing Intensive courses in the majors" (Wayne State University, 2011). Approximately thirty sections are offered per semester. As a writing course and a general education requirement for the Writing Intensive competency, this course provides a strategic environment for information literacy instruction.

135

Seek Opportunities in Liaison Relationships

Curriculum revision projects combined with strong librarian-faculty relationships can introduce opportunities to integrate information literacy into sequenced

FIGURE 7.4
ENG 3010 LibGuide Layout, Wayne State University,
created by Judith Arnold, http://guides.lib.wayne.edu/English

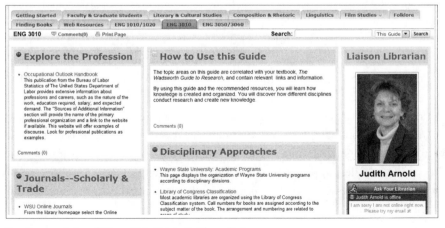

Used by permission of Wayne State University Library System

composition courses, as has been effectively discussed by Holliday and Fagerheim (2006). In our case, an established liaison relationship opened the door to an opportunity to collaborate at the curriculum level, using a syllabus revision project as the entré to incorporating information literacy instruction through a customized LibGuide. Following a discussion with the department's director of composition, the librarian liaison was invited to meet with the department's composition committee to discuss creating a course guide for ENG 3010. The timing was fortuitous. The committee was in the midst of developing a common syllabus for the course and welcomed the opportunity to incorporate the library in a meaningful way as they crafted a plan for teaching this course. The director was particularly interested in creating a teaching tool for the course instructors, most of whom are graduate teaching assistants (GTAs). Her belief was that this guide could provide support for the new common syllabus and specific guidance that would help the instructors to teach research resources to their students.

Collaborate on a Guide Plan

Three meetings were devoted to discussion and planning for the guide. The first meeting involved a discussion of the rationale and goals for the guide and how it might be jointly developed. Primary among the goals was the need to accommodate projects and students in many disciplines, most frequently nursing, pre-med, education, and business. A major objective for the guide was to help students identify databases for their literature reviews and research proposals. A first step was identified: to generate key terms from the text to serve as an organizational structure for the guide and to provide consistent terminology for students. The content was to be limited and focused by the common syllabus and the course textbook, *The Wadsworth Guide to Research* (Miller-Cochran and Rodrigo, 2009). Additionally, the committee emphasized the need for a Help or FAQ section that would offer strategies for students who get stuck. There was agreement that links to relevant instructional videos should also be incorporated into the guide. The committee agreed that the array of disciplinary LibGuides should be incorporated into course assignments that required students to compile a list of journals in the field and select appropriate databases for searching in the discipline. There was also an expressed need for supporting the goal of introducing students to multidisciplinary approaches to research.

Draft Guide and Seek Feedback

Taking the list of suggestions from the committee, the liaison librarian created a draft of the course guide to be presented at the subsequent meeting. The exhortation to "mirror the textbook" led to the creation of content categories and language that took terminology straight from the pages of the text: disciplinary approaches, exploring a topic, the research proposal, the review of research, primary research, and qualitative and quantitative research. This technique implemented the scaffolding efficiency referenced in the first section of this chapter by melding the textbook with the guide. Other categories that the committee suggested after review of the draft guide included core scholarly journals and the annotated bibliography. Supplemental and subordinate to these topics were content areas related to Help: How to Use the Guide, Finding Resources by Discipline, Library Learning Tools and Videos, FAQs, and Help contact numbers.

In the process of developing these defined content areas, these principles reigned:

137

Pedagogical Purpose: Offer content that instructors or librarians can use in teaching.

Limiting Choices: Keep links to a minimum to avoid distraction and overwhelming choices.

One good example of these principles at work is the development of the section on Disciplinary Approaches. Instructors were interested in helping students understand the organization of knowledge. The goal of this section was to expand upon that concept and provide examples of disciplinary perspectives. A listing of academic departments of the university provides one example of how areas of study are organized under different colleges and divisions. Exploring deeper into this structure could help the student see how various programs and degrees relate to the humanities, social sciences, and sciences categories that their course textbook presents. Likewise, the Library of Congress Classification system link places fields of study within a large organizational scheme that helps illustrate how these disciplines are defined, and it serves a double benefit by familiarizing students with the arrangement of library resources. A link to the library Subject Guides (LibGuides) further illustrates the variety of disciplinary study through the specialization and variety of resources featured from guide to guide. The remaining examples included in this content box are citation styles, which also help define how different disciplines approach documentation of sources. All of these links can be used by an instructor as teaching examples to illustrate disciplinary study, with examples that are close to the student's collegiate experience.

The remainder of the guide was created following similar design principles (Arnold, 2011). A content box for Exploring a Topic coordinated with the textbook discussion by offering an online reference portal, the Gale Virtual Reference Library, and a library database featuring current issues, CQ Researcher, as strategies for discovering a topic (figure 7.5).

FIGURE 7.5
Exploring a topic box for ENG 3010, Wayne State University,
created by Judith Arnold, http://guides.lib.wayne.edu/english

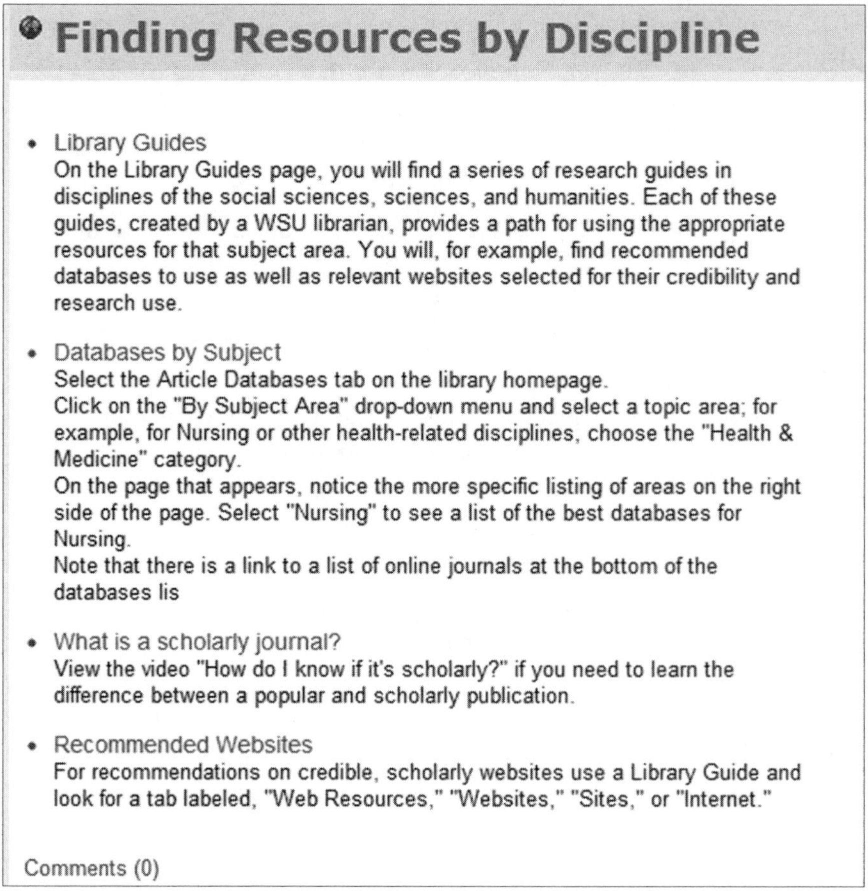

Finding Resources by Discipline

- Library Guides
  On the Library Guides page, you will find a series of research guides in disciplines of the social sciences, sciences, and humanities. Each of these guides, created by a WSU librarian, provides a path for using the appropriate resources for that subject area. You will, for example, find recommended databases to use as well as relevant websites selected for their credibility and research use.

- Databases by Subject
  Select the Article Databases tab on the library homepage.
  Click on the "By Subject Area" drop-down menu and select a topic area; for example, for Nursing or other health-related disciplines, choose the "Health & Medicine" category.
  On the page that appears, notice the more specific listing of areas on the right side of the page. Select "Nursing" to see a list of the best databases for Nursing.
  Note that there is a link to a list of online journals at the bottom of the databases lis

- What is a scholarly journal?
  View the video "How do I know if it's scholarly?" if you need to learn the difference between a popular and scholarly publication.

- Recommended Websites
  For recommendations on credible, scholarly websites use a Library Guide and look for a tab labeled, "Web Resources," "Websites," "Sites," or "Internet."

Comments (0)

Used by permission of Wayne State University Library System

Content boxes for Research Methods, the Research Proposal, and the Review of Research were designed to offer links to sites that define and provide examples. Again, limiting choices with one or two links avoids students being overwhelmed by endless lists, plus instructors appreciate specific examples at hand to help them clarify the points for their students. The composition committee requested the Annotated Bibliography and Core Scholarly Journals as topic areas in order to provide support for course assignments on becoming familiar with the journal literature in the students' majors. The remainder of the page was devoted to Help options: Finding Resources by Discipline, FAQs, a video on Scholarly Journals, a link to the Library videos on YouTube, a link to re:Search, our online learning tool to introduce students to the library, a list of phone numbers for reference desks, as well as the link to the Ask-a-Librarian service. These options were placed on the periphery so as not to detract from the core information related to assignments and textbook content.

139

Integrate Guide into Course

Course instructors were urged to incorporate the guide into their courses. A training session was held to introduce graduate teaching assistants to the ENG 3010 (and the existing ENG 1010/1020) guide as teaching support. The Wayne State University English Department's common syllabus for the course included a substantive section on using the library and its resources, urging that "the Undergraduate Library and its website should be a major resource for teaching research skills in ENG 3010. . . . On the English Guide, there is a special tab for ENG 3010, which has . . . topic areas in the center [that] are correlated to chapters in the Wadsworth Guide" (Wayne State University, Department of English, 2010). In addition, integration of the page was accomplished through the direct link from the Library Resources button in Blackboard, which supported over 800 hits to the page in fall 2011.

Benefits of Collaboration

Informal feedback from course instructors has been positive in relation to use of the guide as a tool for students and as a pedagogical aid for the instructors. Some instructors continue to request live instruction sessions where the liaison librarian provides an orientation to the guide and uses it to teach the session. In a brief survey on course guides, about half of the GTAs expressed reluctance to use the page alone, expressing their view that students benefited from becoming acquainted with and being taught by librarians. Developing the ENG 3010 guide in a collaborative process resulted in a level of curriculum integration that was heretofore unrealized. Similar course guides for the freshman composition sequence have been created in collaboration with course instructors to support key essay assignments. The two-level course guide development is the first step in attempting to sequence and scaffold learning in the writing courses, a goal that is within reach, though not yet realized. Collaboration with faculty at the curriculum level can help reach this goal and transform the LibGuide course guide from a course support resource into a learning tool that is central to the assignments and teaching of the course.

■ ■ ■

CONCLUSION

This chapter began by discussing elements of learner-centered pedagogical design principles such as scaffolding, chunking, and cognitive load. The COM 1010 Case Study showed how integrating these principles, and creating guides that reflect assignment structure, vocabulary, and course resources, can lead students and faculty to embrace the guide as an integral part of the course. The ENG 3010 Case Study illustrated how faculty and librarians working collaboratively on a course page can facilitate the integration of essential resources at the curriculum level, supporting students and providing faculty with a teaching tool. Through these examples, the chapter demonstrated how applying these strategies in guide and page design can transform a LibGuide from a list of links into a dynamic learning tool.

When guides are used in face-to-face instruction and provided to students after the session, they can serve to mediate the recall of memory after the class session. The LibGuide serves as an aid that decreases reliance on memory and provides a place where the goals of completing an assignment and using library resources intersect. Effective LibGuides created for asynchronous use provide sufficient guidance to serve as a scaffold for building student information literacy skills, and provide opportunities for reflection to support self-regulated learning.

The flexibility and infinite design options offered by LibGuides require us to be mindful, in this role of designer, of staying focused on content, providing limited options, and providing basic direction in succinct student-centered language. Schwartz (2004: B-6) addressed the impact of reducing choice in his research, which illustrated this interesting phenomenon, "Students given 30 topics from which to choose to write an extra-credit essay are less likely to write one than those given six. And if they do write one, it tends to be of lower quality." He contends that too much choice can be anxiety-producing and debilitating. We can avoid this by pointing the student to only the most worthy of sources. Being cognizant of good design strategies when developing an assignment or course-integrated guide will ultimately result in a scaffolding tool that will help students stay focused on the learning or information discovery outcome desired. As librarians, we are not doing our students a disservice by severely limiting their choices and guiding their learning. Leading them with direct links to the most appropriate resources, providing videos or other materials that model appropriate processes, and offering tools such as worksheets or other strategies to help them organize their work, support learning and assignment outcomes and allow students to focus on the process of discovering, synthesizing, and producing new content.

REFERENCES

Arnold, Judith. 2011. "ENG 3010 LibGuide." Wayne State University System. http://guides.lib.wayne.edu/content.php?pid=62407&sid=848449 (no longer available).

Befus, Rebeca. 2011. "COM 1010 LibGuide." Wayne State University System. http://guides.lib.wayne.edu/content.php?pid=72657&sid=1482999 (no longer available).

Cooper, Graham. 1998. "Research into Cognitive Load Theory and Instructional Design at UNSW." University of New South Wales, Sydney, Australia. http://dwb4.unl.edu/Diss/Cooper/UNSW.htm.

Elmborg, James K. 2003. "Information Literacy and Writing across the Curriculum: Sharing the Vision." *Reference Services Review* 31, no. 1: 68–80.

ERIC Development Team. 2001. "Learning to Learn: Preparing Teachers and Students for Problem-Based Learning." *ERIC Digests.* ED457524. www.eric.ed.gov/PDFS/ED457524.pdf.

Ford, James E. 1982. "The Natural Alliance between Librarians and English Teachers in Course-Related Library Use Instruction." *College and Research Libraries* 43, no. 5: 379–84.

Holliday, Wendy, and Britt Fagerheim. 2006. "Integrating Information Literacy with a Sequenced English Composition Curriculum." *Portal: Libraries and the Academy* 6, no. 2: 169–84.

Kautzman, Amy M. 1996. "Teaching Critical Thinking: The Alliance of Composition Studies and Research Instruction." *RSR: Reference Services Review* 24, no. 3: 61–65.

Kirsh, David. 2004. "Metacognition, Distributed Cognition, and Visual Design." In *Cognition, Education, and Communication Technology,* edited by Peter Gardenfors and Petter Johansson. Hillsdale, NJ: Earlbaum.

Little, Jennifer J. 2010. "Cognitive Load Theory and Library Research Guides." *Internet Reference Services Quarterly* 15, no. 1: 53–63.

Little, Jennifer J., Moira Fallon, Jason Dauenhauer, Betsy Balzano, and Donald Halquist. 2010. "Interdisciplinary Collaboration: A Faculty Learning Community Creates a Comprehensive LibGuide." *Reference Services Review* 38, no. 3: 431–44.

McKenzie, Jamie. 1999. "Scaffolding for Success." *From Now On: The Educational Technology Journal* 9, no. 4. http://fno.org/dec99/scaffold.html.

Miller-Cochran, Susan K., and Rochelle L. Rodrigo. 2009. *The Wadsworth Guide to Research.* Boston: Wadsworth.

Quinn, Todd, and Jonna Underwood. 2010. "Going Hybrid: Combining In-Class and Online Instruction for Speech 101." Paper presented at the Off-Campus Library Services Conference, Cleveland, OH, April 28–30.

Reiser, Brian J. 2004. "Scaffolding Complex Learning: The Mechanisms of Structuring and Problematizing Student Work." *Journal of the Learning Sciences,* 13, no. 3: 273–304.

Rosenshine, Barak, and Carla Meister. 1992. "The Use of Scaffolds for Teaching Higher-Level Cognitive Strategies." *Educational Leadership* 49, no. 7: 26–33.

Schwartz, Barry. 2004. "The Tyranny of Choice." *Chronicle of Higher Education* 50, no. 20: B-6.

Wayne State University. 2011. *Undergraduate Bulletin 2011–2013.* www.bulletins.wayne.edu/ubk-output.

Wayne State University, Department of English. 2010. "New Common Syllabus for ENG 3010, Intermediate College Writing." Unpublished document.

Wood, David, Jerome S. Bruner, and Gail Ross. 1976. "The Role of Tutoring in Problem Solving." *Journal of Child Psychology & Psychiatry & Allied Disciplines* 17, no. 2: 89–100.

## Chapter Eight

Creating Your First LibGuide

Kenneth Liss

Your LibGuides administrator has set up an account for you. You are now officially a LibGuides author. You are, no doubt, eager to dig in and create your first guide. But how do you begin? This chapter offers everything you need to get started. It will cover:

- Managing your LibGuides profile
- Understanding the basic structure of LibGuides
- Creating new guides (starting fresh or from a template)
- Common box types and how to use them
- Adding, editing, and formatting content
- Publishing your guides
- Getting help.

You will learn more advanced features in chapter 9, but these basics are all you will need to get on your way. The best way to learn to use LibGuides is to get in there and start working. You can create guides without anyone—other than your LibGuides colleagues—seeing the results.

At Boston College (BC), librarians have found LibGuides to be fun—even addictive—to use, and that has made the system easy to learn. BC adopted the software in August 2007 and converted seventy-five single-page, scrolling guides to the new format in four weeks to be ready for the start of the academic year. The number, variety, and quality of our guides have continued to grow as new features and new ideas have been incorporated into the product and the way we use it. More than 2,000 other libraries have joined the LibGuides community since we came on board. Now you can join in, too.

YOUR LIBGUIDES PROFILE

Every LibGuides author has a profile. Your customizable profile lets visitors know who you are and how to get in touch with you. Profile information appears in a box that is shown, by default, on every page you create in the system. You also have a LibGuides profile page—the gateway to your guides and the center of your LibGuides identity. Your LibGuides profile may not say as much about you as some of your other online pages, but you may find it is the first thing that comes up when someone searches your name in Google. You can include links to a personal page as well as Facebook, Twitter, LinkedIn, and other networks if you want people to learn even more about you.

To manage your profile, sign in to your LibGuides account by clicking on Admin Sign In on your library's main LibGuides web page. This will take you to your Dashboard page, which is command central for everything an author does in LibGuides. The first time you sign in, the main page will appear with the command bar at top, announcements and quick links, and a profile box showing only your name and a link, Profile & Guides, to your profile page. Click on Edit at the top of the profile box to customize your profile.

Using the profile editing form (see figure 8.1), enter the following information to create a basic profile:

> **Profile Box Title.** The default title is "Subject Guide" but you can change it to your job title or something else. (It can also be changed later in each guide that you create.)
>
> **Profile Image.** Select Upload a New Image from My Computer to upload a profile image of yourself or of something that you feel is representative of you.
>
> **Display Name.** You can change this to display a different form of your name than the one assigned to your LibGuides account.
>
> **E-mail.** This will not display your e-mail address but will activate an e-mail form which visitors can use to contact you.

FIGURE 8.1
LibGuides profile editing form

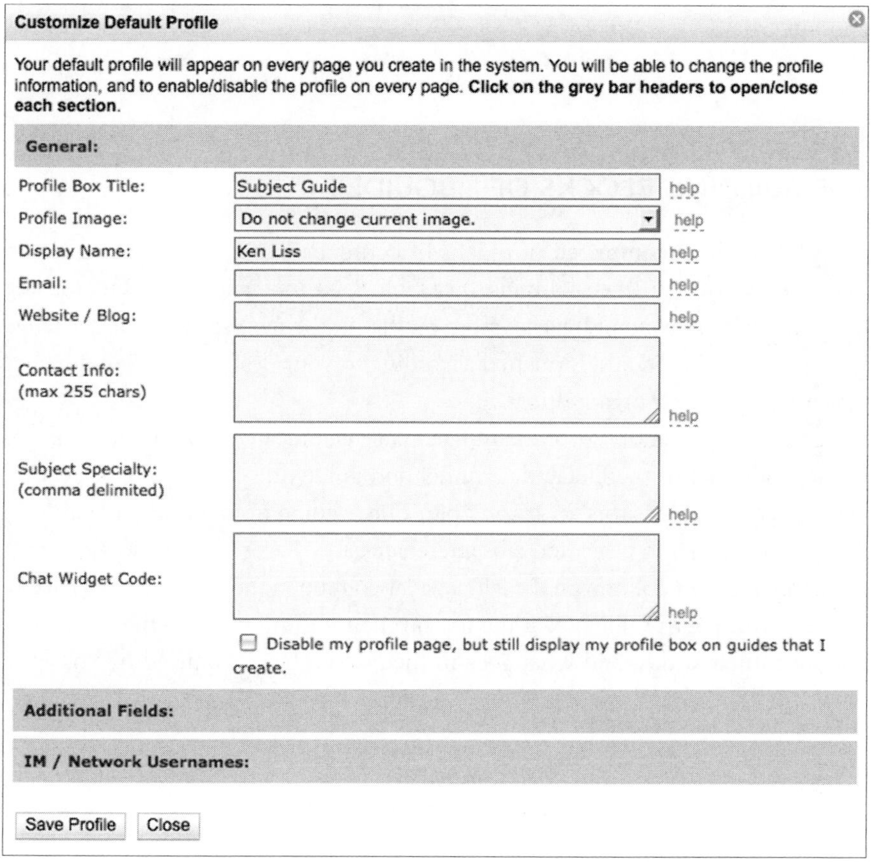

Customize Default Profile   ⊗

Your default profile will appear on every page you create in the system. You will be able to change the profile information, and to enable/disable the profile on every page. **Click on the grey bar headers to open/close each section.**

General:

Profile Box Title:	Subject Guide	help
Profile Image:	Do not change current image. ▾	help
Display Name:	Ken Liss	help
Email:		help
Website / Blog:		help
Contact Info: (max 255 chars)		help
Subject Specialty: (comma delimited)		help
Chat Widget Code:		help

☐ Disable my profile page, but still display my profile box on guides that I create.

Additional Fields:

IM / Network Usernames:

[Save Profile] [Close]

Used by permission of Springshare, LLC

Contact Info. This can include the location of your office, your phone number and mailing address, and any other information you want to include (maximum of 255 characters).

Subject Specialty. Enter your subject or subjects (separated by commas). If you use the subject categories included in your library's LibGuide system they will link to a page with all of the guides in that category.

Additional options you can add to your profile include a website or blog address, code for a chat widget, instant messaging and network user names, or an introductory video. These items can each be changed at a later time. Next we will take a look directly at LibGuides and discuss how your guides will be structured and built.

PAGES, COLUMNS, AND BOXES: THE BUILDING BLOCKS OF LIBGUIDES

Each LibGuide is comprised of blocks of content placed in content boxes on pages of one, two, or three columns. (See table 8.1.) You create the content, using different kinds of content boxes—more on that in the next section—and arrange it on pages organized and formatted according to your design and the guidelines or templates of your organization.

A guide can be one page or many. Each page is indicated by a tab near the top of the guide (below the LibGuides banner and guide title). These tabs appear on every page and let visitors access any part of the guide from anywhere within it. Authors often refer to pages and tabs interchangeably. Pages, by default, have three columns: a narrow column on the left, a wider column in the middle, and a narrow column with your profile box at the top on the right. All of this—the number of columns, their width, and what goes in them—can be customized by you on a

TABLE 8.1
LibGuides terms and definitions

Term	Definition
Column	A vertical division of a page in a LibGuide. Each guide can have 1–3 columns.
Content box or box	An enclosed area on a LibGuides page containing text, images, media, links, and/or other content.
LibGuide or guide	An individual guide consisting of one or more pages.
LibGuides	The underlying software and system provided by Springshare to create, manage, and present individual guides and collections of guides. Also used by individual institutions as the name for their particular sets of guides.
Page	A single screen of content, arranged in one or more columns and boxes within a guide. The words *page* and *tab* are often used interchangeably.
Tab	A navigational element near the top of a guide that links to a particular page.

page-by-page basis. Chapter 6 has some suggestions about resizing the width of columns to enhance content readability and usefulness.

CREATING A NEW GUIDE

Click on Create New Guide on your Dashboard page and you will be given a choice: Start Fresh or Use a Template. If you use an existing guide as a template—one of your own, one of your library's, or one from another organization—everything from that guide will be copied into your new guide for you to work with. If you are starting from scratch, you will begin with a clean slate. There are two key fields to fill in when the Create New Guide form pops up:

> **Guide Title.** The title will appear under your library banner at the top of every page of your guide. It is also how your guide will be listed on your profile page and the index page of your library's LibGuides.

> **Description.** The description will appear under the title on each page of the guide and on index pages.

You can change the title and description later if you need to. After entering the title and description, click on the Create New Guide button and your guide will be ready for your creative hand.

Here are a few things to note about the initial appearance of the new guide:

- The title and description are at the top, below the banner.
- The guide has a three-column setup, with narrow columns on the left and right and a wide column in the center (assuming that your library has chosen the LibGuide default for your guide template).
- The profile box, with all of the information about you that was entered when you set it up, is at the top of the right-hand column.
- There is only one page, or tab, and it has the default name Home.
- There are Add New Box links at the top of the left and center columns and below the profile box in the right column.

The new guide is ready to be filled with content boxes full of valuable information for your users. Some of the most common types of LibGuides content boxes will be discussed in the next section.

LIBGUIDES CONTENT BOXES

As noted above, there are Add New Box links in each column of your new guide. When you add a box, there will be another Add New Box link below it. (You can choose where in the column you want a new box to appear, and you can reorder boxes later.) There are more than twenty different types of content boxes available for use in LibGuides. In this section, we will look at three of the most common types. Chapter 9 will cover several more advanced box types.

- Rich Text boxes
- Simple Web Links
- Links & Lists

Rich Text Boxes

Rich Text boxes—more formally known as Rich Text/Dynamic Content/Scripts boxes—are the most basic and most flexible type of content box in LibGuides. Simply type text in the Rich-Text Editor, click Save and Close and your text will appear. But that is not all. Using the Rich-Text Editor's WYSIWYG toolbar, it is easy to format text in a Rich Text box. You can make text bold, italic, underlined, centered, bulleted, or numbered. You can change font styles, sizes, and colors, and add links and images. Figure 8.2 shows some of the key elements of the Rich-Text Editor toolbar.

A Rich Text box lets you easily create instructions, descriptions, or any kind of narrative information formatted and presented in a way that makes it easy to read. Examples from LibGuides@BC (http://libguides.bc.edu) include

- A definition (with examples) of "primary source" for a guide on Primary Sources in History (http://libguides.bc.edu/primarysourcehistory).

FIGURE 8.2
The rich-text editor toolbar

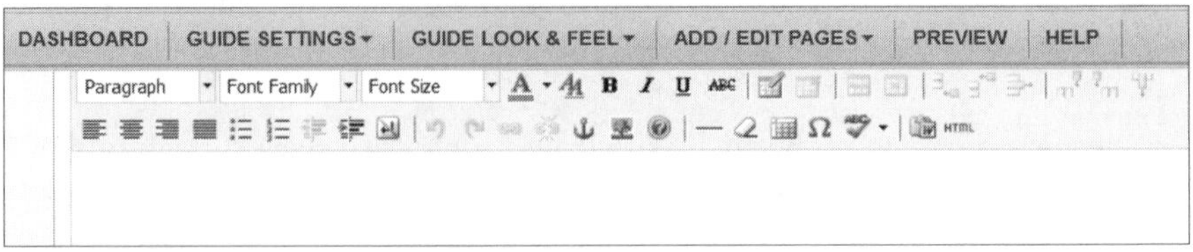

Used by permission of Springshare, LLC

- Instructions (with screenshots) on how to find broadcast transcripts in LexisNexis for a course guide on Crisis Communication (http://libguides.bc.edu/content.php?pid=13647&sid=92385).
- Descriptions of different tools for finding biblical commentary for a Theology guide (http://libguides.bc.edu/content.php?pid=971&sid=610736).
- Instructions for setting up a RefWorks account via the Libraries (http://libguides.bc.edu/content.php?pid=34024&sid=249940).

You can also include descriptive information, using all of the same features, at the top of many other kinds of content boxes, including the next two types we will look at: Simple Web Links and Links & Lists boxes.

One caution about including links in Rich Text content boxes: often during a changeover from HTML to LibGuides, authors will copy the static HTML content of a page and paste it into a LibGuide Rich Text box. Although this is a quick way to get started, it can cause a problem. Although links certainly will work in a Rich Text box, the LibGuides system does not recognize them as links. If your administrator runs the Link Checker tool, any link not in a link box (see the following section) will be ignored.

Simple Web Links and Links & Lists

There are two kinds of link boxes in LibGuides: Simple Web Links and Links & Lists. Both allow you to create lists of resources, presented neatly and consistently without any need for additional formatting. In a Simple Web Links box, you enter the name of the link, the URL, and an optional description of up to 1,000 characters. The links appear in a bulleted list, with the descriptions appearing when you hover the cursor over the name. (See figure 8.3 for an example.) Examples from LibGuides@BC include:

- Quick lists of key resources in different subject areas for subject portals (http://libguides.bc.edu/nursingportal).
- A list of online sources of Irish songs and lyrics for an Irish Music guide (http://libguides.bc.edu/content.php?pid=965&sid=5540).
- A list of popular magazines with advertisements digitized by Google, for a guide on Advertising & Public Relations (http://libguides.bc.edu/content.php?pid=621&sid=1395#965700).

FIGURE 8.3
A simple web links box with mouseover link description

Used by permission of the Boston College University Libraries

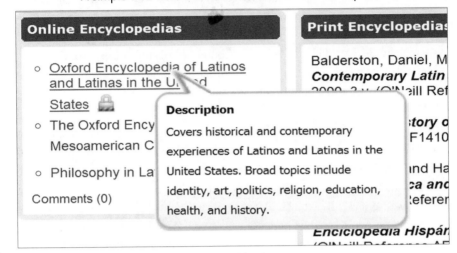

FIGURE 8.4
A Links & Lists box with a "More Information" pop-up

Used by permission of the Boston College University Libraries

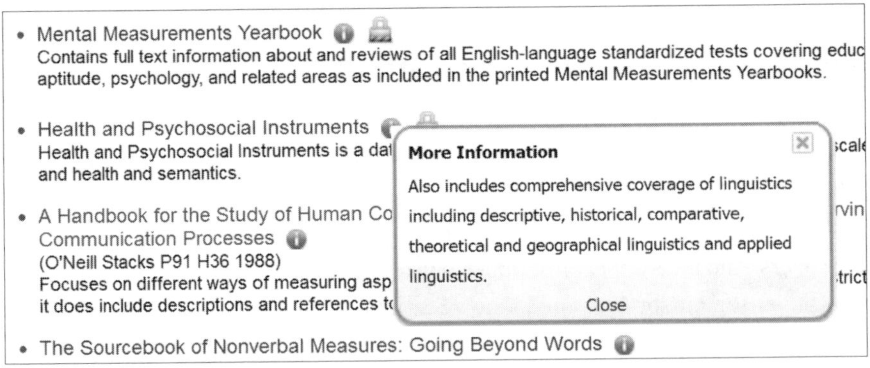

In a Links & Lists box, you enter the name of the link, the URL, an optional description of up to 1,000 characters, and (also optional) additional information of unlimited length. The links appear in a bulleted list with the descriptions beneath the names. If you entered additional information, there will be an information icon that a user can click to bring up that information in a pop-up box. (See figure 8.4 for an example.) Examples of Links & Lists boxes from LibGuides@BC include:

A list of online documents and texts on human rights in a wide center column of a guide on Social Work: Global Practice (http://libguides.bc.edu/content.php?pid=9056&sid=58745).

A list mixing online and print sources of chemical catalogs in a guide on Chemical Laboratory Safety & Methods (http://libguides.bc.edu/content.php?pid=13926&sid=93526#246670).

A list of multidisciplinary databases with biographic information on dramatists, including pop-up information on search techniques specific to each database, for a guide on Theater Studies (http://libguides.bc.edu/content.php?pid=1161&sid=31339).

A Links & Lists box can include both linked *and* unlinked resources. Just include titles and descriptions (without a URL) for the offline sources. However, sources in a Simple Web Links box must include a URL. Table 8.2 outlines the differences between the two kinds of link boxes.

TABLE 8.2
Comparison of simple web links and Links and Lists box types

Simple Web Links	Links and Lists
Description limited to 1,000 characters.	Main description limited to 1,000 characters. Additional information unlimited.
Description appears in pop-up when cursor is moved over link.	Main description appears in box under title. Additional information in a pop-up when icon is clicked on.
Can include online sources only.	Can include online and non-online sources together.
Works well in boxes in narrow columns without lengthening box.	Descriptions below title can cause boxes in narrow columns to be very long.
Automatically puts resources in bulleted list.	Automatically puts resources in bulleted list.

ADDING, EDITING, AND FORMATTING CONTENT

Since we have introduced the most common types of content boxes, we will look at how you can use these, together with pages and columns—the other basic building blocks of LibGuides—to fill your guide.

At the top of your new guide—and of every guide you create—is the LibGuides command bar. (See figure 8.5.) We will focus on the Add/Edit Pages section of the command bar. Click on Add/Edit Pages and you will have these options:

FIGURE 8.5

The LibGuides command bar

Used by permission of Springshare, LLC

Add / Reuse Page. When you first create a guide, it has a single page called Home. To add another page, choose Add / Reuse Page. Enter a page title and an optional description for the page. (The description will be shown when a user hovers the cursor over the tab connecting to that page.) Click the Create Page button and your new page and its associated tab will appear.

Change Page Info. Choose Change Page Info to modify the title or description of an existing page. For example, you might want to change the title of the first page you created from the default Home to Start, for example. Page titles and descriptions can be changed at any time.

Reorder / Move Pages. This option will allow you to reorder the position of the pages you have created. For example, you can make the second page you created (or the third or fourth) the new home page for your guide. Click on Reorder / Move Pages and you can drag any page up or down in the order.

Reorder Boxes. Once you have created content boxes in your guide, you can rearrange them by choosing Reorder Boxes from the command bar. Boxes can be moved up or down in a column, across columns, or even to another page in the guide. Just drag and drop the box where you want it to go.

Resize Columns. The number and width of columns on a LibGuides page can be customized. The LibGuides default page is three columns wide. The center column is wider than the left or the right. (These sizes are defined by pixels. For example, the default page has a left column 230 pixels wide, a center column 520 columns wide, and a right column 209 pixels wide.) Choose Resize Columns to change the number and/or widths of the columns on any page. You can select one of several preset one-, two-, or three-column layouts or use the slider to customize column sizes by changing the number of pixels in each column.

Delete a Page. You may have a page you no longer need. Choose Delete a Page to remove it. (You will be warned several times to make sure you *really* want to delete the page. Once you do, it cannot be recovered.) If you are not sure you want to delete a page or think you might need it again later, you can choose Change Page Info and check a box to *hide* the page. It will not be deleted, but visitors to the guide will not see it.

PUBLISHING YOUR GUIDE

I have discussed how to add content to the most common types of content boxes and how to arrange those boxes in columns and on pages. You will learn more advanced techniques in the next chapter and get other ideas from elsewhere in this book. But you are ready to create your first guide. Remember, no one—except other LibGuides authors at your institution—can see your guide until you are ready for them to see it. Do not be afraid to experiment, to make mistakes, and to learn as you go. But when you are ready, here is how to publish your guide and add it to the collection of guides available to your user community.

Every LibGuide exists in one of three states: Unpublished, Private, and Published.

Unpublished. When you create a guide, its status is Unpublished. That means it is only visible to you or someone who can log in to your institution's LibGuides account.

Private. A Private guide is visible to anyone who knows the guide's URL. It will not show up in your institution's list of guides and will not be found by search engines. You might want to make a guide Private so it can be reviewed by people without LibGuides accounts: faculty members, librarians at other institutions, even friends and family. Private status is also handy if you want your guide to be used by only a select group.

Published. When your guide is Published, it is officially part of your organization's set of guides. It will be listed in the full list of guides, on your profile page, and with other guides in the same subject category. It will be searchable, both within LibGuides and by search engines.

To change the status of a guide, click on Guide Settings on the command bar and choose Change Guide Information. The Guide Title and Description should already be there on the Basic Settings screen. Use the Guide Publication Status drop-down menu to change the status from Unpublished to Private or Published.

On the same screen, you have the option of creating a "Friendly URL." Every guide in LibGuides is automatically assigned a unique address on the web. These URLs are often long and difficult to remember, for example, http://libguides .yourschool.edu/content.php?pid=617. You can simplify the URL by giving it a unique label that is easier to remember, for example http://libguides.yourschool .edu/economics. Your university may have decided on rules to create and organize these Friendly URLs.

On the Subject Associations tab, use the drop-down menu to associate your guide with one or more of your institution's official LibGuides Subject Categories. These are categories which have been previously set up by your local LibGuides administrator. You can create searchable subject words of your own choosing by creating a Tag. On the Assigned Tags tab, add tags—choosing from existing tags or adding new ones—to give researchers more keywords to find your guides. Make sure you click the Save button at the bottom of the screen. Your LibGuide is ready to be used.

GETTING HELP AND LEARNING MORE

This basic introduction to LibGuides authorship only skims the surface of what is possible. You will learn more by doing, by using this powerful and flexible tool to bring your subject knowledge and expertise to users in ways you could not do before.

One of the most powerful aspects of LibGuides is the strength of the LibGuides community. From colleagues at your institution to the staff at Springshare to LibGuides users at organizations around the world, there are many people from whom you can learn. Here are just a few of the resources available for your assistance:

LibGuides Help & Documentation. Get help and support from a LibGuides LibGuide. This set of guides from Springshare covers everything from the basics to customizing the look and feel of your guides to managing your profile to making your guides more interactive. There are also FAQs, a calendar of training events scheduled by Springshare, and connections to Springshare support (http://help.springshare.com).

The LibGuides Community. The LibGuides Community website will allow you to see what other LibGuides users are doing. You can search for institutions by type or location, find existing guides on a subject you want to cover, or discover ideas from other LibGuides authors. You can even use someone else's guide as a template for one of your own: just ask permission first (http://libguides.com).

The Springshare Lounge. Interact with other LibGuides authors and administrators and Springshare staff at this helpful website You can share a problem (or a solution) you are having with other users. At this site you can learn best practices or suggest improvements and enhancements (http://springsharelounge.com).

CONCLUSION

In this chapter you have learned how to get started with LibGuides. Beginning with creating your LibGuides profile, this chapter covered LibGuides terminology, creating a guide from scratch, common content box types, adding, editing, and formatting content, publishing your guide, and getting help. I have also pointed out a number of ways in which Boston College has made use of the various basic components of LibGuides.

At Boston College, librarians moved quickly from being concerned about LibGuides adding to their workload to seeing it, in the words of several staff, as "the best thing that has happened here in a long time." LibGuides empowered our librarians, giving them the freedom and flexibility to engage with end users online in ways that had not been possible before. Now, using what you have learned here, you can have that experience, too.

In chapter 9, you'll learn about advanced features that can add pizzazz to your guides, including customizing the guide layout; adding advanced content with other types of content boxes; reusing content from elsewhere in LibGuides; and more. The best way for you to learn LibGuides is to get started.

## Chapter Nine

Adding Some Pizzazz
to Your Guides

Kathy Gaynor

L ibGuides provides many options for you to add variety and interest to your guides. Changing a guide from one that is textually oriented to one that is more visually engaging and informative is easy to do if you know how to capitalize on LibGuides' more advanced content boxes.

This chapter will demonstrate three general strategies of which you can take advantage to create more dynamic LibGuides:

Customizing layout—LibGuides provides numerous functions that will allow you to enhance the layout of a LibGuide. It is possible to use various colors for title bars and text boxes; column widths can be changed; and pages can be hidden from public view.

Adding advanced content—LibGuide boxes can be populated with many types of content other than text and links. This chapter will discuss the addition of RSS feeds, podcasts, video clips, documents and other types of files, links to your library catalog, forms for user feedback, lists of library events, and Google searches.

Reusing and organizing content—One of the strengths of LibGuides is that boxes, pages, and guides may be reused in other LibGuides. Subpages can be added as an organizational tool. Pages and boxes can easily be reordered within your guide.

Using the skills that you acquired from chapter 8, this chapter will give you the knowledge to add components to your guides that will make them visually more appealing and will be more likely to keep the attention of your audience. As you've discovered, LibGuides is a highly customizable and flexible program with many ways to change the look of your guides. This chapter will not address all of the advanced features, but it will address the more commonly used ones. Most of the strategies in this chapter are as easy to perform as the basic steps discussed in chapter 8. If you have not used LibGuides before, you may want to read chapter 8 before you read this chapter. Springshare also has an excellent introduction to LibGuides in general and adding content to LibGuides in particular. The end of chapter 8 delineated a number of places on Springshare's website to receive introductory help (http://help.springshare.com).

CUSTOMIZING THE GUIDE LAYOUT

This section will cover some of the ways in which you can customize the look and feel of your guides. Everything from the background color to the shape of your content boxes can be changed. However, your local LibGuides administrator has the power to lock down the look and feel for the entire system. Often this is done to ensure that your library's guides have a consistent format for your users. Consult your local LibGuides administrator and find out what customizations are available at your library.

To make any adjustments or customizations to your guides, you need to use the Command Bar located at the top of the screen of the guide that you are editing. (See chapter 8 for a more detailed explanation.) The Command Bar features

> **Dashboard**—The home page for the LibGuide editing system.
>
> **Guide Settings**—This choice allows you to change numerous characteristics of the LibGuide on which you are working.
>
> **Guide Look & Feel**—When enabled at your library you may change colors of guide title bars, background, and so on.
>
> **Add / Edit Pages**—This choice allows you to change numerous characteristics of the page on which you are working.

Preview—This link opens a window where you can see how your guide will look to your users when it is published

Help—Choosing this link sends you to Springshare's extensive knowledge base of FAQs.

Change Color and Shapes

Assuming your local LibGuides administrator has not locked down the colors or box shapes options, click on Guide Look & Feel from the Command bar and select Change Layout / Colors to change the colors or shapes of the content boxes on your guides. The upper bar controls the color of the page background using predefined colors, the shape of the tabs, the color of the tabs using predefined colors, and the font of the tabs and titles of your content boxes.

The second bar of options controls the shape of your content boxes and the color of the headers or titles of your content boxes using predefined colors. Changing the shape of the content boxes is controlled using the Boxes option. LibGuides allows the content boxes to be squared, rounded, or striped. The third bar of options allows you to save your customizations with Save Settings, Cancel any changes made, or Revert to the default design and return to editing your LibGuide. If your Change Layout / Colors menu choice is greyed out, your system has been locked down by your LibGuides administrator.

159

Columns

Often LibGuides administrators or teams may have set up templates or default guides which provide a common column width among an author's creations. Chapter 6 of this book discusses why various column layouts are better than others. However, there will inevitably come a time when you need to deviate from the standard. Chapter 8 goes into more detail discussing how to easily change columns. This section will discuss a bailout strategy if you happen to make a mistake and "lose" the content of a particular column.

If you choose a column layout that removes a column of content, don't panic. Be aware that what you are doing here is simply hiding columns and not deleting the content that was created or placed in those columns. If you've accidentally hidden a column that you didn't want hidden, just revert to the default settings and choose a different layout option. If you have created content in any of the columns that you hide, that content will not be visible to your users. This is a good reason for keeping your guides Unpublished or Private while you are editing. Otherwise, any changes made to a Published guide will be viewable immediately to your users. Later on in this chapter we will go over how to add a new page of content to a Published guide that is hidden from the user until you decide to switch the page from being invisible to visible. Reverting to the default layout is a simple three-step process: (1) Add / Edit Pages, (2) Resize Columns, then (3) click Default.

Page Visibility

Changing page visibility allows you to add or create additional pages of content to a preexisting, published guide without that new page of information being visible to the public until you decide to switch the visibility of that page. This feature is extremely useful when you want to create boxes in a sandbox environment—an area where you are prepping content and polishing the page for inclusion in the published guide.

Adding a page that can be edited without your users seeing it until you are ready is done through a two-step process. At the top of your guide, click on Add / Edit pages and select the Add / Reuse page link. At the bottom left of the Change Page Info screen you will find a check box next to "Hide this page." (See figure 9.1.) When selected, the page will not be displayed on the public version of the guide, but the page will be available to you so it can be edited while hidden. When this box is checked, notice that the title of your page is in italics and at the top of your content is the wording "This page has been flagged as 'hidden' and will not be visible from the public interface." It is also possible to hide an existing page by choosing Add / Edit Pages and then Edit Page Info. You will find the same option that you can check to hide a previously existing page. To make the page visible, uncheck this option.

ADDING ADVANCED CONTENT

Chapter 8 discussed the three most useful types of content that can be added to LibGuides—Rich Text / Dynamic Content / Scripts, Simple Web Links, and Links & Lists. This section covers how to add some of the more advanced content boxes that can give your guide an interactive and Web 2.0 feel. When adding a new box, your choices are on the Content Box Type Menu. (See figure 9.2.)

FIGURE 9.1

Change Page Info screen

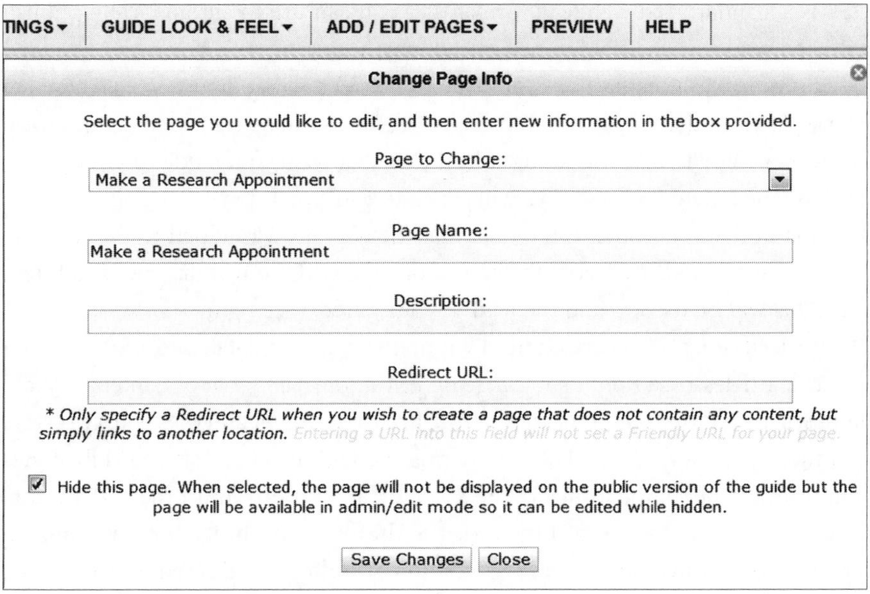

| TINGS ▾ | GUIDE LOOK & FEEL ▾ | ADD / EDIT PAGES ▾ | PREVIEW | HELP |

Change Page Info ⊗

Select the page you would like to edit, and then enter new information in the box provided.

Page to Change:

Make a Research Appointment ▾

Page Name:

Make a Research Appointment

Description:

Redirect URL:

* Only specify a Redirect URL when you wish to create a page that does not contain any content, but simply links to another location. Entering a URL into this field will not set a Friendly URL for your page.

☑ Hide this page. When selected, the page will not be displayed on the public version of the guide but the page will be available in admin/edit mode so it can be edited while hidden.

Save Changes   Close

Used by permission of Springshare, LLC

FIGURE 9.2

Drop-down list of content box types

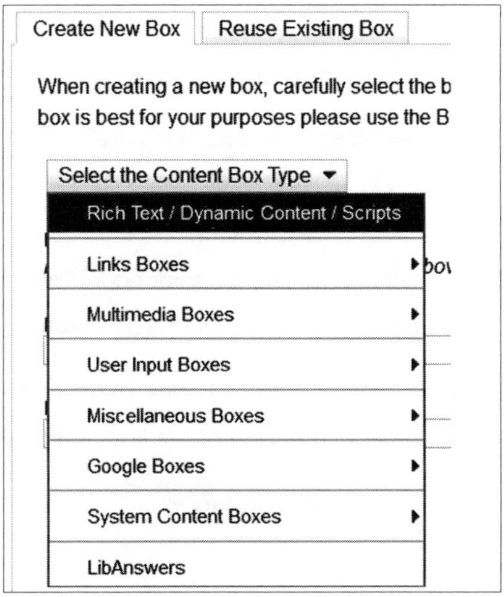

| Create New Box | Reuse Existing Box |

When creating a new box, carefully select the b
box is best for your purposes please use the B

Select the Content Box Type ▼

Rich Text / Dynamic Content / Scripts

Links Boxes ▶

Multimedia Boxes ▶

User Input Boxes ▶

Miscellaneous Boxes ▶

Google Boxes ▶

System Content Boxes ▶

LibAnswers

Used by permission of Springshare, LLC

RSS Feeds

RSS is a standardized web feed format that you can use to automatically publish updated works, such as blogs, news headlines, and so on. RSS boxes can be added by choosing Multimedia Boxes and then RSS Feeds. (See figure 9.2.) There are many places on the Web to find RSS feeds. RSS feeds can be created in online article databases. When you have found a feed that you want to include in your guide, click on the link to the feed. This will generate a stripped-down web page with just the title of the new content, the date that the content was added to the website, and perhaps a brief abstract of the item. Copy the URL from your browser address bar. This will be used to add the feed to your guide. (See figure 9.3.)

RSS feeds are also generated from within many article databases. RSS feeds can retrieve articles based on a subject search or a journal's table of contents. Many libraries use a proxy server to authenticate licensed content and these proxy servers can modify the format of a URL, rendering the URL invalid. Ask your LibGuides administrator about the format of the RSS URL and how to adjust the URL for use.

One of the strengths of LibGuides is the built-in ability for repurposing preexisting information. Within the function of adding an RSS feed to your guide, you can search for other RSS feeds that have been implemented on other LibGuides

FIGURE 9.3
Add RSS Feed URL

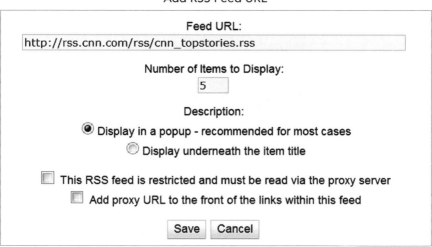

Used by permission of Springshare, LLC

across the system (your library's guides and other libraries using LibGuides) and import those feeds into your guides. When adding an RSS feed to your guide, you will have the opportunity to type in the name of a feed and LibGuides will match your words with preexisting feeds. When you choose one of the existing feeds, LibGuides will pre-populate the URL of the RSS feed for you. Each RSS content box holds only one RSS feed. However, you can have many RSS feed content boxes on your LibGuide.

Some suggestions for the use of RSS feeds are

Current Awareness Alerts—Thompson Rivers University Library— http://libguides.tru.ca/currentawarenessalerts

Making Information Come to You—Popular Feeds—Polytechnic Institute of New York University—Bern Dibner Library—http:// poly.libguides.com/content.php?pid=37279&sid=275466

RSS Feed—Springshare—http://help.springshare.com/content .php?pid =101296&sid=761161

Podcasts

Podcasts add multimedia elements that will enhance your LibGuide. Podcasts are recordings, either audio or video, which are normally issued on a regular basis and are made available for downloading and viewing on portable devices or on your computer. Much like RSS feeds where the content is delivered to you, the same applies for podcasts. Podcasts can be found by searching the Web. Like RSS feeds, they are identifiable with the RSS feed symbol and usually are listed as "podcasts." Once you have located a podcast that you want to add to your guide, you will need to copy the podcast URL from your browser address bar. As you would with an RSS Feed, begin by adding a new content box to your page. Choose Multimedia Boxes and then Podcast.

Examples are:

Finding Podcasts by Discipline—St. John's University—Libraries— http://stjohns.campusguides.com/content.php?pid=36760&sid =277454

Podcast Feed—Springshare—http://help.springshare.com/ content.php?pid=101296&sid=761161

Video

The Embedded Media & Widgets box makes it simple to include a video in your guide. Many instructional video clips exist on the Internet which can be added. Numerous libraries have created short videos on many aspects of information literacy. YouTube is another source of instructional videos which can be added. To add a video, choose the Embedded Media & Widgets box type and click on Add Media / Widget Code and paste in the embed code. Most video sites provide embed code.

Examples include:

Library Video Tutorials—Antelope Valley College Library—http://
avc.libguides.com/content.php?pid=112560&sid=847828

Quick Tips—GateWay Library Video Tutorials—GateWay
Community College—http://libguides.gatewaycc.edu/
Quick_Tips

Documents and Files

The Documents and Files content box enables you to upload files (Word documents, Excel spreadsheets, PowerPoint presentations, PDF files, and so on) to make them available for your users to download. Just as with the other content boxes discussed, begin by adding a box to a page. Choose Select the Box Type; then Multimedia Boxes and then Documents & Files.

Some examples are:

ASA for Users of APA—Printable Handouts—Thompson Rivers
University Library—http://libguides.tru.ca/asastyleguide

Quick Guides—Organizing and Citing Your Research—
Shippensburg University Library—http://library.ship.edu/
content.php?pid=282866&sid=2330046

Books from the Catalog

Book content boxes enable you to enter a list of books and provide links to the book records in your library catalog (or in Amazon). You can display the book title, author, ISBN, URL, and even display the book cover for the item. One of the very useful features of this particular advanced content box is that it allows you to create links directly into your library's catalog, allowing your user to see more detailed information about the item—its circulation status, location, and so on. However, some library catalogs make this direct linking easier than others. Some library catalogs generate a persistent link, while other integrated library systems create a session link to a catalog record. There is a significant difference between these two types of links. A persistent link is a link that remains constant. If your integrated catalog system generates URLs based on sessions or if you are unsure, talk to your vendor or systems librarian for support.

If your catalog uses persistent links, adding a book from your catalog to your guide is as simple as pressing the Add Box link and choosing Books from the catalog from the Multimedia Boxes drop-down list. Pressing the Add New Book link opens a dialogue box which prompts you to add the book title, author/editor, ISBN (this field of information is used to pull cover art from Syndetics or Amazon), URL, cover art URL, cover art size, call number, and description. You will need to decide which of these fields provide you with the display that best suits your needs.

After adding a number of books to the Books from the Catalog content box, you have the ability to sort the books in any order that you deem necessary by clicking and dragging items to different positions. You also have the option to sort books on three predetermined sorting options: by title, by author, or by call number.

You can imagine some of the ways that you could use this box type. In this digital age, we librarians often want to direct users' attention from the website to our paper collections. In many cases the best source of information owned by your library is in paper. Some other examples of this are:

> Books on Environmental History—Thompson Rivers University
> Library—http://libguides.tru.ca/content.php?pid=4561&sid
> =508634

> Nursing—Books to Get You Started—Thompson Rivers University
> Library—http://libguides.tru.ca/nursing

User Input Boxes

The Interactive Poll, User Feedback, and User Link Submission content boxes can encourage user engagement. These content boxes give your users a venue for communicating with your library. Your users will have the opportunity to answer simple poll questions, give you feedback on your guide with predefined questions, or submit their favorite links to you. LibGuides allows only one user input box per content box, but you can have as many user input content boxes as you wish on your LibGuide. Each box type that requests user feedback will send an e-mail including the feedback to the owner of the LibGuide on which they appear.

Interactive Poll, User Feedback, and User Link Submission boxes can be chosen from the drop-down Select the Content Box Type. Choose User Input Boxes. Each box type has a unique usage in LibGuides.

Interactive Poll

The Interactive Poll box allows you to create quick, simple polls to add to your guides. By choosing a User Input box and then by indicating Interactive Poll you can add a box to your page that will allow you to receive audience feedback to one question per box. Choose Add Poll Question and key in the question to which you are seeking a reaction. You can then add up to ten poll prompts which may also have accompanying web pages.

An example is

> Interactive Poll—LibGuides—Ashland University—Library—http://
> libguides.ashland.edu/content.php?pid=33717&sid=256387

User Feedback

The User Feedback box is similar to the Interactive Poll box, but the response prompts are predetermined by LibGuides. The prompts include (1) "Was this information helpful?" (2) "How useful is this content?" (3) "Please provide comments to help improve this page," and (4) "Your e-mail address, so we can get back to you." These prompts are predetermined.

An example is:

> Collaborative Project Resources—EH-300: Business Writing—
> University of Alabama Huntsville Library—http://libguides.uah
> .edu/content.php?pid=31136&sid=1900509

User Link Submission

If you are interested in gathering links of web pages that are used by your audience, the User Link Submission box will allow you to do so. Choosing this type of User Input box gives you an area to explain the purpose of the link request, plus a Submit a Link choice for users. When your guide has been published and users Submit a Link, LibGuides presents them with a form asking for the user's name, e-mail, link title, URL, and a short description. Choosing Submit a Link immediately places the information on the LibGuide. The guide owner is also notified by e-mail when the new link is added.

An example is:

> Star LibGuides – Starting Out—A LibGuides Guide to LibGuides—Ivy Tech Community College Libraries—http://libguides .ivytech.edu/guide

Dates & Events

LibGuides' Dates & Events box allows you to easily create a list of upcoming events in your library. The Dates & Events box is found under the Miscellaneous drop-down category. When creating a box of this type, you are presented with a place to type introductory information, plus an Add New Event link. Choosing this link presents you with an Add Event form, which when filled in formats the information into an agenda layout. The box asks for information including the date and title of the event, plus a description. You can add a URL linking to more information about the event.

An example is

> NLU Library Events—National-Louis University Library—http:// libguides.nl.edu/libraryevents

Google Boxes

Instead of losing your users to Google, why not keep them at your website, but harvest the power of Google on your LibGuide? The Google Book Search, Google Scholar Search, and Google Web Search boxes are extremely easy content boxes to add to your LibGuide. These content boxes facilitate predefined and open Google searches within your LibGuide. Keep in mind that only one Google box can be added to a content box at a time, but you may add several Google content boxes to your guide.

Each of these boxes will allow users to perform searches from inside a LibGuide. The results of the Google Books, the Google Scholar, and the Google Web searches are displayed underneath the Search box on the LibGuide page. As an alternative you can input an initial sample search for each box type as a demonstration. Google Scholar will also allow you to include an initial sample search. Scholar results, however, open up in a new window.

ADVANCED REUSING AND ORGANIZING CONTENT

The ability to reuse content is another strength of LibGuides. After all, why reinvent the wheel? There are two options for reusing content: (1) copying the content into your guide, or (2) linking to the content in another system guide. Each option has its appropriate uses. If linking to other content in LibGuides, any changes made to the original content would be reflected in the content you just added. On the other hand, if you choose to copy content, you can use it as a template. If the original changes, your added copy will remain as you have changed it. It is possible to reuse a LibGuide, a page, or a box.

Linking to a Guide

Sometimes when creating a guide it is useful to create links to other guides within your LibGuides system. For example, if you are making a guide about Lesson Planning, you may want to have that guide also appear on your broader Education subject guide. LibGuides provides you with a content box type called "Link to Guides." Choose Add New Box and then select the Content Box Type. On the drop-down menu choose System Content Boxes and then Link to Guides. A Link to Guides box gives you numerous ways to display related boxes including, among others, (1) Browse by Subject, (2) Most Popular Guides, (3) Guides from a Subject, or (4) Manually Selected Guides.

Linking to a Box

Creating a link to another content box is simple. Choose Add New Box and then Reuse Existing Box. You will be prompted to choose the guide that contains the box you would like to link to. Next you can choose the box you want from a drop-down menu. As usual you have the opportunity to copy it or link to the original.

Boxes are the building blocks of a LibGuide. You will find that the longer your library makes use of LibGuides, the more boxes you will have created that you can use over again. Chapter 3 suggests that it may behoove you to gather these often-used boxes together on a private "Grab" page available to your institution's LibGuide authors.

Linking to a Page

When you link to a page from within a content box, careful attention must be paid to select the correct URL for the link, as LibGuides adds characters to the URL while the page is being edited. After creating a link content box, create a new link by copying and pasting the URL from the browser bar while viewing the page to which you want to link. When you paste the URL from the browser address bar of a page being edited, delete the "ae" from the beginning of the word "content" in the URL. For example, if the URL copied is: "http://libguides.tru.ca/aecontent .php?pid=144949&sid=1232553" remove the "ae" so that the actual link in the URL box is "http://libguides.tru.ca/content.php?pid=144949&sid=1232553." Fortunately, the current version of LibGuides reminds you to remove the "ae" from the link.

To create a tab (representing a LibGuides page) that will link out to an existing LibGuide page, click on Add / Reuse Page from the command bar and select Reuse Existing Page. On the pull-down menu, choose the guide that you wish to link to and you will be prompted to select the page on the desired guide.

If you choose to leave the reused page as a Top Level page, its tab will display beside the tabs you had previously included. However, it is possible when linking another page to a guide to create a "subpage" to an existing page. Instead of leaving the default Add as a Top Level Page, choose the Add Under drop-down menu to add the subpage to the guide. (See figure 9.4.) When the patron views the guide,

FIGURE 9.4
Add/Reuse page and position drop-down menu

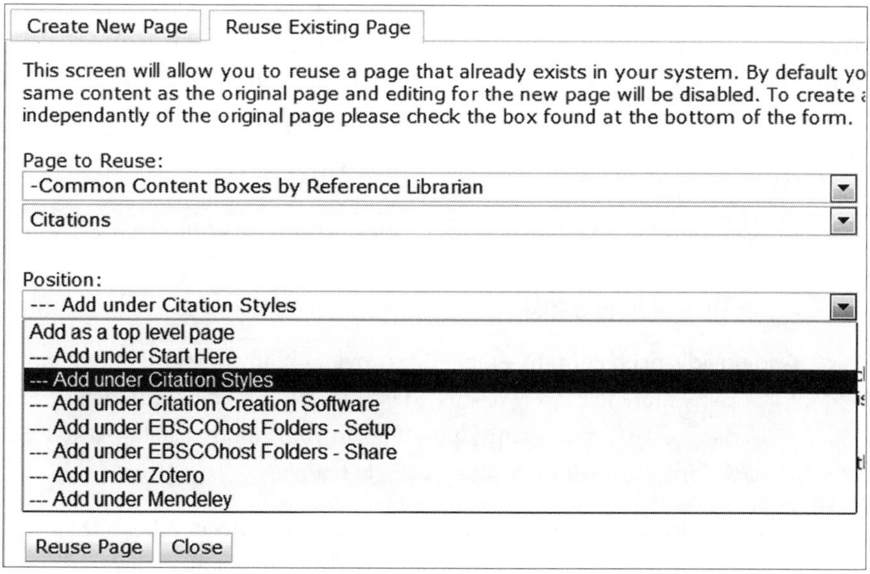

Used by permission of Springshare, LLC

FIGURE 9.5
Tab with "Citations" subpage indicated

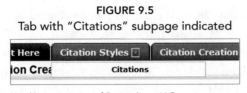

Used by permission of Springshare, LLC

the tab to which the subpage has been appended shows an upside-down triangle next to its name. Hovering over the triangle will display the subpages that can be chosen. (See figure 9.5.)

Moving Content

After creating a LibGuide it is possible to move content around on that guide. To reorder the tabs at the top of your guide, choose Add / Edit Pages and scroll down the drop-down menu and choose Reorder / Move Pages. The order of the tabs can be changed. Choosing Reorder Boxes allows you to move boxes around the page. Chapter 6 discussed the importance of creating a pleasing page layout, by moving boxes.

CONCLUSION

This chapter overviewed many of the advanced options that LibGuides provides with which to add some pizzazz to your guides. Most of these techniques are as easy to use as the more common suggestions in chapter 8. This chapter discussed the following options:

Customizing layout—LibGuides provides various functions that will allow you to enhance the layout of a LibGuide, including colors, column width, and hiding pages.

Adding advanced content—LibGuide provides many types of content boxes —many more than were discussed in this chapter. Boxes can include RSS feeds, podcasts, video clips, files, links to your library catalog, user feedback forms, lists of events, and Google searches.

Reusing and organizing content—One of the strengths of LibGuides is that boxes, pages, and guides may be reused in other LibGuides. Subpages can be added as an organizational tool. Reordering guide content is possible, as well.

By adding a few of these advanced features, your LibGuide is transformed into a guide that is rich not only in content, but rich in features that may entice your users to explore, engage, and participate with the library in ways that haven't been done before. If you have not yet read chapter 6 of this book which discusses the attractive design of web pages, you may want to do so next, as it will provide you with many ideas for adding and moving content that will enhance your page. Also read chapter 7, which will give you instructional strategies for using the various components of LibGuides discussed in chapter 8 and in the current chapter.

PART 4

Making Better Use
of LibGuides

## Chapter Ten

Helping Users Help Themselves
Maximizing LibAnswers Usage

Aaron Tay

Frequently Asked Questions (FAQs) are a commonly seen feature on library websites. Many libraries provide a short list of FAQs on static HTML pages while others employ full-blown knowledge base systems that list the answers to hundreds of questions. In 2010, the National University of Singapore (NUS) Libraries began using Springshare's LibGuides. At the same time, we also moved from a static HTML list of FAQs to Springshare's LibAnswers platform—a database-driven knowledge base system enriched with Web 2.0 features. LibAnswers is a stand-alone but related module to LibGuides. It acts as a tool to allow students to e-mail or text questions to a librarian. LibAnswers tracks and organizes these questions. A librarian can then answer a question and add it to the knowledge base which is accessible through a widget which can be placed on a LibGuide or on a static HTML page. As an added benefit, LibAnswers has a reporting component that allows questions to be tracked and reported. Reference desk questions can be tracked, as well.

Properly employed, the LibAnswers platform can be used to create a knowledge base of FAQs that provides the following benefits:

- Saves the time of users by allowing them to assist themselves
- Saves the time of librarians by allowing users to answer their own commonly asked questions

- Saves the time of librarians by allowing them to easily create and maintain a knowledge base
- Tracks user queries to measure the performance of the knowledge base
- Acts as a repository for those unusual questions librarians answer repeatedly

After reviewing the basic components of LibAnswers, the rest of this chapter will discuss various methods libraries can use to increase the patron use of, plus the efficacy of, the LibAnswers knowledge base. This chapter does assume that you have a basic familiarity with LibAnswers. Depending on your level of knowledge you may want to review Springshare's LibGuide for LibAnswers (www.springshare .com/libanswers) before continuing.

WHAT IS LIBANSWERS?

LibAnswers, at its most basic level, is designed to be a searchable knowledge base. Users can find answers using natural language due to a Google-like auto-suggest feature. If no answer is found or if the user is not satisfied with the answer, they can submit a question to the library. The librarian answering the question can choose to answer the question privately via e-mail, or to convert the question (after suitable modifications for privacy reasons) to a public FAQ. LibAnswers is suitable for collaboration between librarians with different expertise. Questions arriving in the module can be claimed by individual librarians. Librarians can also leave notes for one another or channel submitted questions to appropriate colleagues for their answers.

One of the most useful features in the LibAnswers system is Query Spy. This statistical function allows the library to track the performance of the knowledge base. Using Query Spy, one can see what users are typing into the search and which, if any, of the resident answers are selected. Many other statistics are also available, including what Springshare module the query is coming from (e.g., Mobile, LibAnswers, LibGuides, and so on), the referring page, date and time, and IP address. You can export the statistics to a comma-separated values (CSV) spreadsheet file or use the built-in system to generate charts and tables.

The optional reference analytics module provides even more statistics allowing you to store and track all kinds of reference transactions, including chat, phone, and face-to-face. Another optional module is the SMS/Texting module, which allows libraries to provide SMS reference service.

WHY USERS DON'T WANT TO USE FAQS AND WHAT TO DO ABOUT IT

Unfortunately, libraries face an uphill battle to get users to use knowledge bases, as it has been my experience that most users do not like to read help files and prefer to figure things out themselves. So what can librarians do? Arguably to improve usage of FAQs, librarians have to consider the following issues:

- Can users find the knowledge base?
- Does the answer to what the user is looking for exist in the knowledge base?
- If the answer exists, can the user find it by searching or browsing the knowledge base?

LibAnswers includes many features that can be used to help control these three issues.

Can Users Find the Knowledge Base?

The best knowledge base in the world, packed with all the answers that a user could want, would be useless if it could not easily be found. Besides putting a link to the knowledge base on the library home page, links can also be placed at the point of need. Point of need refers to places or points in users' workflow where they may be stuck and would naturally look for help. This could be anywhere from the library-controlled systems such as the library catalog to other systems such as university courseware pages.

Besides linking to LibAnswers at various levels (home page, topic pages, specific FAQs, and so on), LibAnswers also provides additional options in terms of different widgets that enable answers to be searched without leaving a web page. Librarians should discuss and consider the following:

- Where are users most likely to be looking for help (points of need)?
- Should a widget or link be included? If a widget, which type of widget? If a link is included, should it be linked to the LibAnswers home page, an appropriate LibAnswers topic page, or to a specific FAQ?
- Should all Contact Us points be channeled through LibAnswers first?

In the section "Placing LibAnswers at Points of Need" I will discuss the various points of need at which librarians can embed links or widgets to LibAnswers.

Does the Answer Exist in the Knowledge Base?

The importance of populating the knowledge base with questions for which users actually need to know the answers may seem obvious, but Jakob Nielsen (2002), a noted usability expert, observed that

> too many websites have FAQs that list questions the company wished users would ask. No good. FAQs have a simplistic information design that does not scale well. They must be reserved for frequently asked questions, since that's the only thing that makes an FAQ a useful website feature.

Users who find that the knowledge base does not have what they need are unlikely to return; hence it is important to create FAQs within the patron's realm of confusion. One reason why most knowledge bases do not list questions that are actually being asked is that there is often no easy way to determine what users really want to know.

LibAnswers helps to reduce this problem in three ways:

- The Query Spy feature tracks what users are searching for and whether they find the answer.
- Users are able to submit questions directly to the library if they are unable to find the answer they need; librarians can answer directly and post an edited version of the question on LibAnswers.
- Users can comment on existing FAQs.

Librarians should discuss and consider the following:

- What type of FAQs should be included, for example, policy-related, subject-related? What should not be included?
- Should information be placed in LibAnswers, or elsewhere, for example, a LibGuide or on a library page rather than an FAQ?
- What question sources should be used to create FAQs, for example, e-mail, chat?
- Should all questions asked by users be listed publicly?

In the section "Setting Up and Pre-Populating LibAnswers with Questions" I will discuss what sources to use to populate the LibAnswers system and how to select which FAQs to include. The section "Maximizing Hit Rates and Adding More Questions" will provide tips on how to use LibAnswers' Query Spy system to measure the performance of existing FAQs and how to include FAQs that users are looking for but are not in the system.

If the Answer Exists, Can the User Find It?

While LibAnswers provides features for browsing and searching, most users are "search dominant" (Nielsen, 2011). Nielsen defines "search dominant" users as users who go straight to the search button, as opposed to "link dominant" users who browse the site via links. As most librarians are aware, searching, in general, often fails, not because the information doesn't exist but because the keyword searched for does not match the term used. This is often called the "synonym problem" (Beall, 2008). The same problem exists when patrons search a library knowledge base.

To improve the likelihood of users finding the FAQ needed, librarians should use the keyword function in LibAnswers in combination with the Query Spy system to add appropriate synonyms to the FAQ to enhance its retrieval probability.

Though most users are "search dominant" (Nielsen, 2011), some thought should also be given to organizing FAQs by topics, as topics allow librarians to create a more context-aware environment by leading users to the FAQs for which they are likely to be looking. For instance, users who are seeking help on the library catalog web page are likely to be looking for only a specific subset of FAQs. Instead of linking to the LibAnswers home page, they can be linked to a LibAnswers topic page for that area, which will list the most frequently asked questions for that topic, increasing the chance of users finding what they need.

Librarians should discuss and consider the following:

- What topics should be created?
- How should FAQs be phrased to increase their ability to be found?
- How often should Query Spy be monitored to check for FAQs not included in the knowledge base?

The section "Maximizing Hit Rates and Adding More Questions" will provide tips on how to use LibAnswers' Query Spy system to refine existing FAQs to ensure that they can be found by users.

PLACING LIBANSWERS AT POINTS OF NEED

The LibAnswers system allows users to help themselves and, as such, an obvious place to add a link to the system is at points just before users want to contact the library to ask a question. In many libraries clicking on a Contact Us link results in an electronic form for submitting questions. This would be a good place to include a LibAnswers widget to encourage users to search the knowledge base before sending a question.

A slightly more intrusive way to encourage usage would be to link all Contact Us pages to the LibAnswers home page. As this page includes a "more ways to ask questions" box, which lists all the communication channels provided by the library, all queries could reasonably be routed to the main LibAnswers home page first, where users can choose either to use the knowledge base or choose one of the communication options.

Besides points where users want to contact the library, libraries can consider adding access to LibAnswers at various points, including

- Library home page
- Every page of the library portal in a menu-bar or as a button on the far left of a page by using the LibAnswers pop-up widget
- Library catalog
- Courseware (e.g., Blackboard, Desire2Learn, and so on)
- Databases (e.g., EBSCOhost databases)
- Social media sites (e.g., Facebook, Twitter, wikis, blogs)
- All LibGuides
- Library toolbars, such as the LibX toolbar (http://libx.org) or the Conduit toolbar (www.conduit.com)
- Library e-mail loan notices and e-mail signatures of library staff

Libraries should embed Google Analytics (see chapter 11 for more information about Google Analytics) into LibAnswers to track how users are accessing the FAQs, thus allowing greater customization. Academic libraries should consider linking from courseware, catalogs, and databases as these tend to be high-volume, high-traffic web pages where users often get stuck.

Where Should You Put LibAnswers Access Points?

At the National University of Singapore, access to LibAnswers is available from such web pages as the library catalog. (See figure 10.1. "Library FAQ" is at the bottom

FIGURE 10.1
Library FAQ link on the library catalog search page,
National University of Singapore, http://libencore.nus.edu.sg

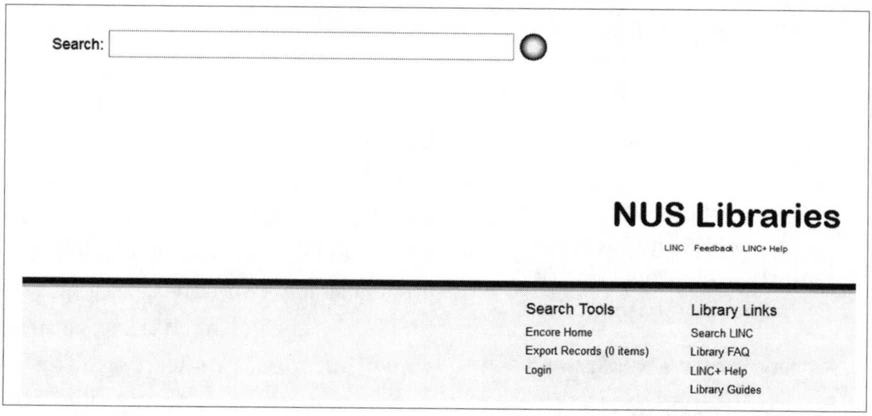

Courtesy of National University of Singapore

right of the search screen.) LibAnswers is also available from our courseware page, on the menu bar of all library pages, and our page on Facebook. (It takes a bit more work to embed LibAnswers into library Facebook pages; refer to www.springsharelounge.com/forum/topics/libanswers-and-facebook for how this is achieved.)

According to recent statistics at NUS Libraries, most of the incoming traffic to LibAnswers comes unsurprisingly from links on the library home page. The next highest source is LibGuides (34 percent). The third highest source comes from the link on the Blackboard page, which accounts for 13 percent of all incoming LibAnswers traffic. The library catalog is fourth highest at 5 percent.

Considering the Context of the User

Once you have determined the points of access to LibAnswers, you can provide entrance to it in several ways. The most obvious thing to do is to create a plain HTML link to the home page of LibAnswers, but a more customized approach can be taken. For example, you can:

- link to a specific LibAnswers topic page
- link to a specific LibAnswer FAQ

- use an embedded widget with popular and featured questions
- use a pop-up widget as a button on the left of every web page
- link to a related LibGuide on the topic with a LibAnswers box with predefined questions

Figure 10.2 shows an example of an auto-suggest widget that has been customized by Lehman Library's LibGuides administrator, Aaron W. Dobbs.

FIGURE 10.2
Shippensburg University "Instant Answers" widget, http://Library.ship.edu

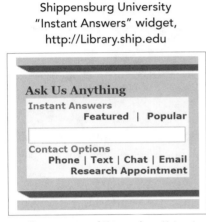

Used by permission of Shippensburg University Library

Figure 10.3 shows an example of the landing page that greets users at NUS when they click on the Help link from the library catalog. Our library has a specific LibGuide about the library catalog which introduces its features. This is supplemented by a LibAnswers box with predefined questions drawn from the system. This allows users to have quick access to the FAQs they are likely to use, on top of the possibility of exploring the LibGuide for more information about the features of the catalog.

What are the advantages of giving users this extra information? In the case

FIGURE 10.3
National University of Singapore landing page, http://libguides.nus.edu.sg/lincplus

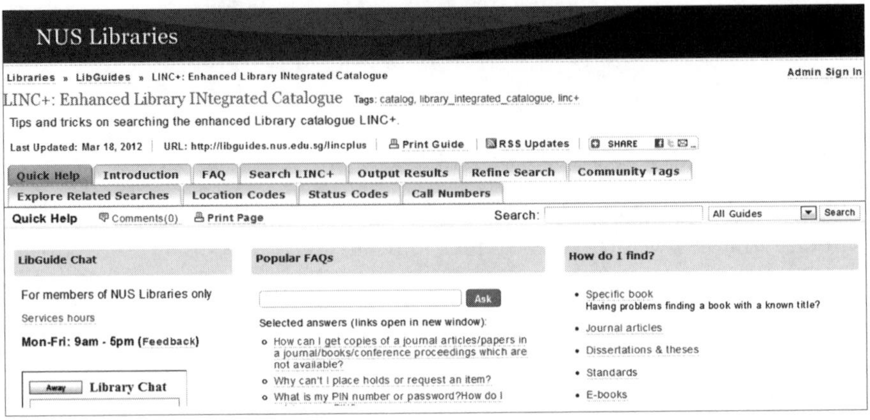

Courtesy of National University of Singapore

of the embedded widget, it allows users to get instant satisfaction by searching directly without leaving the page. While searching for FAQs is important, the predefined or featured questions option, if properly deployed, allows users to quickly access required FAQs without even searching. This saves them time and improves the possibility of their finding the right FAQ.

How Do You Decide Which Predefined Questions to Add?

Properly handled, predefined questions or featured questions can predict user needs and display the FAQs they are mostly like to seek without their searching (see table 10.1). But how do you know what questions to list? In many cases because you are channeling in users from specific places, you have a very good guess regarding what types of questions users are looking for by considering the context of use. For example, users who are clicking the FAQ link from the library catalog will most likely be looking for FAQs related to loan services, searching for items, and so on.

In our library, we also employ chat boxes by Libraryh3lp (http://libraryh3lp .com) embedded in both LibAnswers and LibGuides systems. The questions asked by users from chats are tracked, giving us potential FAQs to add to the knowledge base. For instance, we found that one of the most common chat questions asked by users coming through a link from the catalog was a question about our "marked for export" function. We quickly added the answer as an FAQ and added it as a predefined question in a LibAnswers box.

SETTING UP AND PRE-POPULATING LIBANSWERS WITH QUESTIONS

It is often difficult to predict what users will look for, hence it is important to base FAQs entered into the system on actual questions that have been asked by users. If you are populating the LibAnswers system from scratch, some good sources of preexisting data can be found in e-mail transactions or chat transcripts.

Sources for Pre-Populating FAQs

At NUS library, we studied a year's worth of e-mail queries and divided them into major categories. As queries often reflect difficulties in navigating the library

TABLE 10.1

Pros and cons of different methods of linking to LibAnswers

Method	Pros	Cons
Link to LibAnswers home page	No extra work need	No customization possible per source
Link to LibAnswers topic page	Shows group of similar Q&As, with no LibGuide necessary. Better targeting, ability to highlight and feature specific FAQs based on placement of widget	LibAnswers topic page is less customizable than main LibAnswers home page.
Link to specific LibAnswers Q&A	Specific, gives the user exactly what he wants.	Rare, that you can predict exactly what specifically user wants.
Embedded widget with featured answers	Instant gratification, users enter search without leaving page. Better targeting, ability to highlight and feature specific FAQs based on placement of widget	Takes up space Not possible to add on certain pages that allow only links, not JavaScript
Pop-up widget as a button on the left of every web page	Can be embedded on every page Saves space	Unknown if users will use
Link to related LibGuide with a LibAnswers box (with up to 10 predefined questions)	Informs users of the existence of an appropriate LibGuide for more information Better targeting, ability to highlight and feature specific FAQs based on placement of widget	No suitable LibGuide might be available.

website, it is not worthwhile to study transactions that go too far back due to various changes. We also used word visualization tools like Wordle (www.wordle .net) to create word clouds that helped us understand which words were being used in the transactions.

While this data excluded questions asked in person, we could have supplemented this analysis by librarians brainstorming about typical questions that were asked at the desk. This was not done however, because we already had a substantial number of questions both from this analysis and also from transferring existing FAQs from our previous knowledge base.

Another method to begin populating the knowledge base would be to channel all Contact Us links to the LibAnswers embedded question form widget. This would allow the capture of every online query sent to the library that could then be converted into FAQs if desired. As the knowledge base fills up, it might be worthwhile to switch to other widgets that allow searching the knowledge base first before submitting the question.

Should Information Be Kept in LibGuides, LibAnswers, or on the Library Website?

The same piece of information can reside in LibGuides, LibAnswers, and on the library web page itself. To avoid duplication, whenever possible, it is advisable to put the same information at only one place. You may have already begun answering this question if you have clearly defined what information you will place within a LibGuide as compared to what information goes onto the library web pages. To ensure the likelihood that FAQs are found, make sure that your site search (which could be a Google Search App or a simple Google Custom Search) covers all three areas.

In general, LibAnswers is suitable for brief answers; if you need to describe a library service, such as the full details of document delivery, it might be better to put a brief description in LibAnswers but link to the full details on a LibGuide or a library web page created for that purpose.

In the other direction, you can use a LibAnswers box in LibGuides to embed related FAQs from LibAnswers in the relevant LibGuides. Another option would be to use a widget with appropriate questions embedded in a library web page.

What FAQs Should Be Listed?

An analysis of questions asked by users is likely to result in hundreds of potential questions that can be listed. In most cases, the more you list, the greater the chance of the users finding what they need. As patrons use LibAnswers, they will submit more questions which can then be converted into more FAQs. The question facing libraries is this, "What should be added to LibAnswers?"

There are two main approaches. The first approach is to create an FAQ for every actual question asked. The other is to be more selective, listing entries in LibAnswers based on certain criteria. The first approach has the advantage of requiring little judgment on deciding what to list; however, there is the potential for the LibAnswers system to grow to an unwieldy size.

NUS library decided on the more selective approach, listing only items that we believed were most likely to be searched. The 80-20 rule is an economic truism which states that 80 percent of the effects stem from 20 percent of the causes. As applied here, the 80-20 rule implies that we can answer most questions by selecting just a smaller proportion of the most popular questions.

The 80-20 rule or Pareto principle has been studied in the library context. For example, it has been used to study whether articles downloaded in Emerald were mostly drawn from a small subset of journal titles (Evans and Peters, 2005). An interesting question is whether this holds true for FAQs. Table 10.2 shows the results drawn from a survey of six libraries with LibAnswers systems of varying sizes.

As shown in table 10.2, the 80-20 rule doesn't quite hold for FAQs but it comes close. For four libraries, roughly 70 percent of views come from the top 20 percent of FAQs, while for the remaining two, the top 20 percent account for 50 percent of views. In either case, it does show that the distribution of views is highly skewed, with the top few FAQs accounting for most views. More in-depth research should be done, although the results do suggest that libraries seeking to maximize return on investment on creating and maintaining FAQs can focus on including the most popular FAQs.

At NUS library we gave higher priority for providing answers in cases where users

- can help themselves without intervention from librarians, for example, "How do I reset my password?" (An automated way to reset this exists.)
- can be guided to contact the right specialized departments or persons directly when time is of the essence, for example, "What do I do if I lose my library card?"
- have been asking or searching numerous times in the past.

TABLE 10.2
An informal survey of six libraries with LibAnswers

Library	No. of FAQs	% of Total Views from Top 20% Popular FAQs
Library A	1,662	71
Library B	1,030	54
Library C	427	56
Library D	376	71
NUS	188	70
Library E	109	68

FIX ROOT CAUSES

Another benefit of studying user questions is that patterns may point to a design flaw in your website structure. As you study past transactions to look for FAQs to add you will start noticing patterns—questions that are asked over and over again. Try to understand the root cause. Why are these questions being asked repeatedly? Is the wording on the web page unclear? Is the mechanism for reserving books obscure? If so, fix the problem, so that the FAQ is no longer necessary. You may be able to preclude future questions by fixing the root cause of the question.

Organizing Topics in LibAnswers

Besides populating the LibAnswers system, you can also group FAQs under different topics. LibAnswers search widgets give patrons the possibility to browse the knowledge base as well as to search it. The question remains: how often do users browse for questions as opposed to searching? As suggested previously, the answer is "not often" as searching is the dominant practice (Nielsen, 2011). In NUS libraries our analysis of the LibAnswers home page shows that while the top ten most popular questions on the home page are clicked 45 percent of the time, the topics box which exposes the categories for browsing is not used as much. Despite being placed very prominently just under the search box, it is clicked only 20 percent of the time. Users probably do not want to spend time figuring out the categorization system.

187

But topics can be used to channel users to specific pages when you can predict what they are looking for. When adding a question to the knowledge base the librarian has the choice to assign the FAQ to a specific topic. These topics can be used to organize FAQs. For instance, a link for help on an electronic online form for requesting interlibrary loans can be linked to a LibAnswers topic page covering that. Alternatively, in a LibAnswers box in LibGuides, you could select a topic to automatically list all FAQs from that topic.

Another result of putting FAQs into topics is that the topics affect the Related Question list at the bottom of each FAQ. If the FAQ is tagged with multiple topics, it will only show one topic—alphabetically the first topic you assigned. For example, if you assigned both "Loans" and "Passwords" to an FAQ, only "Loans" will display as it comes before "Passwords" in the alphabet.

MAXIMIZING HIT RATES AND ADDING MORE QUESTIONS

Understanding how LibAnswers matches search queries with FAQs created is critical in ensuring users can find what they are looking for. As time passes, even a well-adjusted knowledge base will need to be tweaked as things change. For example, new services may be added, and library pages could be redesigned, making some features less obvious while exposing others that will result in new queries. This section will provide tips on how to ensure your knowledge base continues to be useful. But first, we need to understand how LibAnswers matches queries.

How Does a LibAnswers Search Match Questions?

Currently the search component of the LibAnswers knowledge base is quite similar to that of a typical search engine. Understanding how the system searches can help you to circumvent potential answers being missed by patrons. The following are basic functions of the search software:

1. Direct Matching via auto-suggest is akin to auto-complete in Google searches; all characters typed will have to match characters entered in the questions fields or defined keywords in the order they were typed.
2. If a typed query finds no Direct Match, the software tries to match all search terms in any order and may even match questions where not all the search terms are in the same order. Potential matches will match text in questions, keywords, and answers with priority given to the first two.
3. There is some simple stemming that occurs. For example, typing the term "Room" will match a question that has the word "Rooms" for both auto-suggest and potential matches.
4. Hyphens are not handled so "inter-library" is different from "interlibrary."

The LibAnswers Keyword function can assist in avoiding some of the problems listed above. For example, use keywords to add synonyms and variant forms for matching. Even if the text is in the question or answer already, one can add keywords to further improve the ranking of FAQs in the relevancy ranking. For even more targeted keywords you can add phrases such as "borrow books."

Putting this all together, try to use the terms that you expect users to use in searches when phrasing questions. Going through e-mail queries and Query Spy will help with the correct phrasing. In general use plurals (e.g., "Rooms" rather than "Room") to increase hit rates. Synonyms should also be added by the Keyword function to help improve search results. For example, add "inter-library" as a keyword if the main body of your FAQ uses the term "interlibrary."

LibAnswers currently does not allow the setting of stopwords, hence it is a good idea to also use common words like "library" or "book" sparingly in the question and answer as users like to type those in the search queries and, as such, FAQs that use the word "book" or "library" multiple times in answers and questions will float to the top of results even if they may not be most relevant.

Reviewing Performance with Query Spy

Users have the option of submitting questions via the system when no answers are found; this theoretically allows LibAnswers to be self-adjusting when you post those answers directly into the knowledge base. In practice, we find that the vast majority of users do not submit a question when they cannot find the answer in the knowledge base. At NUS, we found only 35 submitted questions from January to May 2011. This is less than 2 percent of the unsuccessful queries (queries where users did not click on any answers).

This makes it important to manually review the Query Spy logs to pick up failed queries. Here in NUS Libraries we review such logs weekly at a minimum. We monitor Query Spy to detect two types of failures:

1. The query fails because the FAQ matching the search does not exist.
2. The query fails despite the fact the FAQ matching the search exists.

The first case requires the creation of a new FAQ. To determine how often a query has been searched, simply search Query Spy with the appropriate keyword. While the first case does not necessarily require action, the latter case almost always does. If a query fails because of a synonym-matching problem, a keyword could be added or the FAQ could be edited to include the synonym.

CONCLUSION

This chapter discussed a number of methods that libraries using LibAnswers to create a knowledge base of FAQs can utilize to maximize the efficiency of the software. Much of what was discussed centered around understanding how users typically search and in understanding the fine points of LibAnswers. In summary, the following actions were reviewed.

First decide where to place links or widgets at points of need. For academic libraries, other than on the library's main page, we recommend putting links or widgets in LibGuides, courseware, and the library catalog. Databases are the next obvious points.

Next, start populating LibAnswers. There are two approaches. One can start seeding the knowledge base with questions and answers before releasing to the public or one can just start accepting questions. In the first case, FAQs can be created from many sources, including e-mail and chat transcripts or recorded transactions at the desk. The golden rule here is to always use actual questions asked by users in the past as a guide to creating FAQs. In the second case, one can start LibAnswers with almost no questions and try to quickly build up a bank of FAQs by directing all online queries to the embedded question form widget, so all inquiries can be placed into the knowledge base. One major decision when populating LibAnswers is to decide on criteria for including an FAQ. We believe that the 80-20 rule suggests that libraries should be selective in listing only the most common FAQs rather than trying to answer everything.

Lastly, monitor LibAnswers using Query Spy to ensure that the knowledge base is working well. In particular, our experience at NUS Libraries is that when a search fails at LibAnswers, very few users bother to submit the question. As such, it is critical to monitor Query Spy to see what users are failing to find.

LibAnswers is a very flexible and powerful tool that can be used by libraries to maximize usage of FAQs. By using the full set of LibAnswer features one can ensure that users find the FAQs they are looking for with few problems.

REFERENCES

Beall, Jeffrey. 2008. "The Weaknesses of Full-Text Searching." *Journal of Academic Librarianship* 34, no. 5: 438–44.

Evans, Paul, and John Peters. 2005. "Analysis of the Dispersal of Use for Journals in Emerald Management Xtra (EMX)." *Interlending & Document Supply* 33, no. 3: 155–57.

Nielsen, Jakob. 2002. "Top Ten Web-Design Mistakes of 2002." *Useit.com.* www.useit .com/alertbox/20021223.html.

———. 2011. "Incompetent Research Skills Curb Users' Problem Solving." *Useit.com.* www.useit.com/alertbox/search-skills.html.

## Chapter Eleven

Using Statistical Gathering Tools to Determine Effectiveness and Accountability

Lora Baldwin and Sue A. McFadden

Assessment is commonplace in academia and libraries are among the academic units on which scrutiny is placed. Shrinking budgets, mixed with growing database and journal costs, force libraries to carefully consider and justify every expense. Librarians may think that LibGuides are wonderful and a needed expense, but how does a library evaluate, assess, and ultimately justify the product's worth?

Little has been published about assessment and LibGuides; most publications discuss the positive qualities of the software and how to implement and make use of it. After surveying faculty locally as well as librarians across the nation, the authors considered ways to discover the value of LibGuides beyond the opinions voiced in surveys. Because of the need to assess LibGuides, the authors developed a rubric for librarians to help justify LibGuides' acquisition and continued use. In this chapter we will provide librarians with this rubric, which we believe to be a useful assessment tool of objective data. We will look at how to find statistical information, using LibGuides' statistical tools and Google Analytics, and discuss how to apply those statistics to the rubric, thus determining value and justifying continued use of LibGuides.

A RUBRIC TO ASSESS LIBGUIDES' VALUE

Rubrics are tools that are used to make subjective decisions objective by defining criteria. In recent years, they have increasingly been used for assessment in libraries.

Megan Oakleaf, for example, has provided instructive guides in the areas of information literacy instruction and decision making in libraries that utilize rubrics (Oakleaf, 2007, 2009a, 2009b). Rubrics also provide assessment for individual assignments and complex programmatic evaluations. "Rubrics can also be used to evaluate programs as a whole, as well as specific aspects such as courses, faculty, and delivery systems" (Cook and Farmer, 2011: 137). A library should not continue using a product that is ineffective just because librarians like it. We need to ask: "Are students using the product? Are faculty encouraging use of the product?" The LibGuide Rubric (see table 11.1) consists of goals that librarians can use to measure the effectiveness of LibGuides in their library. Librarians completing the rubric will be able to analyze the areas that need to be improved to get maximum value out of the product.

When we were creating our rubric, we had a brainstorming session about what information would be important and how we could get that information. We arranged the questions we had into four specific categories: (1) economic value, (2) instructional role value, (3) value in distance education, and (4) incidental value. We feel that this rubric helps libraries make well thought-out decisions about the LibGuide product. Further, some of the information necessary to complete the rubric can be determined using the statistical package that comes with LibGuides. Other information will need to be garnered from outside sources like Google Analytics. The rubric in table 11.1 contains an abridged description of goals. For a more detailed version of this rubric, visit http://iue.libguides.com/LGAssessments.

Economic Value

In a world where cost is everything, librarians need to determine economic value before looking at other criteria. So, how does a library determine this? The Economic Value section of the LibGuide Rubric looks at five criteria.

1. Cost per Use
2, Goal Values
3. Increased Database Usage
4. Visits and Path
5. Subscription Traffic

Perhaps the most important indicator is cost per use. This can be determined by looking at total cost of the product (including administrative, creation, and

TABLE 11.1
Rubric assessing LibGuide value as an organizational tool

VALUE Viewed:	LOW		MEDIUM		HIGH	
Economic Value—LibGuides are a great product, but are they worth the money? Is your library receiving a value worthy of the cost?						
Cost per use	☐	Cost per use is greater than $30.	☐	Cost per use averages between $10 and $30.	☐	Cost per use is less than $10.
Goal values	☐	0–33% of all users reach an end goal.	☐	34–67% of all users reach an end goal.	☐	68–100% of all users reach one or more end goals.
Increased database usage	☐	0–33% of users leave the LibGuide and access a database.	☐	34–67% of users leave the LibGuide and access a database.	☐	68–100% of users leave the LibGuide and access a database.
Visits and paths	☐	0–33% of users leave the LibGuide and follow a suggested link.	☐	34–67% of users leave the LibGuide and follow a suggested link.	☐	68–100% of users leave the LibGuide and follow a suggested link.
Subscription traffic	☐	0–33% of users leave the LibGuide and go to a supported library tool.	☐	34–67% of users leave the LibGuide and go to a supported library tool.	☐	68–100% of users leave the LibGuide and go to a supported library tool.
Instructional Role Value—LibGuides are a great instructional tool. Is your library utilizing them to their highest potential?						
Use in instruction session	☐	0–33% of instruction sessions use a LibGuide.	☐	34–67% of instruction sessions use a LibGuide.	☐	68–100% of instruction sessions use a LibGuide.
Percentage of use in class	☐	0–33% of the instruction session is focused on the LibGuide and its components.	☐	34–67% of the instruction session is focused on the LibGuide and its components.	☐	68–100% of the instruction session is focused on the LibGuide and its components.
Active engagement	☐	0–33% of the students are looking at the LibGuide and its pages during the instruction session.	☐	34–67% of the students are looking at the LibGuide and its pages during the instruction session.	☐	68–100% of the students are looking at the LibGuide and its pages during the instruction session.
Assess learning modules	☐	Post session poll scores increase 0–33%.	☐	Post session poll scores increase 34–67%.	☐	Post session poll scores increase 68–100%.
Survey/poll faculty	☐	0–33% of the faculty provide input for their classroom session.	☐	34–67% of the faculty provide input for their classroom session.	☐	68–100% of the faculty provide input for their classroom session.

(cont.)

TABLE 11.1   Rubric assessing LibGuide value as an organizational tool (cont.)

VALUE Viewed:		LOW		MEDIUM		HIGH
Value in Distance Education—LibGuides can be linked-to from classroom management software. Identical LibGuides can be made unique by adding a section number to collect statistical information. Does your institution use LibGuides in their distance education/ online classes to help students in the research process?						
Are online classes using	☐	The number of unique page views divided by students is <1 page use.	☐	The number of unique page views divided by students is between 1 and 5 page uses.	☐	The number of unique page views divided by students is >5 page uses.
Return visits	☐	In the six months following the class, the number of unique page views divided by students is <1 page use.	☐	In the six months following the class, the number of unique page views divided by students is between 1 and 3 page uses.	☐	In the six months following the class, the number of unique page views divided by students is >3 page uses.
Incidental Value—These are other units of measure to determine the success of the LibGuide.						
Visits, return visits per guide	☐	The number of unique page views for two weeks following instruction divided by students is less than 1 page use. Divide the number of page views by the number of students in class.	☐	The number of unique page views for two weeks following instruction divided by students is 1 to 5 page uses. Divide the number of page views by the number of students in class.	☐	The number of unique page views for two weeks following instruction divided by students is greater than 5 page uses. Divide the number of page views by the number of students in class.
Inbound and outbound traffic	☐	0–33% of users arrive from a direct link.	☐	34–67% of users arrive from a direct link.	☐	68–100% of users arrive from a direct link.
Student feedback polls/ surveys	☐	0–33% of students respond to a poll during an instruction session.	☐	34–67% of students respond to a poll during an instruction session.	☐	68–100% of students respond to a poll during an instruction session.
Total the checks in each column and multiply by the value assigned to that column		__ × 1 = _____		__ × 3 = _____		__ × 5 = _____

Add the three sums together.

A score of 0–15 indicates that there is a lot of room for improvement in your LibGuide program. You are not getting much value from the LibGuides or are not utilizing them to their full potential.

A score of 16–35 means that there is room for improvement. Look at where you scored lowest and try to improve in those areas

A score of 36–55 shows that you are incorporating LibGuides into your instruction routine, but need to encourage more usage from faculty and students.

A score of over 56 shows that you are on target to using LibGuides successfully.

maintenance costs), and dividing that number by the total of page views. Libraries can set up measurable goals using the Google Analytics Goals feature. Results can determine how successfully a goal was reached. Examples of measurable goals might include having students fill out an evaluation, use a database, or look at a website. The final three criteria are based upon analyzing website traffic. Using LibGuides, libraries can direct students to use expensive databases, recommend useful websites, and encourage usage of library products like RefWorks. LibGuide Statistics can show which links are used within a guide, but to get more detailed information, you will need to use Google Analytics.

Instructional Role Value

LibGuides can be very helpful in the library instruction process. The Instructional Role Value section of the rubric looks at five criteria to determine if libraries are utilizing LibGuides to their highest potential.

1. Use in Instruction Session
2. Percentage of Use in Class
3. Active Engagement
4. Assess Learning Modules
5. Survey/Poll Faculty

The first two criteria are derived from a library's own record keeping. The first criterion asks how many library instruction sessions use a LibGuide and the second asks to determine how much of the session is spent using the LibGuide to direct students. Google Analytics can provide information about where users go when they leave a web page. Ideally, librarians would like students to go to the sites they are demonstrating in class. It is possible to determine how engaged students are by tracking their searching and seeing if they are staying on task. LibGuide Polling is a way of assessing if students grasp major ideas and determining if learning is taking place. Pre-session polls can alert students to content that will be covered, and post-session polls can reveal if students have an understanding of the new content. Ideally, library instruction sessions should be designed with input from the requesting faculty member. Faculty members happy with the instruction and the LibGuide will direct students back to the guide. We need to ask: "Are faculty responding to polling questions about the value of the LibGuide?"

Value in Distance Education

Distance education students pose a unique challenge to librarians. How do librarians have an impact on students that are physically removed from the campus? There are two criteria examined in this section of the LibGuide Rubric.

1. Are Online Classes Using LibGuides?
2. Return Visits

LibGuides can be linked to and from classroom management software, but the guides need to be written and displayed clearly enough so that a student can use them without detailed direction. Librarians question whether students are using the guides designed specifically for their online classes and if students return to the guide for help with later research or classes. The first criterion takes information from the LibGuide Statistics to determine if the online students are using the guide. Divide the number of total page views of the LibGuide by the number of students in the class. The second criterion looks at whether students who found a LibGuide helpful return to that guide for future assignments. This can be tracked by looking at the guide's statistics for the six months following the class.

Incidental Value

Incidental value looks at other measures to determine the success of the LibGuide. There are three criteria examining usage, access, and student/faculty feedback.

1. Visits, Returns, Visits per Guide
2. Inbound and Outbound Traffic
3. Student Feedback, Polls/Surveys

Ideally, students should be returning to a class LibGuide as a starting point for their research. Using Google Analytics, you can determine more specific information about LibGuide usage after an instruction session. You can look at a specific time frame following an instruction session, for example the two weeks following the session, and see if students are using that particular guide. Another question that librarians need to ask is how students access LibGuides. Are they using a direct link (URL), coming from the library's website, linking from an online course management system, or using a search engine? Google Analytics will show the path your students are using to get to LibGuides.

LibGuides makes it easy to use surveys, assessing either the quality of the LibGuide or the usefulness of the library instruction. However, surveys are not useful unless students are responding. Determine survey response rates to answer the third criterion in the Incidental Value section. This rubric (see table 11.1) allows librarians using LibGuides to gather measurable data and to combine it in a meaningful way. These data sets, when studied together, will allow librarians to place a value upon apparently useful software packages, and will ultimately help to justify related expenditures to library managers. Later in this chapter a case study will be used to further display the value of this rubric.

GATHERING STATISTICS ABOUT LIBGUIDE'S USAGE

This section of the chapter will focus on how to locate statistics that can be used to complete the LibGuide Rubric. LibGuides has a built-in statistical program that can provide information necessary for assessment. Statistics are available from within the My Admin/Dashboard section and can be accessed by clicking on Statistics on the Command Bar. As a LibGuide author, you can view your own guide statistics as shown in figure 11.1. However, only a LibGuide administrator can view all of the LibGuide Statistics. Table 11.2 compares statistics available to administrators and authors.

There are four different components to the administrator's Statistics menu (see figure 11.2). Select Your Report allows you to choose from General System Reports or individual guide reports. There are three display formats: (1) web browser, (2) a plain text version that can easily be incorporated into another document, and

FIGURE 11.1
Author view of statistics

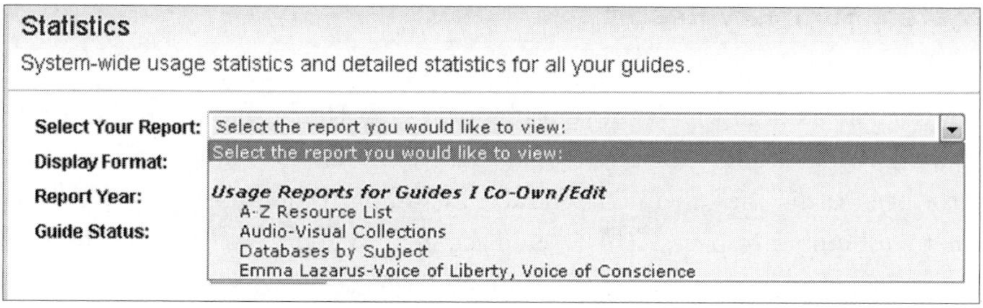

Statistics
System-wide usage statistics and detailed statistics for all your guides.

Select Your Report:	Select the report you would like to view:
Display Format:	Select the report you would like to view:
Report Year:	*Usage Reports for Guides I Co-Own/Edit*
Guide Status:	A-Z Resource List
	Audio-Visual Collections
	Databases by Subject
	Emma Lazarus-Voice of Liberty, Voice of Conscience

Used by permission of Springshare, LLC

TABLE 11.2

Statistics available to administrators and authors

LibGuides Stats	System Summary	Content Box Types	Home Page Hits	Guide Hits ALL	Guide Hits by Author
Usage stats available to all guide authors					X
Usage stats available to administrators	X	X	X	X	X

FIGURE 11.2

LibGuides statistics menu

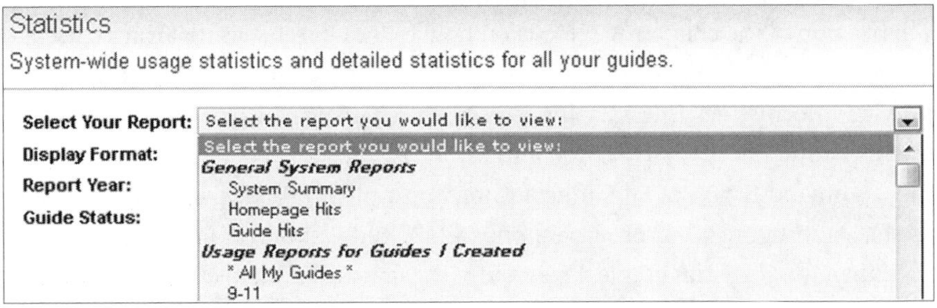

Statistics

System-wide usage statistics and detailed statistics for all your guides.

Select Your Report: Select the report you would like to view:

Display Format: Select the report you would like to view:

Report Year: *General System Reports*

Guide Status: System Summary
          Homepage Hits
          Guide Hits
    Usage Reports for Guides I Created
       * All My Guides *
       9-11

Used by permission of Springshare, LLC

(3) an Excel version. The Report Year Option lets you choose statistics by year. The final component lets you select published guides, unpublished guides, private guides, or all guides.

System Summary Report

The System Summary Report (see figure 11.3) provides you with general information about LibGuides at your library. It gives Homepage Views and Guide Views for the current year; remaining statistics are for the entire time that you have been using the LibGuide product, including the number of guides and the total number of pages. The System Summary Report is a good example of how LibGuides displays statistical information. As such, we will not include an illustration of each report discussed.

FIGURE 11.3

Indiana University East System summary report

System Summary *(generated: 2012-02-10, guide status: All statuses)*

# Guides	# Pages	# Content Boxes	# Accounts	Homepage Views (2012)	Guide Views (2012)
269	1663	6395	17	1636	9325

Content Box Types *(generated 2012-02-10, guide status: All statuses)*

# Rich Text	# Simple Web Links	# Links & Lists	# Documents & Files	# RSS Feed	# Dates & Events
2498	356	1752	98	31	3
# Embedded Media & Widgets	**# Podcast Feed**	**# Interactive Poll**	**# Linked/Reused Box**	**# Delicious Tag Cloud**	**# Books from the Catalog**
370		20	818	3	164
# User Submitted Links	**# Remote Script**	**# Google Web Search**	**# Feedback**	**# Google Book Search**	**# Google Scholar Search**
14	7		142	97	1
# LibAnswers	**# Links to Guides**	**# Partner Links & Search**	**# User Profile**		
9	1		10		

Courtesy of Indiana University East

Each tab within a LibGuide is considered a page. When you have stacked tabs (subpages), each one of those is considered a page. In the example provided, the average IU East LibGuide has just over six pages. LibGuides has a main page that directs users to the individual guides and that statistic is listed under Homepage Views. Total Guide Views includes Homepage Views and all of the pages within each guide that have been viewed.

Each LibGuide consists of content boxes and there are a variety of content boxes available. The System Summary includes the total number of content boxes as well as giving a breakdown of all of the types of boxes and the number of each. The System Summary also includes the total number of accounts. This refers to the total number of individuals who have been given administrator or author access. Collaborators are not included in this number.

Homepage Hits and Guide Hits

Homepage Hits is a monthly breakdown of hits to the LibGuide main page and can be viewed by year. The Guide Hits Report lets you view monthly usage of individual guides by year. You can select to view all guides, published guides, private guides, and unpublished guides. This report provides an easy way to determine the most popular guides.

Individual Guides

Statistical information is available for individual guides by year. Select the guide you want to view and the year. Figure 11.4 shows a monthly usage breakdown for each page of the Social Work Resources guide. While guide authors can only view statistics for guides that they own, administrators can view all guide statistics. There are also breakdowns for Widgets and APIs (under Widget & API Hits) and individual links within the guide (Link Hits).

LibGuides Statistical Reports (as viewed by LibGuides authors and administrators) display usage statistics for a particular guide or for a group of guides. In order to gain more detailed data Google Analytics must be installed.

FIGURE 11.4
Social Work Resources Guide report

"Social Work Resources" Page Hits 2011 *(generated 2012-01-02)*

Page	Jan	Feb	Mar	Apr	May	Jun	Jul	Aug	Sep	Oct	Nov	Dec	Total
Articles	43	37	13	30	117	39	-	1	106	55	31	17	489
Books & E-Books	27	5	4	10	18	5	-	3	47	13	6	3	141
Getting Started	38	45	25	45	149	52	4	10	232	123	46	24	793
If Not @ IUE	16	1	-	-	13	-	-	-	16	1	1	-	48
Need More Help?	12	-	-	-	10	-	-	-	9	-	-	-	31
Reference Sources	15	13	6	8	15	4	-	2	66	53	14	5	201
Web links & RSS Feeds	-	-	-	-	-	-	-	-	15	3	5	-	23
Writing & Citing	22	18	5	3	42	9	-	-	44	5	2	3	153
Totals	**173**	**119**	**53**	**96**	**364**	**109**	**4**	**16**	**535**	**253**	**105**	**52**	**1879**

Courtesy of Indiana University East

GOOGLE ANALYTICS IN LIBGUIDES

Google Analytics is a valuable assessment tool. Fortunately for the LibGuides administrator, the setup of the Google Analytics feature requires only a few steps to implement. Google Analytics allows libraries to track users, and more important, to determine which pages and links are used within the LibGuide. The information collected from the standard setup of Google Analytics provides basic statistics, including visits, bounce rate (defined as leaving site with no other action with the exception of media and flash links), time on site, page views, page visits, and the percentage of new visits. The detail is extensive and may be used to infer deeper understanding of the visits. An example of how a guide is being used is accomplished by analyzing the sum of information segments such as time-on-page, bounce rate, and number of new visits.

Setting up Google Analytics

Google Analytics is a free product available from Google. To use Analytics you will need a free Google Analytics account. To create an account, go to www.google.com/analytics. Once on the website, select the "Sign Up Now" link to begin (located under the blue Access Analytics button). Creating a new account requires the website address you wish to track, in this case your institution's LibGuides URL, and a unique name for your account. The next step asks for contact information and user agreement acceptance; and the final step provides the standard tracking code which you will paste into LibGuides. The Google Analytics system provides explanations and instructions to which you will want to refer.

Installing Google Analytics into LibGuides

The Google Analytics feature is set up by the library LibGuides administrator. From the LibGuides Dashboard, the administrator should choose Admin Stuff on the Command Bar and then select System Settings. The analytics coding information box is found toward the bottom of the System Settings screen. Paste the code from Google Analytics in this box.

USING GOOGLE ANALYTICS

After creating a Google Analytics account and after adding the code as discussed in the previous section, logging into Google Analytics will display the Overview screen. (This description is based on the newest version of Google Analytics.) Select the report that you want to view. This will take you to the Analytics' Dashboard menu.

Analytics' Dashboard opens to the Visitors Overview of the data returned. There is a chart detailing the total visits, with the default being the past month; however, you can change the time being viewed by the pull-down date option at the top right. There is a pie chart showing new visitors and returning visitors. A breakdown providing total visits, unique visitors, page views, pages/visits, average time on site, bounce rates, and new visits is also provided.

The Map Overlay (under Demographics: Location) shows geographically where visitors originate. The Traffic Sources: Overview shows the links visitors followed to arrive at your site. Each component of the Dashboard can be broken down for more in-depth analysis by clicking on the links to the left. If the terms and usage of Google Analytics are unclear there is a Help link at the top right of the screen. You may search for a term(s), example "bounce rate," or use the content links provided.

Analysis of Google Analytics

Deeper analysis of the data reveals other details: you can go beyond looking at site information to looking at individual guide statistics. Each area offers the opportunity to drill down farther to find more specific information. The date box, on the top right of the page, lets you select a specific time period. The example shown demonstrates the change in usage when the LibGuides' A-Z List replaced a list of databases on the external library website. The first six months of LibGuide usage for 2011 (see table 11.3) are one tenth of the total uses for the year.

TABLE 11.3
Google Analytics page views, by month, for the A-Z List—2011

Google Analytics Data	JAN	FEB	MAR	APR	MAY	JUN	JUL	AUG	SEP	OCT	NOV	DEC
A-Z List LibGuide 2011	44	64	53	91	25	82	456	572	1779	2752	2029	987

If an event such as instruction is being measured then the data can be viewed previous to the event, on the day of the event, and post-event. This requires the guide/event URL to have three separate views of the data by changing the date/time frame on the screen.

Included in the navigational bar on the left is an additional feature—Conversions: Goals: Overview—which is available after the administrator completes a second setup. Goals can be set based on URLs, time on site, or pages/visits. This setup does not have to be done initially and may be added after the administrator gains more experience with the tool.

The Full Report, found by selecting Content: Overview and clicking on the View Full Report link (located bottom-right corner of the page) provides an in-depth look at the entire site. From the Explorer tab, you can view the statistics per LibGuides page. If the addresses are confusing, you can view by Page Title. The Navigation Summary tab lets you view entry and exit paths. The In-Page tab lets you look at individual pages and see where users clicked. Graphical interpretation of the data is depicted in the main window using balloons, showing percentages, hovering over the links.

LIBGUIDES AS ASSESSMENT

LibGuides allow guide creators or owners to incorporate feedback boxes, interactive polls, and surveys to assess users of each guide. Your overall approach to gathering feedback can be enhanced by a little creativity and ingenuity. Consider all the capabilities of the LibGuide boxes and evaluate all possibilities to include non-LibGuides resources to provide a program of assessment. Table 11.4 provides a summary of internal LibGuides boxes that can be used for assessment.

INTERNAL LIBGUIDES OPTIONS FOR ASSESSMENT

The LibGuides product has several built-in features that can be used to create your own assessment tools. These tools can be designed specifically to assist you to gather information under the Incidental Goal of the LibGuides Rubric. The Feedback Box uses a predefined survey. Interactive Polls and User Link submissions ask for input about specific individualized questions. Librarians can also include

TABLE 11.4
LibGuide assessment boxes

LibGuide Box Type	System Assessment	Where Data
Feedback	Summarize student learning over time—supports programmatic LibGuide usage. Student feedback is important.	Captures data in e-mail
Interactive polls	Summarize student engagement and task completion over time. Are students providing responses to opinion polls? Additionally this is data to establish Goal Value.	Data on LibGuide page Goal Value in Google Analytics
User-link submission	Student engagement in LibGuide environment over time demonstrates worthiness of the LibGuides as continued tool.	Capture data in e-mail
Survey box—Campus Guides subscriber/ Springshare	Surveys allow several measures: Answering = engagement. What percentage of students is actively engaged during the instruction session? Follow instructions?	Data in LibGuides Goal Value in Google Analytics
Embed or RTF- Survey-Free or other survey tool	Surveys allow several measures: Answering = engagement. What percentage of students is actively engaged during the instruction session? Follow Instructions.	Goal Value in Google Analytics

specialized surveys to get more detailed information. Each of these options is discussed in greater detail in Chapter 9.

Feedback Boxes

The Feedback box has three predefined types of questions to gain feedback. The first question is a simple "Yes" or "No" response to the direct question, "Was this information helpful?" The second question, "How useful is this page?" is answered with a Likert Scale defining "1 = Not Useful" and "5 = Very Useful!" The third question asks the individual to provide comment for improvement with an open text box for data entry.

The Feedback box's responses are sent to the guide "owner" or to designated recipients. This basic feedback information helps guide developers understand usage from an individual user's perspective. The analysis of these data as a group provides anecdotal sources of information useful for guide redesign and correction.

Incidentally, we replied to a student's feedback comments who had initially rated one of our LibGuides as poor. The student was looking for more information on a topic that our resources do not cover well. A response to the student helped her find the needed information. In this way the LibGuide helped identify a resource need, in addition to the Incidental Value portion of the rubric. Using the Feedback polling, students can confidently identify areas that need improvement in the LibGuide.

Interactive Polls

The provision of interactive polls as a box option can be used resourcefully to create various forms of assessment. Poll choices can be presented as words, phrases, or sentences. When creating responses, the guide owner can make each response a live link.

A simple learning assessment is demonstrated at our Web Page Evaluation guide's Analysis tab (see http://iue.libguides.com/content.php?pid=206673&sid=1723917). At this point assessment of this data goes beyond just the individual instructional level. If there is evidence that the students are responding following the instruction session, then there is evidence that the LibGuide is being actively used and students are actively engaged. The guide's theme is web page evaluation, and the analysis page includes five basic questions regarding the mock-up websites. While the responses do not provide individuals' potential grades, it does provide an overall measurement of the learning materials. This kind of interactive poll could be used to assess pre- and post-test learning for individual guides or for a system of guides. Access to the collection of data is easy; click View Results in the Poll box and numbers and percentages are already calculated. Any user can view the results. These results appear automatically when a user clicks on Submit Vote. Only the guide owner has the ability to clear the count. In this way the results may be counted over specified periods and provide a breakdown for comparison.

User Link Submission

LibGuides offers a third type of user input box, User Link Submission. This box type can be used in a question format, asking users to enter URLs to measure understanding of the guide's instruction. The question could be entered as the box title or as a text field of the box. Text comments, entered under Description, are a part of the box's setup. The links and collected information go to the guide owner's e-mail, and he or she decides whether to post and reuse the information. Anecdotal information and inferences from the data generated are useful in the overall analysis. If this box type is used in an assignment format the measure could be, "Did the student follow through?" This information could be used to add to the data gathered for the LibGuide Rubric subgoal for Student Engagement

Adding Assessment to LibGuides Using Other Software Applications

Institutions that also subscribe to Springshare's product CampusGuides have another option available under the User Input Boxes—a survey box. The software prompts you as you create forms, write the embed codes for forms, and capture the information. The data is automatically organized and processed for further analysis. If students are responding to a survey, they are in some measure actively engaging in the instruction and adding to the data used in the LibGuide Rubric's Incidental Value measure.

If you want to design a survey without purchasing Campus Guides, free applications, such as Google Drive—formerly Google Docs—(http://drive.google .com) are available to create surveys. Users must have a Google account in order to take advantage of this option. After you have logged in, choose Create and then Form. Google provides excellent instructions to assist the author in creating the form that participants will later fill out. When the form is finished, a Google Spreadsheet is automatically created to hold the data. After you have created a survey, Google will produce an embed code for the survey. To get the actual survey to show up, click on the Form pull-down menu option when viewing the survey template. Select Embed from underneath the More Actions menu. This code can be pasted into LibGuides by adding a new box, then selecting the content box option, Multimedia Input—Embedded Media & Widgets. The created box has an option to Add Text and a link to Add Embed/Widget Code. Paste the code from Google into the Embed Code box. If the code works, the survey will appear immediately. The single-column page option will be the best one to present the survey. An example of a survey is available from http://iue.libguides.com/lkbsurvey.

207

FILLING OUT THE RUBRIC: A CASE STUDY AT EASTLAND

In this chapter we have discussed our rubric consisting of fifteen evaluative criteria. We then described how to use LibGuides' statistical tools and Google Analytics to answer statistical questions posed by the rubric.

To assist you in filling out the rubric for your own institution, we will be doing the same with a fictional library called Eastland University Library (EUL). Eastland is a small campus with a full-time equivalent of 2,300 students. (See table 11.5.) Our examples of useful data will provide actual numbers and values to complete the rubric. Each criterion response is broken down into three levels, representing "high," "medium," and "low" identified with percentages. As we work through each criterion, we will indicate which section EUL falls into.

Economic Value

We will start with the Economic Value section. The yearly cost to EUL for LibGuides was $1,158. There were 13,047 guide views and 54,020 page views for 2011. Without considering other factors, cost was $.09 per guide view and $.02 per page view. However, there is more expense to LibGuides than purchase price. (See table 11.6.) EUL published 83 new guides in 2011 and averaged seven hours per guide creation. The hourly salary for the instruction librarian is $28. Assuming she produced all of the guides, the creation costs would be $16,268. There are also administrative costs associated with LibGuides. EUL determined that a senior librarian spends approximately five hours per week on administrative duties. At a cost of $32 an hour, the administrative costs are $8,320. Adding all these amounts, the total LibGuides cost is $25,746. Considering labor, total cost per view is now $1.98 and total cost per page view is now $.48. This places EUL in the third column for cost per use being less than $10. (See table 11.6.)

The LibGuide product is not the only assessment going on at the Eastland Library. Library instruction is also being assessed. At the end of each instruction session, students are encouraged to fill out a survey evaluating the class. A goal was formulated to see how many students actually completed the survey. Two hundred and seventeen students, out of 279 who landed on the page, actually completed the survey, which represents 78 percent. This places EUL in the third column for goal values.

The third criterion for economic value is Increased Usage of Databases. These resources comprise a major expense and librarians need to direct students to use appropriate databases. The most popular of all of EUL's LibGuides is our A-Z list, an alphabetical listing of all of our databases, which received almost 30 percent of the total page hits for 2011.

TABLE 11.5
Rubric-assessing LibGuide value as an organizational tool—Eastland: A case study

VALUE Viewed:	LOW		MEDIUM		HIGH	
Economic Value—LibGuides are a great product, but are they worth the money? Is your library receiving a value worthy of the cost?						
Cost per use	☐	Cost per use is greater than $30.	☐	Cost per use averages between $10 and $30.	X	Cost per use is less than $10.
Goal values	☐	0–33% of all users reach an end goal.	☐	34–67% of all users reach an end goal.	X	68–100% of all users reach one or more end goals.
Increased database usage	☐	0–33% of users leave the LibGuide and access a database.	X	34–67% of users leave the LibGuide and access a database.	☐	68–100% of users leave the LibGuide and access a database.
Visits and paths	☐	0–33% of users leave the LibGuide and follow a suggested link.	X	34–67% of users leave the LibGuide and follow a suggested link.	☐	68–100% of users leave the LibGuide and follow a suggested link.
Subscription traffic	X	0–33% of users leave the LibGuide and go to a supported library tool.	☐	34–67% of users leave the LibGuide and go to a supported library tool.	☐	68–100% of users leave the LibGuide and go to a supported library tool.
Instructional Role Value—LibGuides are a great instructional tool. Is your library utilizing them to their highest potential?						
Use in instruction session	☐	0–33% of instruction sessions use a LibGuide.	☐	34–67% of instruction sessions use a LibGuide.	X	68–100% of instruction sessions use a LibGuide.
Percentage of use in class	☐	0–33% of the instruction session is focused on the LibGuide and its components.	☐	34–67% of the instruction session is focused on the LibGuide and its components.	X	68–100% of the instruction session is focused on the LibGuide and its components.
Active engagement	☐	0–33% of the students are looking at the LibGuide and its pages during the instruction session.	X	34–67% of the students are looking at the LibGuide and its pages during the instruction session.	☐	68–100% of the students are looking at the LibGuide and its pages during the instruction session.
Assess learning modules	☐	Post session poll scores increase 0–33%.	X	Post session poll scores increase 34–67%.	☐	Post session poll scores increase 68–100%.
Survey/poll faculty	☐	0–33% of the faculty provide input for their classroom session.	X	34–67% of the faculty provide input for their classroom session.	☐	68–100% of the faculty provide input for their classroom session.

(cont.)

VALUE Viewed:	LOW		MEDIUM		HIGH

Value in Distance Education—LibGuides can be linked-to from classroom management software. Identical LibGuides can be made unique by adding a section number to collect statistical information. Does your institution use LibGuides in their distance education/ online classes to help students in the research process?

Are online classes using	☐	The number of unique page views divided by students is <1 page use.	☐	The number of unique page views divided by students is between 1 and 5 page uses.	X	The number of unique page views divided by students is >5 page uses.
Return visits	☐	In the six months following the class, the number of unique page views divided by students is <1 page use.	X	In the six months following the class, the number of unique page views divided by students is between 1 and 3 page uses.	☐	In the six months following the class, the number of unique page views divided by students is >3 page uses.

Incidental Value—These are other units of measure to determine the success of the LibGuide.

Visits, return visits per guide	☐	The number of unique page views for two weeks following instruction divided by students is less than 1 page use. Divide the number of page views by the number of students in class.	X	The number of unique page views for two weeks following instruction divided by students is 1 to 5 page uses. Divide the number of page views by the number of students in class.	☐	The number of unique page views for two weeks following instruction divided by students is greater than 5 page uses. Divide the number of page views by the number of students in class.
Inbound and outbound traffic	☐	0–33% of users arrive from a direct link.	☐	34–67% of users arrive from a direct link.	X	68–100% of users arrive from a direct link.
Student feedback polls/ surveys	☐	0–33% of students respond to a poll during an instruction session.	X	34–67% of students respond to a poll during an instruction session.	☐	68–100% of students respond to a poll during an instruction session.
Total the checks in each column and multiply by the value assigned to that column.	1 × 1 = __1__		8 × 3 = __24__		6 × 5 = __30__ TOTAL = 55

Add the three sums together.

A score of 0–15 indicates that there is a lot of room for improvement in your LibGuide program. You are not getting much value from the LibGuides or are not utilizing them to their full potential.

A score of 16–35 means that there is room for improvement. Look at where you scored lowest and try to improve in those areas

A score of 36–55 shows that you are incorporating LibGuides into your instruction routine, but need to encourage more usage from faculty and students.

A score of over 56 shows that you are on target to using LibGuides successfully.

TABLE 11.6
Worksheet representing total LibGuide costs

LibGuides Economic Value	Cost	Guides	Page Views	Cost per Guide/Page
Cost per year	$1,158/year	13,047 guide views	54,020	$.09/guide $.02/page
New guides in 2011	$28/hour @ 7 hrs/guide = $16,268 / year	(in 2011 there were 83 new guides)		
Administrative costs	$32/hour @ 5 hrs = $8,320 / year			
Subtotal	$25,746	13,047 guide views	54,020	$1.98/guide $ .48/page

TABLE 11.7
Number of links to Academic Search Premier from LibGuides

Guide	Tab Links	Database	Database Links	% EASP Users
A-Z List : A-Tab total links	1158	(EASP) Academic Search Premier	638	55%
Fairy Tales Guide	743	(EASP) Academic Search Premier	446	60%
Average % of EBSCO Academic Search Premier usage (total percent divided number of observations)				57.5%

LibGuides tracks the number of times links created correctly are followed. In this example specific databases are identified to illustrate the value principle. EBSCO's Academic Search Premier (EASP) is found on the A page of the A-Z List. EASP was accessed 638 times of a total 1,158 visits to the A-Tab of the A-Z guide in 2011. This means that 55 percent of A-Tab users went to EASP. This simplification identifies the statistics available to formulate measures of value. Ideally, the real value would be a cumulative result for all access to specific databases targeted. (See table 11.7.)

In addition to the A-Z List usage of the EASP link, other EUL guides demonstrate database usage. As an example, the EUL LibGuide for Fairy Tales shows users linking to EASP 446 times out of 743 visits, or about 60 percent of page visits in 2011. To calculate the value for a total view of EASP use encouraged by LibGuides, we then add the values and divide by the total number of guides represented, resulting in 57.5 percent. While these examples are oversimplifications of usage, they provide data to begin a model of value assessment. This places Increased Database Usage in the middle column for 2011. An EUL goal for 2012 would be to increase the number of times users access EASP through LibGuides.

While LibGuides software provides basic statistical data, Google Analytics captures more complete sets of data. Using Google Analytics Outbound Links, a goal may be created for each database. Each outbound link can have a set of conditions to describe referral URLs, paths, and time. This is not a simple administrative setup, but requires JavaScript editing skills. This provides a third option to add to the data for this criterion and allows counting by date and date ranges other than the year used in LibGuides. Google Analytics has many resources to help the individual, including videos available online. (See http://support.google.com/analytics/?hl=en.)

LibGuides connects users to subscription services and free web-based services. As developers of LibGuides we thoroughly research topics and find relevant resources to support the needs of researchers. Does this work have value for the resources in our institutions? We will use Google Books to represent our free website for this example. Again, the statistics from LibGuides' A-Z List for EUL identifies 223 uses of the G-Tab, and then 55 links to the free website, Google Books. (See table 11.8.) The 24 percent of uses of Google Books in the A-Z List combined with the aggregate use of the other LibGuides will provide a value for the rubric. A Women's History LibGuide is identified that included research links to Google Books. Of the 381 uses of all resources on the LibGuide page, 247 used Google Books links, or 64 percent of the users went to Google Books. We will simplify the math, add the percentages, and divide by two in this example, for a summary score of 44 percent. This puts the criterion 4 score in the middle column, identifying it as an area needing more support or review.

The value for subscription traffic (in this case as measured by use of services such as ILLiad, RefWorks, and URL resolvers) is measured in a similar way to the third criterion, Increase Database Usage. Using RefWorks as an example, data shows that 22 users clicked on the RefWorks Link out of a total of 111 users that went to the R-Tab of the A-Z List. This represents a 19.8 percentage and places the

TABLE 11.8
Number of links to Google Books from LibGuides

Guide	Tab Links	Database	Database links	% GB Uses
A-Z List : G-Tab total links	223	Google Books (GB)	55	24%
Women's History Guide	381	Google Book (GB)	247	64%
Average % of Google Books usage (total percent divided by number of guides/ observations of data)				44%

measure in the 0–33 percent or first column. If the LibGuide author has created links correctly in a Link and List box, other uses of RefWorks links will be captured. Because of an error at EUL, other data on RefWorks have not been captured. In our case some anecdotal information about RefWorks may add to the value score for this resource. (See table 11.9.) RefWorks is accessible through other databases and is a built-in for ProQuest databases. For the fifth criterion the rating represents an area that needs improvement. An ideal score would include analysis of all subscription components from the LibGuides using these services.

TABLE 11.9
Number of links to RefWorks from LibGuides

Guide	Tab Links	Database	Database links	% of Uses
A-Z List : R-Tab total links	111	RefWorks	22	19.8%

Instructional Role Value

There are five criteria under instructional role value. The first looks at the usage of LibGuides during instructional sessions. Eastland Library is very dedicated to using LibGuides as an integral part of the instruction process. Of 122 instructional sessions in 2011, all but one used a LibGuide. The second criterion is percentage of use in class, and because most instructional sessions focus on teaching content using a LibGuide, the majority of sessions use a LibGuide for 90–100 percent of the time. Therefore, EUL places in the third column for the first two criteria listed under Instructional Role Value.

The third criterion looks at how actively students are engaged during the instruction session. Are students following along with the instructor as they demonstrate various databases? Using the Visitors Flow, listed under Audience in Google Analytics, you can get an indication of where students are going. (See table 11.10.) For our rubric, we chose three classes to analyze: a marketing class, a social work class, and an informatics class. Visitors Flow allows you to track interactions, up through the 12th interaction. It is easier if you select dates where there was only one instruction session so there can be no confusion as to which usage is being studied. For the rubric, we looked at where students were in the 10th interaction. The social work class started with 15 students and ended with 13 students by the 10th interaction. Marketing and informatics started with 17 and 16 and ended with 13 and 5 respectively.

TABLE 11.10

Table representing visitors flow data from Google Analytics

Marketing Guide Interactions	Start	1st	2nd	3rd	4th	5th	6th	7th	8th	9th	10th
Home	38	31	14		6	1	1	2	4		
A-Z List	18	3	7			2					1
M301	15		17	5	11	2	7	7	5	9	5
DB-Subjects	5			2		3		2			
Guide/Articles Databases+		24	11	30	15	20	13	13	12	5	9
Search				3	3	3					

While this demonstrates that the majority of students were on task, it fails to disclose that the students were not always on the same pages at the same time. For example, by the 10th interaction, the social work students were in six different locations. However, one wrong click would mess up the count.

You can also use Google Analytics' In Page Analysis to see where students are going during an instruction session. Bubbles (little balloons filled with numbers) show up over links that have been clicked on. The number represents the percentage of clicks/users that went to the link. If someone were to note each link the instructor used, and in what order, you would have a better chance of knowing whether the class was on task. Because students in the three example classes were not always at the same place, but were in the neighborhood, EUL scores in the second column for active engagement.

LibGuides interactive boxes gather pre- and post-session learning data that can be used for assessment. For example, librarians, like any other professionals, tend to use jargon and assume that students know what we are talking about. To make sure students understand the important terminology, a brief quiz is used at the beginning of instruction sessions for introductory classes. The terms on the quiz are "database," "record," "subject heading," and "abstract." After allowing a minute to take the quiz, the librarian goes over each term. At the end of the class, students are asked the same questions, but the responses are arranged differently. Scores between the two quizzes increase by 50 percent on average, placing EUL in the second column on assessing learning. These concepts are important to LibGuides usage because students need to successfully understand the composition of databases because LibGuides lead students to databases.

The final criterion under Instructional Role Value deals with faculty response with using LibGuides as part of the instruction process. When asked if they would use a LibGuide again for their class, 78 percent of the responding faculty said "yes." When asked how useful they thought LibGuides were, 43 percent responded "extremely useful" and "more useful." Another 33 percent responded "useful" or "some usefulness," while the remaining 23 percent said "not useful at all." However, when asked if they would recommend LibGuides to other faculty, 82 percent said "yes." There were 30 faculty who responded out of 71 who had library instruction sessions, for a 42 percent response rate. This places EUL in the second column. (See table 11.5.)

Value in Distance Education

Distance education is a term used to describe a variety of instructional experiences at Eastland and includes online courses, courses taught in a different city than the main campus, and video courses. We will examine two courses for this rubric measure. Both courses were entirely online. One was an accounting course, where the instructor provided the LibGuide link to the students. The other class, a women's history class, had an embedded librarian, who monitored discussions and was available within the course for online consultation and e-mail. The accounting course had 29 students and had a total page view of 113 pages. The history class had 47 students and 551 pages viewed. The scores, determined by dividing the number of unique page views by the number of students, were 3.89 for the accounting class and 11.72 for the history class. In this rubric value, the accounting class fits into the medium level while the history class fits into the high level. Averaging the two scores together gives a score of 7.8, placing it in the high level. There appears to be a relationship between having an embedded librarian in the class and a greater usage of LibGuides. EUL needs to think about adding more active embedded librarians to raise this score.

The second value under distance education is whether students found the LibGuide of value and return back to the guide when assigned future research projects. The accounting class had 58 page views by the 29 students, recorded for the six months following the class. The history class had 50 page views by their 47 students. As we did in the previous section, scores are determined by dividing the number of unique page views by the number of students. This gives us scores of 2 and 1.06 respectively, placing EUL in the middle level for this criterion. The librarians at EUL will need to find ways to encourage online students to return to the LibGuides. It should be noted that while the scores for any one particular LibGuide may appear low, one cannot assume that students are not using other LibGuides in their academic tasks. LibGuides and most external statistical packages cannot track specific students, so one cannot know if they are using other LibGuides to direct them to their research tools.

Incidental Value

The first criterion for incidental assessment is the number of return visits students make to a LibGuide after instruction using the LibGuide. Many factors enter into the total view of returning visits; some may be discounted, others overlooked. An administrator can use Google Analytics to look at origination of traffic, traffic dates, kind of devices used to access, and so on. Assumptions are made in these calculations and interpretations of the data. At EUL we will use three courses to represent traffic. Our formula is the number of unique pages viewed divided by the number of students in the instruction session two weeks after the class presentation. For this criterion, levels range from less than one to greater than five.

In EUL's marketing course instruction there was a specific LibGuide demonstrated to the class, and there were 333 page views on the date of instruction by the 17 students. In the two weeks following instruction, the guide was used an additional 101 times. This gives a score of 5.94 in the two weeks following instruction, representing an average of almost six page views per student.

The social work class of 15 students had 388 unique page views during the instruction section and 324 in the two weeks afterwards. This gives a score of 21.6. In the informatics class of 16 students there were 147 unique page views during instruction, but only four page views in the two weeks preceding instruction. This gives an extremely dismal score of .25.

The three classes provide an interesting look at return visitors. Scores can be skewed for a variety of reasons. Two of the guides used were course-specific, and the social work LibGuide is a subject guide. General subject guides seem to show higher usage than course-specific guides. Another factor that could skew the results is whether there is an assignment associated with the library instruction session. Students working on a research assignment are more likely to go back and use the LibGuide to access the resources. Because of the diversity of the scores for the return criterion, EUL scores in the second column. A goal for librarians would be to try to align scheduled instruction with research assignments.

A second criterion under incidental value uses site traffic to help visualize use of the LibGuides. By selecting Sources—All Traffic in Google Analytics, librarians can have an indication of how students are getting to your LibGuides. Ideally, it would be terrific if students had the direct address memorized. However, since that is not the case, the library's website and other resources should provide obvious links. We do not want our students accessing our LibGuides by searching on the Web. In 2011, EUL LibGuides were reached from a direct link 14,311 times and from an indirect link 524 times. For this criterion we are defining direct as access from within an EUL LibGuide, from the EUL's website or campus website, or typing the address in directly. Indirect would include access from a search engine or a link not affiliated with EUL. With 14,835 total points of access, EUL scored 96 percent and ranks in the third column. Libraries wanting to increase this score need to make their direct links more visible. EUL created business-size cards that had a QR code directing students to LibGuides and also used our Facebook page and library blog to highlight guides.

The third criterion under incidental value is student feedback, polls, and surveys. Students, as users of LibGuides, can provide assessment to help libraries measure user experience, impact, and opinion. EUL uses the default feedback survey on guides not using the instruction survey. The feedback is sent to the guide developer or an e-mail address designated to receive the e-mails. In 2011, one of the guide administrators for EUL received 37 feedback responses from 11 noninstructional guides. Twenty-nine of the respondents rated their experience on a Likert scale of 1 (low) to 5 (high) as 5; three respondents scored the guide with a 3; and three respondents had a rating of 1. Positive responses are calculated as 78 percent, placing the value in the rubric's right, top-scoring column. The information received from polls and surveys can be interpreted in many ways. Using the LibGuide Polls Box students can provide "yes" or "no" responses to in-class answered opinion questions about the guides. In 12 EUL course guides the question, "Did you learn from the LibGuide?" was asked of a total of 197 students. The responses were 113 "yes," 73 "no," and 11 did not answer. For this use of polls, 57 percent self-reported they had learned, placing the rubric measure in the middle column and adding to EUL's goal of using the comment information available to inform LibGuide creation and revision. We review the comments, looking for immediate needs, and then later transpose to numeric values to inform the overall response measure.

Totaling the Rubric

Looking again at table 11.5, score a "1" for every response in the first column, a "3" for the second column, and a "5" for the third column. Total the scores in each column to determine a final score.

- A score of 0–15 indicates that there is a lot of room for improvement in your LibGuide program. You are not getting much value from the LibGuides or are not utilizing them to their full potential.
- A score of 16–35 means that there is room for improvement. Look at where you scored lowest and try to improve in those areas.
- A score of 36–55 shows that you are incorporating LibGuides into your instruction routine, but need to encourage more usage from faculty and students.
- A score of over 56 shows that you are on target to using LibGuides successfully.

In tallying scores for Eastland Library, we received a 55, meaning that there is work that can be done to better utilize our LibGuides. While we are getting obvious value from the program, we need to work to improve return visits and response to polling/surveys. We also need to make sure our links to databases and other library subscription products are coded correctly to accurately reflect usage.

In many of the calculations for this fictional library we chose only a few LibGuides to represent the total traffic on the website. It would obviously be impossible to include data from every LibGuide into your calculations. Each time we used the rubric we would use different LibGuides for this process, depending on what our goals were for that time.

CONCLUSION

This chapter discussed and demonstrated a rubric created to be a useful LibGuide value assessment tool, allowing librarians to objectify data that is often very anecdotal. The rubric addressed four important categories 1) the economic value of LibGuides, 2) the instructional value of LibGuides, 3) the value of LibGuides in distance education, and 4) the incidental value of LibGuides. Each category included measurable subcategories. The second part of this chapter explained how data for the rubric could be collected from LibGuides and from Google Analytics. Finally the use of the rubric was demonstrated through a case study of a fictional university library—Eastland University Library.

Assessment is vital in academic libraries. While librarians like and use LibGuides it is important in the current academic climate to provide a variety of measurements for the resource. The value of LibGuides can be assessed on a continuum with value gained at both ends, from the individual to the library/institution, and then reaching the LibGuides community. The rubric presented will help libraries in their decision making regarding particular areas of the library environment that are touched by LibGuides. This rubric will also give overall information to library administrators regarding the actual value of LibGuides to the institution.

REFERENCES

Cook, Douglas, and Lesley S. J. Farmer, eds. 2011. *Using Qualitative Methods in Action Research: How Librarians Can Get to the Why of Data.* Chicago: Association of College and Research Libraries.

Oakleaf, Megan. 2007. "Using Rubrics to Collect Evidence for Decision-Making: What Do Librarians Need to Learn?" *Evidence Based Library and Information Practice* 2, no. 3: 27–42.

———. 2009a. "The Information Literacy Instruction Assessment Cycle: A Guide for Increasing Student Learning and Improving Librarian Instructional Skills." *Journal of Documentation* 65, no. 4: 539–60.

———. 2009b. "Using Rubrics to Assess Information Literacy: An Examination of Methodology and Interrater Reliability." *Journal of the American Society for Information Science and Technology* 60, no. 5: 969–83.

Using LibGuides to Promote Information Literacy in a Distance Education Environment

Barbara J. Mann, Julie Lee Arnold, and Joseph Rawson

When students are virtual and located all over the world, finding ways to proactively help them to understand how to locate, evaluate, and effectively and efficiently use information provides a host of challenges. Junk, Deringer, and Junk (2011: 2) state that "the goal of an online program should be to provide an environment which actively engages students in the learning process and promotes independent learning where students take ownership of their work." LibGuides serves as an important resource in this process. LibGuides, as will be explained in more detail in this chapter, can serve as a platform to provide "self-service" information literacy instruction as well as focused research resources in an educational environment where students are accessing resources and services both at a distance and at all times of the day and night, often without any librarian mediation.

While not much has been written about the use of LibGuides in the distance education environment, what has been written pertains to the overall effectiveness of LibGuides because they can be updated quickly, keeping the content "fresh," as well as having the ability to incorporate the ever-changing Web 2.0 technology and providing standardization in "look and feel" (see e.g., McMullin and Hutton, 2010; Robinson and Kim, 2010). This chapter will focus on how these characteristics make LibGuides an ideal delivery system for information literacy instruction in the distance education environment.

BEGINNING THE PROCESS

The first step in the process of creating a LibGuide is determining user need. This can be done through discussions with faculty, examination of syllabi and assignments, determination of learning outcomes, or from user information queries. It is important to determine the specific need in order to create a resource that is relevant and useful for the population it serves, in this case the needs of distance education faculty and students. Because it takes a lot of time and effort to create a guide, ensuring that it will meet the needs of those who are being served, before embarking on the project, is important.

Understanding faculty and student needs and expectations is crucial to the success of the LibGuide. Communication begins when a faculty member asks for a resource, when a librarian offers a resource to a faculty member or administrator or a group of faculty, or when multiple queries are made for the same information. Based on these communications, determination can then be made regarding which type of LibGuide resource will best meet the needs of the users it will serve.

Once a LibGuide resource type has been determined, examine the syllabi for any courses related to the guide being created. This may be a single course, or a series of courses for a particular academic program. The course syllabus will give information on assignments and research topics in the course(s). Knowing the course outcomes and assignments will help the librarian determine relevant sources for guide inclusion. Finally, defining the knowledge and skills the user should have as a result of using the resource will help determine the content of the guide.

Because the focus of this chapter is on using LibGuides as a tool to reach distance education learners, four main types of LibGuides will be discussed:

- Embedded stand-alone library instruction modules
- Course resources guides
- Subject-specific guides
- Tutorials

Explanation of Guide Types

Embedded Stand-Alone Library Instruction Module
In 2008, the University of Maryland University College (UMUC) library liaison to the Management, Accounting, and Finance Department in the Graduate School (GS) created stand-alone library modules for a high-enrollment online management

course as a way to provide scalable library instruction as a vehicle for information literacy skill-building in the asynchronous environment of distance education. This stand-alone module, where no librarian is present in the classroom, proved very successful, and is now offered at UMUC in dozens of courses in various departments, at both the graduate and undergraduate level. Since the original inception, the library modules have been transferred to the LibGuides platform, which makes them more visually appealing, easier to navigate, and provides an opportunity for assessing the usage of the modules. They are customized for each course and include all of the content the UMUC Library uses for all of its asynchronous online library instruction sessions. An embedded library module models the research process and typically includes the following pages:

- Topic Development Tips
- Search Tips and Techniques
- Locating and Using Library Databases
- Locating and Evaluating Scholarly Articles
- Locating and Evaluating Websites
- Finding Books
- Plagiarism Avoidance Using [insert citation style for example APA, MLA, Chicago] Citation Style, usually abbreviated with just the citation style name on the page tab

In addition, some guides, depending on the course need, also include

- Creating Annotated Bibliographies
- Finding Case Studies

Figure 12.1 is the home page of the LibGuide for the graduate-level course MGMT 610, Organizational Theory, which is a stand-alone module. In this embedded library module, the Topic Development page gives tips on developing a topic through background reading and refining the topic to create a valid research question that is focused and specific. The Search Tips page gives information on Boolean searching, phrase searching, keyword searching, truncation, subject searching, and thesauri. The Scholarly Articles tab gives information on locating, retrieving, and evaluating scholarly articles.

The remaining pages provide information such as how to search for and evaluate databases, websites, books, and case studies, as well as how to create annotated

FIGURE 12.1

Library Module for MGMT 610, University of Maryland University College

UMUC Information and Library Services » UMUC Subject Resources » Library Module for MGMT 610: Organizational Theory   Admin Sign In

Library Module for MGMT 610: Organizational Theory

This module is designed to show you how to access and use the resources and services available to you through the UMUC library.

Last Updated: Aug 26, 2011 | 🖨 Print Guide

| Home | Topic Development | Search Tips | Databases | Scholarly Articles | Web Sites | Books | Case Studies | APA Style |
| Annotated Bibliographies | Secrets of My Research Success |

Home 🖨 Print Page

■ Technical Help

Technical Help

■ Welcome!

Welcome to the Library Module for MGMT 610, Organizational Theory. The research topics covered in this module include:

- Topic Development Tips
- Search Tips and Techniques
- Locating and Using Library Databases
- Locating and Evaluating Scholarly Articles
- Locating and Evaluating Web Sites
- Finding Books
- Finding Case Studies
- APA Citation Format
- Creating Annotated Bibliographies

Please link to each research topic by clicking the corresponding tab at the top of the module.

You will find that the material covered in this guide complements and reinforces information presented in UCSP 611. Like anything else, good research skills take practice, and this guide is intended to help you become more comfortable with finding, evaluating, and citing material in various formats.

You may also ask for help anytime (24/7) by using our Ask a Librarian service.

Ask a Librarian

Have a quick reference question?
IM us using the form below.
The IM widget below works best in IE8, Firefox, Chrome & Safari.

Chatty   UMUC

Type here to chat.
Press ENTER to send.

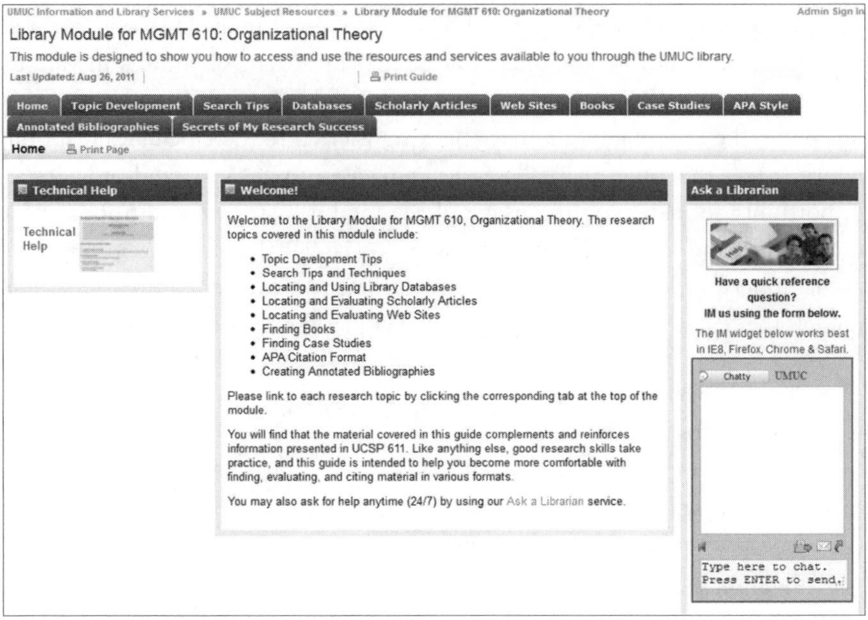

Courtesy of University of Maryland University College

reference lists. Not every guide includes every topic, as the content is based on the requirements of the course. The citation style page gives information on academic integrity, including plagiarism, and rules and examples of in-text and reference list citations in the citation style appropriate for that class.

Included throughout each section of a guide are appropriate research helps in the form of links to short tutorials, some in multimedia formats, as well as technical assistance. Each page also includes point-of-need reference assistance via the UMUC Information and Library Services instant messaging/texting widget. Other information may be included in stand-alone modules based on the needs of the instructor or department. Some instructors ask for a link to UMUC's plagiarism tutorial, or to the library's "Secrets of My Research Success" research process tutorial. The academic director for UMUC's Biotechnology Department, for example, asked for information on patent searching for the capstone course.

Course Resources Guide

A course resources guide is customized to a particular online course with links to research materials to provide the user with a smaller microcosm of relevant

FIGURE 12.2
Resource Guide for HIST 156, University of Maryland University College

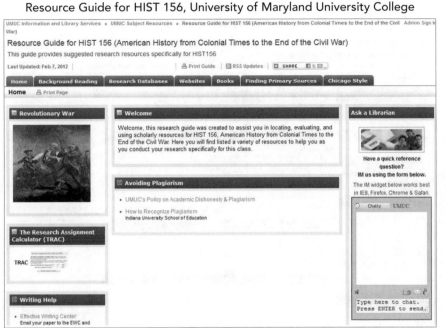

Courtesy of University of Maryland University College

resources tailored to the research needs of a specific class. This type of guide complements the stand-alone module because its main purpose is to lead users to resources relevant to specific assignments in a course. This is particularly useful for distance education students who need focused, assignment-related research help. Figure 12.2 is the home page of a course resources guide for HIST 156, American History from Colonial Times to the End of the Civil War. Undergraduate students who are new to research and need specific help for assignments in a particular course will find these guides particularly useful.

Subject-Specific Guide

Many libraries have created subject-specific guides, using the LibGuides platform, as has UMUC. These guides, created and maintained by library staff members, contain a wide variety of research materials and web links relevant for specific subject areas, based on the curricular needs of the subject area after an examination of course syllabi and assignment descriptions. Distance education students coming to the library website with a subject-specific need will find these guides useful as a beginning point in order to more efficiently and effectively find various types

FIGURE 12.3
Guide to Business and Marketing Resources,
University of Maryland University College

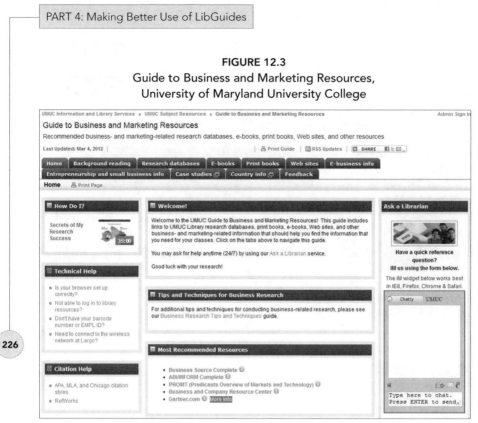

Courtesy of University of Maryland University College

of resources related to a particular topic, especially if they are unable to obtain research assistance at the time. When building a subject-specific guide, the UMUC librarian follows a Best Practices document that was created by a Subject Guide Task Force when LibGuides was decided on as a medium (see http://libguides .umuc.edu/best_practices to access the UMUC Best Practices guide). The types of resources and best practices will be discussed in greater detail later in the chapter.

Figure 12.3 is from the highly used Guide to Business and Marketing Resources and shows an example of subject-specific LibGuides featuring pages pertinent to the students in the course. To further demonstrate their popularity and usefulness in 2011, this guide was viewed more than 76,000 times.

Tutorial

A LibGuide tutorial should meet a very specific research need providing users with step-by-step instructions on how to perform a certain research task. Tutorials

FIGURE 12.4

Business Research: Tips and Techniques tutorial home page,
University of Maryland University College

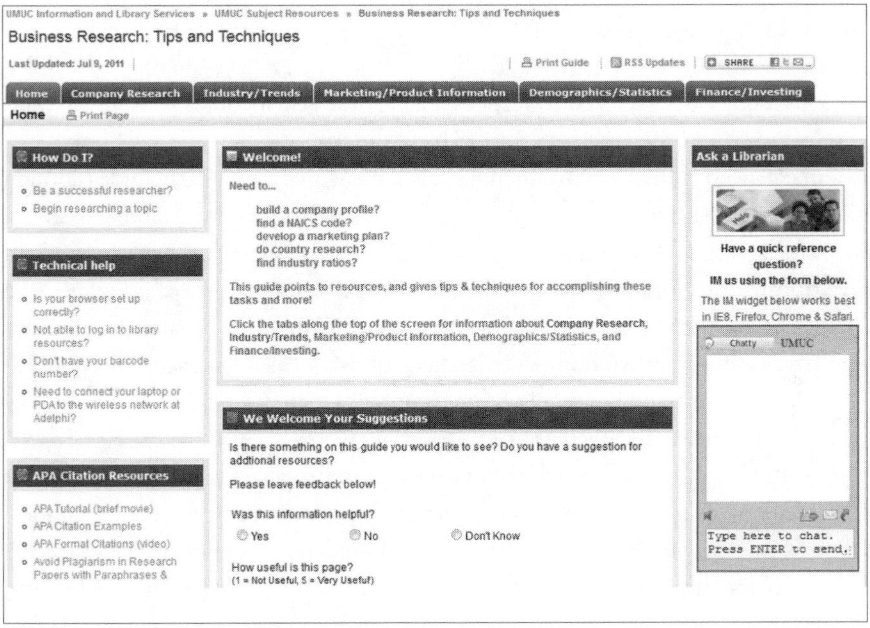

Courtesy of University of Maryland University College

that provide quick, point-of-need instruction are very useful in the asynchronous distance education environment when reference assistance may not be available. For example, a student may be asked to find a country report or a financial profile for a particular company. The UMUC Library's Business Research: Tips and Techniques tutorial has multimedia presentations created using Adobe Captivate on company research, industry and trends, marketing and product information, demographics and statistics, and finance and investing. Figure 12.4 displays the home page of the tutorial.

Because the main purpose of a tutorial is to provide point-of-need instruction, the tutorial needs to be well placed on the library home page for easy access. It is also important to link to it from other LibGuides and other course materials where instructions on that research task are needed. Talking to the faculty in the department will help determine what research tasks students or faculty will have to perform.

BUILDING THE GUIDE TYPE

When beginning to build subject-specific and course-specific LibGuides, the UMUC Library decided early on that certain resources should always be included in order to establish consistency. The standard resources include relevant books, e-books, library databases, and websites. Each guide also includes relevant citations and technical and research assistance. This standardization is especially important in a distance education environment because it ensures that all LibGuides contain a similar set of resources and can be navigated by students in a similar fashion, helping to eliminate confusion as to where certain resources can be located. In addition to the required elements, other various Web 2.0 media may also be included, depending on the guide's topic and purpose. There are some guides that have been topically arranged by certain subject areas. Guides such as political science and information technology are examples where users are better served by accessing resources arranged around a topic area.

Because books are a key source of research information, as a best practice at UMUC, there is a main-page tab designating books in each of these LibGuides. In the distance education environment print books may not always be accessible because of the inability of students and faculty to visit the physical library. However, the distance education book delivery program at the UMUC Library enables books to be mailed to students in the continental United States, making it an important resource to be included. Help links to tutorials on the book delivery process are also provided on this LibGuide page so that students are aware of what is required in order to have a book delivered and how to return the book to UMUC when it is no longer needed.

Instead of including a listing of books that may become outdated quickly with the arrival of new publications on a particular topic, the books tab contains a box that provides links to the catalog subject headings relevant to a particular guide's topic area. This is especially important in a distance education environment because the user is not able to physically access the library and browse the shelves looking for similar content. Because these are Library of Congress subject headings students and faculty can also use them to locate books at libraries that may be closer to them.

Library staff have been provided with instructions on how to insert a subject heading into the LibGuide box using special HTML code that creates links to subject terms in the catalog. When clicking on these links, a subject search on those areas is automatically performed. The print books box may also provide additional examples of subject headings that can be used based on the topic covered in the

LibGuide. Also included is the catalog search box so that students can directly perform a search on any subject, title, or author of their choice.

E-books are an important resource for distance education students, especially for those overseas, for whom print book delivery is not an option. The e-book page lists book titles as well as providing links to relevant e-books in the collection that relate to the subject covered in the LibGuide, along with possible search statements that can be used to find other e-books on the topic. Help on using the e-book collection is also provided here.

One specific tab relating to e-books that is included in these LibGuides is Background Reading. Because distance learners are not able to physically visit a library and access the rich storehouse of background reading found in a traditional print reference collection, including e-sources such as subject encyclopedias and dictionaries provides such an experience electronically. Students are guided here to begin exploration of a topic in order to further develop their topic and determine possible search terms.

The database tab lists relevant databases on the topic covered in the LibGuide. This may be broken down into general and subject-specific databases. If the LibGuide is very broad, there may be a tab for databases on specific subtopics. For example, the course resources guide for BEHS 365, Individuals, Society, & Sustainability, contains specific tabs for databases relevant to the subject areas of environment, sociology, psychology, and so on. (See http://libguides.umuc.edu/ BEHS365.)

Guides that have a more specific subject focus may only have one tab for databases. The databases are one of the most essential resources for distance education students because they contain full-text resources that are scholarly and current, and subsequently the database page of each LibGuide is accessed the most, which makes it necessary to be as comprehensive as possible. Another tab included on each LibGuide is for websites. This tab links to websites relevant to the topic and can be subdivided into various subject-specific areas. These websites have been prescreened by the guide creator for authoritativeness, accuracy, currency, and bias. Web resources are an important resource for distance education students, so having a comprehensive list of relevant websites is vital.

In addition to the resources listed above that are included in each LibGuide, various other Web 2.0 media can be included depending on the topic, such as podcasts, RSS feeds, and videos. These media can be integrated into the existing pages and put on the LibGuide home page or on a page of their own depending on the topic and the type of resource. Some of these resources, such as RSS feeds,

FIGURE 12.5
Resource Information Management System (RIMS),
University of Maryland University College

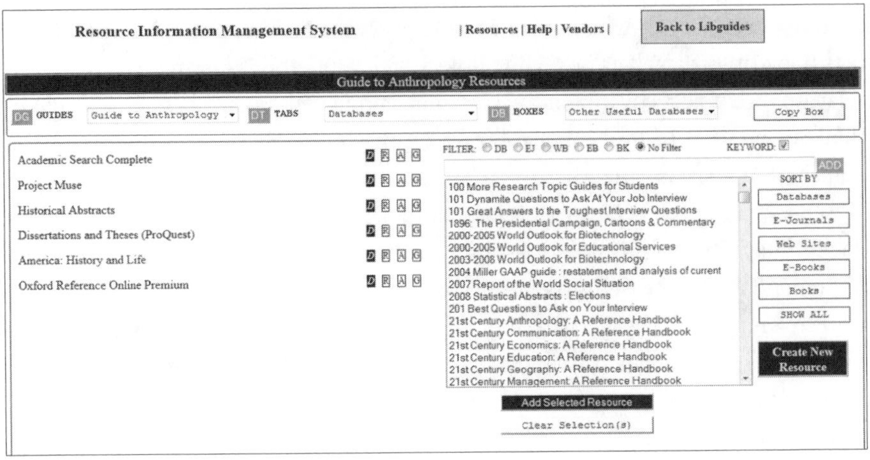

Courtesy of University of Maryland University College

are automatically updated to keep the LibGuide "fresh" and can help drive traffic to the guide.

The resources used in the various guides can be shared among all staff through the use of a common database, RIMS (Resource Information Management System), developed in-house in the UMUC Library. (See figure 12.5.) Each resource, whether a database, book, e-book, or website, is entered into the shared database only once, along with a resource description and link. Then, when that resource is needed in another guide, it can be easily accessed and placed in the new LibGuide without having to create it again. This shared database of resources also ensures that if a change is made to the record of a particular resource, the change is replicated wherever that resource is used in a particular LibGuide, so that individual updates of numerous guides do not have to be made. Because each resource listed in the shared database has a description attached, that description appears as a pop-up box next to each resource in the LibGuides when moused over. These descriptions serve to help the user to select appropriate resources, while saving space in each guide that might have otherwise been taken up by descriptions.

As previously noted, help is integrated into each page at point-of-need. For example, links to database help will be found on the databases tab, searching the catalog on the books tab, and so on. Each guide provides links to the appropriate citation style help on the home page or other applicable page. Technical help links are also provided throughout the guides. These help links are especially important to distance education users because many are not able to physically visit the library to obtain assistance. In designing a LibGuide it is especially important to keep in mind your users' various learning styles and make sure that you include graphics, multimedia, and audiovisual tutorials (transcripts provided), videos, and podcasts in addition to text. This is a key best practice at UMUC in working with distance education students in order to ensure that the content is understandable in a variety of learning contexts.

In order to provide point-of-need assistance, the instant messaging widget is built into each page along with the link for e-mail research assistance. Having instant messaging/texting and e-mail help available at point of need is important so that users do not have to find the appropriate place on the website when seeking assistance. For UMUC the addition of the instant messaging widget to each page has greatly increased the number of questions received via instant messaging.

Individual librarians should have some flexibility when creating LibGuides and be allowed to show creativity in their works. However, a balance needs to be maintained so that each resource has some consistency and can be identified as a particular organization's LibGuide. At UMUC, a style guide was created that listed the elements to be included in each guide, along with colors, box shapes, placement of boxes, language to be used in titles and headings, where to place help, and so on. This allows users to easily navigate through individual LibGuides, regardless of the topic. The Style Guide included in the UMUC Library Best Practices document (see http://libguides.umuc.edu/best_practices) provides suggestions to guide creators about other types of materials to consider for inclusion into their guides. UMUC decided to lock down certain features, such as color and box shape, for consistency while leaving other options open for their LibGuides authors.

TECHNICAL IMPLEMENTATIONS

One of the benefits of using LibGuides as a delivery mechanism for instructional purposes, especially in the distance education environment, is the fact that the URL for each guide is stable. Because of this each guide can be considered a "living document," that is, it can be revised as needed to keep the content fresh without having to change the URL. Therefore, using these guides as a vehicle for any kind of instruction can be accomplished through inserting the guide link into a learning management system (LMS)/course management system (CMS), providing point-of-need resources, services, as well as technical and research help at the fingertips of the user. The following paragraphs will provide more specifics on how to embed a LibGuide into some of the more popular systems and is provided via expertise from librarians at other institutions, some of whom responded to a request for information that was posted on the ILI-L electronic discussion list, hosted by the Instruction Section of the Association of College and Research Libraries.

Blackboard

Loyola Marymount University in Los Angeles is an example of an institution that has been integrating LibGuides into Blackboard. (See appendix C.) Their library and their Information Technology Services Department have created a database that includes course codes (subject-number-section) and LibGuide URLs. Within each Blackboard course, a dynamic link is created with Blackboard-generated code that includes the database link and the course ID. When a user clicks the link in a Blackboard course, there is a process "to translate course ID to subject-number-section" which then references the LibGuide URL in the database and forwards the user to that LibGuide page. If no LibGuide exists for that specific course, then the user is forwarded to a generic LibGuide page (Joe Russo, e-mail interview, May 5, 2011).

Moodle

Moodle, another popular course management system, also allows for LibGuides insertion. Phillips Library of Aurora University has created a LibGuide entitled "For Faculty," which provides a variety of helpful information. (See http://libguides .aurora.edu/content.php?pid=52421&sid=1198765.) Of special note is the page which provides step-by-step instructions for faculty on "how to import a course- or subject-specific LibGuide widget into their Moodle course shell." These instructions are the same for any Moodle user (Amy Schlumpf Manion, e-mail interview, July 14, 2011). Phillips Library reports that not only have many faculty been successful in integrating LibGuides into their courses, they have also found that faculty "are very appreciative of this research tool made easily available to their students (Amy Schlumpf Manion, e-mail interview, July 14, 2011).

Angel

Angel, another CMS, also makes this process easy. The first step is to click on the Lessons tab within Angel. Once this area has been accessed, click on Add Content, which leads to the Create an Item section. One of the choices under Create an Item is Link. Clicking on the Link heading opens the New Link section where the LibGuide URL will be pasted into the Link URL box, a title provided in the Title box, and finally clicking on Save will complete the process (Rhonda Fisher, e-mail interview, July 13, 2011).

Desire2Learn

Desire2Learn (D2L) allows the inclusion of a stable URL, such as those used by LibGuides, into a course shell. In general, to add a resource to a D2L course, "add a new Topic (item) to a Module (folder). Also, in general, add the new content as a Quicklink" (Doug Cook, personal interview, May 10, 2012). Shippensburg University has created a LibGuide for faculty that provides examples of placing resources into D2L. One page of the guide gives specific instructions for including LibGuides (see http://research.library.ship.edu/D2L).

There are a wide variety of LMSs/CMSs available. Each individual system has its own way of providing linkage to URLs. Those who are unfamiliar with how to integrate LibGuides into the system being used will want to consult the technical departments that handle such requests within an individual institution.

233

CONCLUSION

LibGuides is an invaluable tool in meeting students, faculty, administrators, and staff at their point of need for research and other assistance in the distance learning environment, most of whom will never see the physical library. Providing help at point of need and presenting the content in ways that meet a variety of learning styles are crucial to the resources being utilized. Communication with faculty regarding the instructional opportunities and added educational value these guides provide to their classes is vital in this promotion. Just creating guides of various types is not enough because they need to be utilized by faculty in their classes as an aid to students.

The value of using LibGuides can be promoted via library newsletters, faculty meetings, and communications with department heads and individual faculty members. Faculty need to actively advocate for the use of the LibGuides by their students through classroom announcements and online discussions. They must also continually assess how well the LibGuides are adding value to the class and communicate the need for changes to the LibGuides to the librarians. LibGuide creators also need to assess the value of the guides they create and continue to keep the content fresh and relevant.

REFERENCES

Junk, Virginia, Nancy Deringer, and William Junk. 2011. "Techniques to Engage the Online Learner." *Research in Higher Education Journal* 10: 1–15. www.aabri.com/rhej.html.

McMullin, Rachel, and Jane Hutton. 2010. "Web Subject Guides: Virtual Connections across the University Community." *Journal of Library Administration* 50: 789–97.

Robinson, Julie, and Don Kim. 2010. "Creating Customizable Subject Guides at Your Library to Support Online, Distance and Traditional Education: Comparing Three Self-Developed and One Commercial Online Subject Guide." *Journal of Library & Information Services in Distance Learning* 4, no. 4: 185–96.

APPENDIX C

LibGuide/Blackboard Integration at Loyola Marymount University

Appendix text and images contributed by Joe Russo, instructional technology analyst, and Ken Simon, reference and instruction technologies librarian, from Loyola Marymount University, Los Angeles.

Background

In late 2010, Loyola Marymount University's (LMU's) William H. Hannon Library and the Information Technology Services group initiated a project to integrate LibGuides into LMU's Blackboard 9.1 course management system. The desired outcome was to have a direct link to a subject- or course-specific LibGuide within each instructor's Blackboard course. The following is a description of how LibGuides was integrated into Blackboard.

Each semester at LMU, courses scheduled by the registrar are uploaded to Blackboard using a common course template. The courses are blank "shells" that do not contain any course information. It is each instructor's responsibility to add content to the course and make the course available to the students. Additionally, outside of the Blackboard environment and residing on the library's website, LibGuides exist for all course subjects (PSYC, MATH, BIOL, and so on). The instructors may also request a LibGuide specific to their course (PSYC-101) or section (PSYC-101-02). Prior to the integration project, instructors who wanted a link from Blackboard to their LibGuide were provided instructions on how to manually add the link to their course. The project sought to automate this by adding a LibGuide link to every Blackboard course. The LibGuide link in Blackboard forwards students to a custom application created using Java and an Oracle database. The custom application translates the course ID to a LibGuide URL, using mapping stored in the database.

Integration

The LibGuide/Blackboard integration requires three key elements:

- Dynamic code provided by Blackboard that automatically generates a course ID when a page is loaded in Blackboard.

235

- A database link to the registrar's system (Banner) to translate course ID to subject, course number, and section.
- A custom application that links subject, course number, and/or section to a LibGuide URL.

With these three elements in place, a LibGuide content area and link can be created in Blackboard, and the content area can be included in the course template when courses are created. Thus, every course created with the template contains a link to the LibGuide associated with that subject, course number, or section. Every course contains the same base link, with dynamic code appended that automatically translates to the current course's course ID. The link is as follows (dynamic code in bold):

http://<database_url>/redirect?courseID=**@X@course.course_id@X@**

For example, for PSYC-101-02, this link translates to:

http://<database_url>/redirect?courseID=**12345.201130**

When a student chooses this link, he or she will be redirected to the LibGuide associated with that course. Several database lookups occur in the background prior to the redirect, but to the user the redirect is instantaneous. First, the course ID is cross-referenced in Banner, and the course subject, number, and section are returned. Then the LibGuide database is queried for the course subject, number, and section. The query is nested such that a LibGuide is found for one of three combinations: subject-number-section, subject-number, or subject. This query is represented in figure 12.6.

Figure 12.6 shows that a generic LibGuide page will be displayed if no custom LibGuide exists for course section, number, or subject. LMU's objective is to have a LibGuide for each subject as a minimum. However, the link to a generic page is included as a backup and to prevent database errors.

LibGuide Database Maintenance

LMU's librarians maintain the LibGuide database. Each row in the database includes fields for subject, number, section, LibGuide name, URL, and comments. In addition, a field for active/inactive is included so LibGuides can be temporarily deactivated if, for example, a faculty member is on sabbatical and may want to use the LibGuide in the future. A sample from our LibGuides database is shown in figure 12.7.

FIGURE 12.6

Database lookups as a result of a student choosing a link in Blackboard

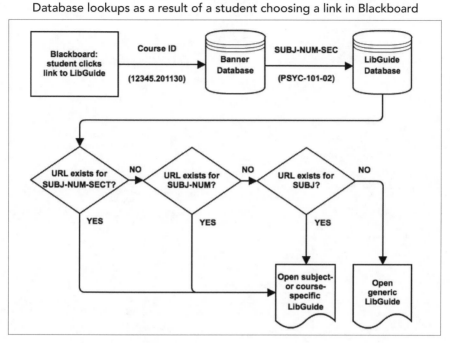

FIGURE 12.7

Database created to redirect students to the correct LibGuide

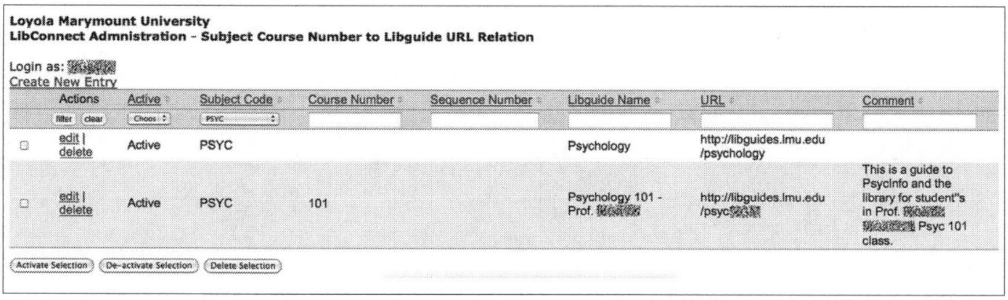

Loyola Marymount University
LibConnect Admnistration – Subject Course Number to Libguide URL Relation

Login as: ▓▓▓▓▓
Create New Entry

Actions	Active	Subject Code	Course Number	Sequence Number	Libguide Name	URL	Comment
filter clear	Choos ⬦	PSYC ⬦					
☐ edit | delete	Active	PSYC			Psychology	http://libguides.lmu.edu /psychology	
☐ edit | delete	Active	PSYC	101		Psychology 101 - Prof. ▓▓▓▓	http://libguides.lmu.edu /psyc▓▓▓	This is a guide to PsycInfo and the library for student"s in Prof. ▓▓▓▓ ▓▓▓▓▓ Psyc 101 class.

(Activate Selection) (De-activate Selection) (Delete Selection)

Figure 12.7 shows that LibGuides exist for PSYC-101 and PSYC. So if students in a PSYC-101 class click the LibGuide link in their Blackboard course, they will be forwarded to the "Psychology 101" LibGuide. Alternately, if students in any other psychology course click the link in their Blackboard course, they will be forwarded to the "Psychology" LibGuide.

## Chapter Thirteen

Why Go Mobile?

Mark Ellis, Leslie Adebonojo,
and Kathy Campbell

The smartphone revolution has changed the way we find information. A smartphone is generally defined as a cell phone with more improved connectivity, greater memory, and more advanced Internet applications. These improved cell phones allow us to access the Internet anytime and anywhere. It is quickly apparent to anyone who uses a smartphone that traditionally designed websites do not translate well to a mobile device as they can be slow to load, hard to read, and hard to navigate. As smartphones have become more popular, developers have realized that they need to create websites that are responsive to these devices.

Recent research has shown that there has been a shift in how people communicate and access information over the Internet. According to the 2010 Pew Research Center's Internet and American Life Project, 40 percent of adults use the Internet, e-mail, or instant messaging on a mobile phone, and 65 percent of young adults access the Internet through a mobile application (Pew Research, 2010). Mobile use is growing as smartphone producers develop more and more powerful and versatile devices. In a May 2011 survey on smartphone usage, the Pew Internet Project found that 83 percent of U.S. adults own a cell phone, and 42 percent own smartphones (Pew Internet, 2011).

A recent Google study revealed that mobile users have several characteristics that cross all demographic categories (Pham, 2011):

- They access information while on the move to satisfy an immediate need.
- They plan on the go and are apt to take action within a day of their search.

- They are multitaskers. A majority of those surveyed reported using other media, such as watching television or reading the paper, while using their smartphone.

According to these statistics, librarians can expect to have many more, busy smartphone users attempt to access our websites. Particularly in academic libraries, our patrons tend to be young adults, many of whom carry their smartphones with them at all times. We need to ensure that the many hours we spend in creating websites also benefit this ever-growing population of smartphone users. As will be discussed later in this chapter, LibGuides easily lends itself to smartphone use.

Another item of interest to website developers is the changing popularity of the various types of smartphones. This breakdown changes from season to season as telecommunications companies compete to produce new, more powerful devices. Providers have recently begun touting the newer, faster 4G-compatible smartphones which may bring about another change in the way patrons use smartphones. As of August 2011 (Kellogg, 2011) the most popular smartphone platforms are Android, iPhone, and Blackberry. Android is the top-selling smartphone with 43 percent of the market share. Apple smartphones follow with 28 percent of all users owning these devices. Blackberry users represent 18 percent of total smartphone ownership. Each of these phone types works a bit differently and has different characteristics that need to be considered as we plan for mobile accessibility.

Also, new products are constantly appearing with increased memory and capability. Patrons are able to access the Internet on Nooks, Kindles, and, of course, tablet devices such as the Galaxy or iPad. These devices will add another dimension of concern as we test access to our library websites with them. Follow the developments, read reviews, and look at the new devices when they are launched by the retailers. For you, as a LibGuides author or administrator and therefore an application developer, this means that you will have to stay current on what your patrons use and make sure your LibGuides are accessible.

This chapter will be of particular interest to LibGuide creators who want to ensure that their patrons who use smartphones will have ready access to usable guides. The rest of this chapter will discuss why you need to create new LibGuides specifically for use on smartphones, outline decisions you will need to make before beginning to create mobile guides, discuss how to make a mobile LibGuide, explain why you might want to add QR codes to your site, and finally we will take a brief look at the LibGuides add-on, Mobile Site Builder.

CAN USERS ACCESS MY LIBGUIDE ON THEIR SMARTPHONES?

In general, smartphones will reformat a web page to fit the phone's screen. Smartphone screens are small and vary in size across platforms. For example, Android allows for variation depending on the size of the device. In the case of Android smartphones such as the HTC Evo 4G, the screen has a 4.3-inch diagonal display with a resolution of 800 × 480 pixels. The iPhone has a 3.5-inch diagonal display with a 960 × 640 pixel resolution, and the Blackberry Storm has a 3.25-inch diagonal display with a 480 × 360 pixel resolution. How the smartphone handles the website display depends on the platform, the particular style of phone, and the website itself. Some websites convert automatically to a mobile version; others offer a mobile alternative from the main website; and many others, unfortunately, cannot be converted and are difficult to read on the smartphone screen.

Figure 13.1 is a smartphone image of one of Sherrod Library's LibGuides which did not convert to the smartphone screen format. It is usable, but would be frustrating for most smartphone owners. In order for the entire image to be viewed, the patron would need to move the full image across the screen. Many smartphones allow the user to zoom in and out on images. Zooming this website, however, still would not make it much easier to use. Fortunately, you can create usable mobile LibGuides by following a few easy steps.

FIGURE 13.1

A nonmobile website that is not easily readable on a smartphone, East Tennessee State University

Reprinted by permission of East Tennessee State University

241

DO-IT-YOURSELF MOBILE LIBGUIDES

Using the LibGuides basic program, we will build upon the page-authoring skills you learned in chapter 8 and chapter 9. In this section, we will guide you through basic steps of mobile site development from planning, through selecting content, and through formatting content.

Planning

As with standard LibGuides, you need to make decisions at the start about format, content, visuals, videos, and so on. Smartphones place a number of restrictions on both format and content. Since it is impossible to tell what phone features a particular user will have, how a user has configured a smartphone, or what new features and capabilities will appear in the near future, you need to design your mobile LibGuide to run effectively on as many devices as possible. The key is simplicity. The less complex your guide is, the more likely it will be able to be viewed on a smartphone. The following includes some of the elements that affect how a website will load on a smartphone.

Content Requirements

Certain formats of material may require special add-ons or drivers to run well. Think about using simple programs and links that are straightforward and easy to use. You don't want to frustrate users by linking to material and databases that will require their own downloads to run.

Device Memory

Since the newest generation smartphones are almost like small computers, the available memory can have a great effect on performance and how quickly your LibGuide will load. Smartphones can have as little as 2 GB of memory or as much as 32 GB (as of this writing) or more depending on the model and how much the user has paid. At the same time, a user may have loaded programs, games, videos, and music, drastically reducing the amount of available memory. How does this affect your planning? Avoid including complex graphics in your mobile LibGuide that might make it difficult or impossible for users to download the LibGuide without deleting other programs. On the other hand, you might want to include streaming video since it uses little memory, and therefore plays well on most mobile devices.

Telecommunications

Smartphones use several forms of telecommunication, and the type of connection can have an effect on how your mobile LibGuide will work. Basic cell phone service uses radio waves from networks of towers to transmit calls, data, and so on. Newer smartphones are capable of using several types of networks together, including G3 and G4 (Generation 3 and Generation 4) networks, and secured and unsecured wireless networks, allowing users to search and communicate over the Internet. Speeds depend on having the current generation of smartphone or a good wireless connection. Of course, you and the user have no control over the telecommunication connection, beyond the user's choice of network. How does this affect your planning? Again, simple is usually the best choice.

Proprietary Databases, Intellectual Property, and Authentication

Yet another important consideration when creating mobile LibGuides is the ownership of the links you include. If you link to a database licensed by your institution, you will have to determine how to authenticate users when they are not using your institutional network. Authentication is the way that a licensee shows that the user has the legal right to access the licensed database, text, video, and so on. Typical methods of authentication using sign-ons and passwords may be too cumbersome for smartphone users. Also, depending on the type of connection, authentication may not work at all. How does this affect your planning? An easy solution to this problem is to choose open source or open access links. There are many available open access databases that can serve users just as well as the proprietary databases licensed by institutions. Two examples that come quickly to mind are PubMed and Google Scholar.

Mobile Versions of Websites

No matter how clear and simple the main page of your mobile LibGuide may appear, you can quickly make it unusable if you link to a standard website rather than a mobile version. Linking to a standard website can put the user in a screen with print so small that it is unreadable, or into a screen with a web page that resembles the pieces of a puzzle (see figure 13.1). How does this affect your planning? With the increased use of smartphones, many website designers have created easy-to-find mobile versions. WorldCat (www.worldcat.org/m) and EBSCOhost (available on iTunes and the Android Market) have applications that you may want to refer to in your LibGuides.

Layering

Think about the number of layers of links that you will have in your mobile LibGuide. Since smartphone users are multitaskers who are on the move and looking for information fast, they will not take the time to find material buried under five layers of links. The smartphone itself may also have difficulty loading more than two or three layers. How does this affect your planning? When creating menu navigation, try to link to only one website for each menu item.

Survey Your User Group

Each group of users is different. How do your students use smartphones? What would students on your campus want to find on the library's website? How does this affect your planning? You may want to survey your patrons. For example, our undergraduate student services librarian recently conducted an informal survey of 150 randomly selected students at the campus activity center at East Tennessee State University (Adebonojo, 2010). Students were asked, "What type of information would you be looking for if you were using your handheld?" Here are their answers:

- "Look up a word/concept while professor is talking"
- "Only a snippet"; students can go back later and get more info
- "Look up a drug"
- "Check course reserve"; students would read it later
- "Check how to cite sources"

More often than not students use handheld devices to rapidly find quick bits of information so that they can complete a task or go on to another task. Keeping this in mind, simplicity is the key to designing websites that mobile users will use and return to again and again. It is obvious that the simplest version of a mobile LibGuide will run better than a complex, layered site with a lot of text, links, and pictures. Remember the purpose of the mobile LibGuide. If you want to include a long list of links and documents, save the unabridged version for a standard web page.

Start Working on Your Mobile LibGuide

To make this process easier for you to imagine, let us assume that you received a request from an English instructor for a mobile LibGuide for a class. Listed below are the steps that you would need to follow in order to create the guide.

Step 1: Log in to My Admin

On your Dashboard click on Create New Guide. If you are making your first mobile LibGuide, select Start Fresh because you will be creating a new template that will be compatible with a typical smartphone's display. After you have made one, you can use the template for other mobile LibGuides. Name your guide and click on Create New Guide.

Step 2: Resize the Columns

Your first task will be to resize your LibGuide's columns. So that the mobile LibGuide will appear in the correct position you will have to resize the columns from the default three columns to one column. Changing to one column is necessary for the text to be readable on the mobile device. On the top toolbar choose Edit Page and then Resize Columns. From the options in the menu, choose 1 Column—Center Column Only.

Step 3: Add a Box for Linking

In your one-column guide, click on Add New Box. If you are creating a simple mobile LibGuide with only links to websites or databases, from the Box Type drop-down menu, choose Links Boxes, then Simple Web Links. Type in a title for the box. In this case, we are calling it Research Tools. Then click Create Box.

Step 4: Place Links in the Box

Click on Add New Link. Now you are ready to add links to databases and websites. In the Link Title box, give the databases brief, easily understood titles. Descriptions are not necessary since they will take up space. Also, remember to use the mobile versions of the databases and websites to which you are linking. Select open access websites and free databases whenever possible.

Step 5: Preview Your Mobile LibGuide

There are several ways to preview your mobile LibGuide. You can click on Preview in the toolbar at the top of the page (see figure 13.2). This will let you see the functionality of your mobile LibGuide, but it does not give you a good idea of how it will look on an actual smartphone.

Step 6: Preview Your LibGuide with an Emulator

Springshare recommends using Google Chrome to test mobile LibGuides; however, the display will not completely resemble an actual mobile display. A more accurate representation can be viewed using a device emulator, which is a software

FIGURE 13.2

Finished mobile LibGuide seen on the admin side in preview mode, East Tennessee State University, http://libguides.etsu.edu/ENGL1020Mobile

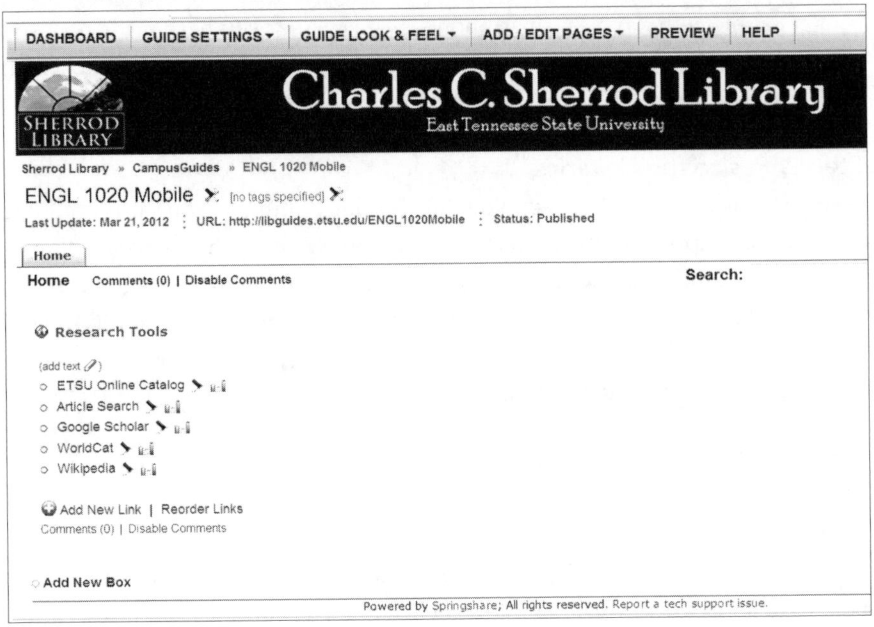

Reprinted by permission of East Tennessee State University

application that can accurately imitate a mobile phone and run software from that computer. TestiPhone (www.testiphone.com) is an easy tool to use because it does not require you to download a program or to register. An Internet search will identify emulators to use with other types of smartphones. Of course, the most accurate preview with full functionality would be to type in the mobile LibGuide's URL in a smartphone and test all of the links (see figure 13.3). You should be able to easily see if your mobile site works or needs improvement.

Step 7: Adding Communication Functionality

One of the best ways for students to share a mobile LibGuide is with a QR code on the site (see figure 13.4). This code allows anyone with a QR reader to open a LibGuide without having to type in a URL. QR code is an abbreviation for "quick response code." It is a type of matrix bar code, originally used in manufacturing. QR codes are readable by dedicated QR readers (similar to bar code readers) and many smartphone applications, such as Google Goggles (www.google.com/mobile/

FIGURE 13.3

The LibGuide previewed on a smartphone, East Tennessee State University, http://libguides.etsu.edu/ENGL1020Mobile

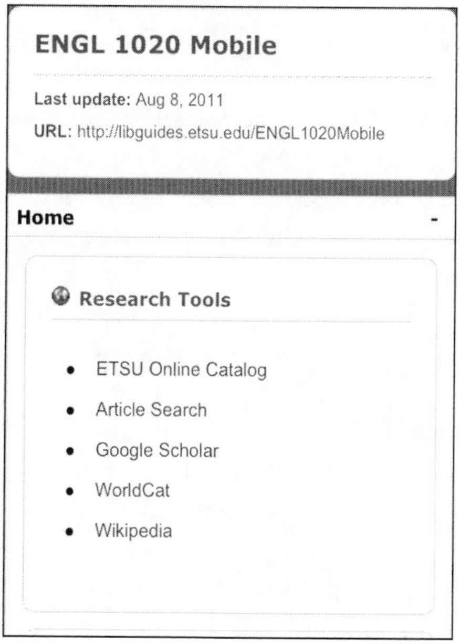

ENGL 1020 Mobile

Last update: Aug 8, 2011

URL: http://libguides.etsu.edu/ENGL1020Mobile

Home −

🌐 **Research Tools**

- ETSU Online Catalog
- Article Search
- Google Scholar
- WorldCat
- Wikipedia

Reprinted by permission of East Tennessee State University

FIGURE 13.4

The QR code for this mobile LibGuide, East Tennessee State University, http://libguides.etsu.edu/ENGL1020Mobile

Reprinted by permission of East Tennessee State University

goggles). The QR code consists of black modules arranged in a square pattern on a white background. The information encoded may be text, a URL, or other type of data. These codes are becoming increasingly popular and appear on retail store aisles, in newspapers and magazine ads, and so on. If your mobile LibGuide has a QR code, it can easily be shared between smartphones. Figure 13.4 is a QR code created for the mobile LibGuide described in this chapter.

QR codes are simple to produce. Many code generators are available on the Web that allow you to input a URL. The program then outputs a graphic file which you can include in a LibGuide (http://qrcode.kaywa.com is one code generator). After you have saved the QR code JPEG to your computer, go to your mobile LibGuide. You have two options: you can either add the QR code before your links or create a second box. If you create a second box, click on Add New Box. For content/box type, select Rich Text/Dynamic Content/Scripts. Give the box a title, and click

FIGURE 13.5
The finished mobile LibGuide on a smartphone (to see the QR code you would need to scroll down), East Tennessee State University, http://libguides .etsu.edu/ENGL1020Mobile

Reprinted by permission of East Tennessee State University

on Create Box. In the new box, click on Add Text. In the toolbar, click on the icon for Insert/Edit Image. (The icon looks like a picture of a small tree.) Click on the red message: "Click to upload an image from your computer. . ." Click on the QR code and then insert it. (The ability to upload images from your desktop is an add-on program from Springshare that you will need to purchase.) Now you have a mobile LibGuide with a QR code (see figure 13.5).

MOBILE SITE BUILDER ADD-ON

During the summer of 2011, Springshare launched its Mobile Site Builder Add-on module. For an additional fee, you can purchase the module to create new mobile LibGuides (the module does not convert existing LibGuides to a mobile format). Springshare offers default choices for building a mobile guide, but you can also customize any or all sections. Following the site instructions, Mobile Site Builder: Create a Mobile Library Website in 3, 2, 1! (http:// help.springshare.com/msb), you can make format, color, and content choices that allow you to brand and customize your mobile version differently from your basic Lib-Guides program. The module allows the placement of headers, footers, two links for each tab, and ten top-level items. You can select a setting in the Mobile Site Builder that will direct the smartphone to choose the mobile version of a website. With a few additional instructions from the site for LibGuides Help & Documentation (http://help.springshare.com/content.php?pid=263775&sid=2177856), you will be able to build a simple mobile site in a few hours (see figure 13.6).

Compare figure 13.6 to figure 13.3. The links are larger and easier to see. Also a small graphic can be associated with each link. A mobile main page for any LibGuide will improve the users' ability to quickly access the headings or tabs in your guide. However, keep in mind that any web pages connected to this main page will not show up in a mobile format unless they were designed as mobile sites or can be automatically converted to a mobile site on your smartphone.

MORE POSSIBILITIES

Emphasized in this chapter is the basic mobile guide functionality provided to you by LibGuides. There are further possibilities to add to the mobile accessibility of your guides. For example, it is possible for you to create an app for your mobile site. There are many programs available that will enable you to create an app and link it to the URL for your mobile LibGuide. You can also add a wide range of information formats to the mobile LibGuide. Newer smartphones are capable of handling audio files and YouTube and other video file types. These files can be easily included in any LibGuide. The search box for LibAnswers (an add-on from Springshare that includes a knowledge base, covered in chapter 10) can also be included in a mobile LibGuide. This will give smartphone users 24/7 access to the most frequently asked questions about your library as well as give them an opportunity to ask questions through a feedback function.

FIGURE 13.6
Finished mobile LibGuide created with Mobile Site Builder Add-on, East Tennessee State University

Reprinted by permission of East Tennessee State University

249

CONCLUSION

This chapter discussed the rapidly increasing number of smartphone users who access our websites. With the strong presence of smartphones in the hands of our users, as well as the recent upsurge of e-readers and tablet devices which can access the Web, it is important that we do not ignore this ever-growing clientele base. A solid understanding of the functionality of mobile devices is important as you plan how you will provide access to your website. Since smartphones have less memory and access the Internet through technology different from the typical laptop, awareness of these details will help you accommodate mobile access. Keeping abreast of the latest mobile technology will help you to adapt to new user demands.

The Pew Research Center's Internet and American Life Project (Pew Research, 2010) reinforces what we know anecdotally—that more and more people are using smartphones to access the Internet. With 40 percent of adults and 65 percent of young adults using mobile devices to find information, libraries must develop websites that work well with these devices or they will lose opportunities to serve their patrons. LibGuides is an adaptable, inexpensive, easy-to-use tool that librarians can employ to create smartphone-friendly research guides. With the information contained in this chapter, you can make informed decisions about what to include in your mobile guides—whether using the Mobile Site Builder or the traditional LibGuide builder. Since mobile devices are here to stay, we hope you will take advantage of all the tools LibGuides offer to serve this growing population of library patrons.

REFERENCES

Adebonojo, Leslie. 2010. Unpublished survey. Charles C. Sherrod Library. East Tennessee State University.

Kellogg, Don.. 2011. "In U.S. Market, New Smartphone Buyers Increasingly Embracing Android." *NielsonWire* (blog), September 26. http://blog.nielsen.com/nielsenwire/online_mobile/in-u-s-market-new-smartphone-buyers-increasingly-embracing-android.

Pew Internet and American Life Project. 2011. "Smartphone Adoptions and Usage." http://pewinternet.org/Reports/2011/Smartphones.aspx.

Pew Research Center Internet and American Life Project. 2010. "Mobile Access 2010." http://pewinternet.org/Reports/2010/Mobile-Access-2010.aspx.

Pham, Dai. 2011. "Smartphone User Study Shows Mobile Movement Underway." http://googlemobileads.blogspot.com/2011/04/smartphone-user-study-shows-mobile.html.

5

PART 5

Technological and Pedagogical Exemplars from Academic, K–12, Public, and Special Libraries

## Chapter Fourteen

Showcase of Exceptional LibGuides

Sharon Whitfield and Claire Clemens

L ibGuides is a content creation platform that assists both technical and non-technical librarians to create interactive, dynamic content for their patrons. As an institution begins to establish a collection of basic LibGuides, it is important to consider the level of standardization of content, appearance, and functionality across the library organization. It is imperative to plan navigational and usability strategies within individual LibGuides, as well as the overall look and feel of the LibGuides home page. At the same time, the function of LibGuides in reference service should also be part of the planning. The library must consider how to maximize the teachable moment to make each guide an effective instruction (and public relations) tool. To aid in the discussion of these important issues, this showcase chapter provides LibGuides examples featuring excellence in technological and pedagogical design. The authors independently reviewed and selected examples for each area and then collaborated to compile a list of best LibGuides in both aspects. Finally, to spark your imagination, a list of unique LibGuides for special purposes is included in Appendix D.

The chapter authors chose guides to showcase from each of the four major library types: academic, public, school, and special. For each library category, three exemplary LibGuides for technological design and three for pedagogical design were selected. The review of LibGuides for technological design excellence considered the layout and navigability of individual LibGuides and the overall design features of the LibGuides website. The review of LibGuides for pedagogical design excellence considered elements of good online instruction. For this reason, only institutions with ten or more LibGuides were evaluated. The authors visited over 500 LibGuides sites to arrive at the showcase entries. The LibGuides websites were identified using Springshare's LibGuides Community web page, a "master list" of LibGuides institutions. The list may be sorted by library type, location, and product (http://libguides.com/community.php?m=i&ref=www.libguides.com). On this page Springshare stated in early January 2012: "search and explore 213,193 guides by 39,624 librarians at 2,765 libraries worldwide!" By examining the list, approximate numbers of institutions in each category can be calculated: public libraries (60), special libraries (85), K–12 libraries (430), and academic libraries (1,760). This means that roughly 2,335 institutions have chosen LibGuides. For each library type, there are institutions that have not yet created LibGuides. All public libraries, special libraries, and school libraries that have ten or more LibGuides were visited. Over 200 academic library LibGuides sites were reviewed. Not all individual LibGuides at a given site were evaluated. In the case of some academic libraries, hundreds of LibGuides have been published.

254

In October 2011 the Springshare Support Blog reported reaching the milestone of 200,000 LibGuides and CampusGuides with 1.3 million pages and described the time line of the phenomenal growth: "it took almost 3 years to hit the first 100,000 guides, but only 1 year to double that amount" (http://support .springshare.com/2011/10). The chapter authors think that it is time to look ahead by collaborating with colleagues to make LibGuides' valuable assets available to the user community. By collaborating we can provide accessible, responsive tools that will not only promote library resources and services, but also foster the development of independent, information-literate researchers. We trust that this chapter will provide you with the motivation to contact your library colleagues of like interest and collaborate with them rather than reinventing the wheel.

BEST PRACTICES IN TECHNOLOGICAL DESIGN

Designing an effective LibGuide requires more than just gathering relevant information and posting it. LibGuide authors must pay careful attention to the selection, organization, and presentation of text and graphics to ensure that patrons can easily find and retain their desired information. Yet, a LibGuide must also be both clear and engaging so that patrons return to the LibGuide for assistance with their research.

TABLE 14.1

Checklist of major criteria for technical design evaluation of LibGuides

Criteria	Definition	Characteristics
Information architecture	The overall design and organization of the LibGuide	• Purpose of the LibGuide is defined • Audience consideration • Hierarchy of information is clear (Use of headings) • Does not overly divide information
Navigation	The interface and directional aids should logically assist the user to move around the LibGuide.	• Navigation is consistent throughout website • Multiple entry points for content
Text	The textual information on the LibGuide should aid the usability of the site.	• Easy to read and understand • There are no more than 10–12 words across • Text is big enough to read and scan
Graphics and interactive content • Graphic design • Screen design	The graphical additions to the LibGuide should serve a specific purpose.	• Graphic design is relevant and has a clear focal point • Balance achieved by following the rules of thirds • Appropriate use of columns and white space
Colors	Colors should complement each other and increase the page's readability.	• Colors are compliant with accessibility standards • Colors are consistent
Links	The links should be able to be easily recognized.	• Link colors coordinate with page colors • Links are easy to follow and easy to recognize
Help and documentation	Assistance should be available on each page.	• Users are given a clear way to seek assistance

The "Checklist of major criteria for technical design evaluation of LibGuides" (see table 14.1) was created based on a review of the literature filtered through years of service as information professionals. When analyzing a website, an information professional should look for certain characteristics to aid the website user. These same analysis techniques applied to a website should also be applied to a LibGuide.

In order to be considered for analysis, the LibGuide site must have had over ten guides available to the public. Once it was determined that the LibGuide site warranted analysis, the checklist was applied. Those LibGuides displaying most of the characteristics on the checklist were pooled. Further reflection brought these LibGuides to the top.

Sound technological design of a LibGuide follows the same fundamental principles of website design, which are outlined in table 14.1. These areas of consideration included

- Information architecture
- Navigation
- Text
- Graphics and interactive content

- Colors
- Links
- Help and documentation

Further explanation of these principles will be provided as each LibGuide site chosen is annotated in the next sections. Chapter 6 of this book explores LibGuide design in greater detail.

Top Three Academic Library Choices for Exceptional Technical Design of LibGuides

Virginia Commonwealth University,
VCU Libraries, Richmond, Virginia

The VCU Subject and Course Guide site excels because of its simplicity and ease of use. By customizing the header and footer of the standard LibGuides interface,

FIGURE 14.1
Virginia Commonwealth University, LibGuides home,
http://guides.library.vcu.edu

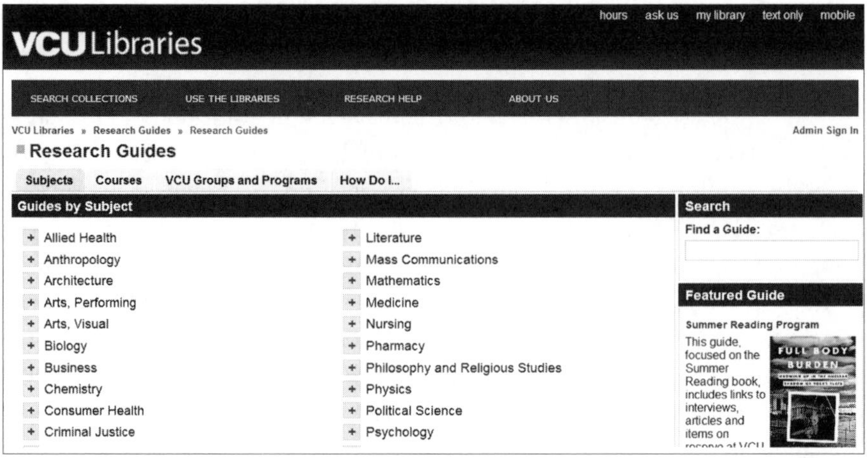

Courtesy of Virginia Commonwealth University Libraries

there is a continuation of the VCU library brand and navigation. The presence of limited color draws the users' attention to key areas of the LibGuide. The color also allows users to quickly read the content on the LibGuide and determine if the guide's content is applicable to their research or if they will need more assistance. If further assistance is needed, there are four different locations that allow the guide users to seek help from the guide author.

VCU has clearly established a template that assists their users to find the desired content. Yet, the template does not restrict LibGuides authors to meet the informational needs of their intended audience. Each LibGuides author has his or her own established writing and content delivery style that allows the LibGuides user to digitally connect to their subject librarian. My only caveat to this recommendation is that often VCU guide authors do not use multimedia objects, which would add to the visual impact of their guides.

Heidelberg University, Beeghly Library, Tiffin, Ohio

With the pace of breaking news, maintaining current events LibGuides is extremely challenging. By utilizing a suggested topic form, the guide author appears to have

FIGURE 14.2
Heidelberg University, Current Events,
http://libguides.heidelberg.edu/CurrentEvents

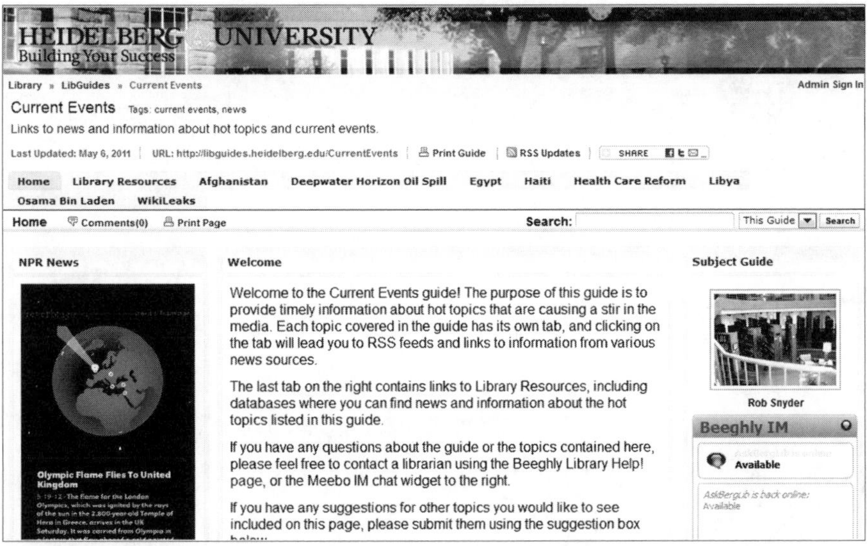

Courtesy of Heidelberg University, Beeghly Library, designed by Robert J. Snyder, currently Reference and Instruction Librarian, Bowling Green State University

reached a balance between the desired informational needs of Heidelberg's audience and breaking news. The welcome message walks the clearly defined intended audience to their desired information. By providing access to the resources, the author enables the user to move beyond the tabbed topics.

The guide author follows basic web page design by utilizing an eye-catching image to draw the audience to the guide. Utilization of dynamic media and RSS feeds allows the page to display fresh content that is intended to lure repeat visits. The Twitter search feed also allows for the delivery of instant updates on the user's specific topic; however, the author missed an opportune moment to remind users about evaluating these resources.

The users do not lose focus on content and can quickly navigate to their desired informational needs, even though the guide's colors are difficult on the eyes. Furthermore, users are encouraged to offer comments, leave messages, and ask for help on each LibGuides page, which increases the level of usability.

Georgia Tech Library, Atlanta, Georgia

The description text of Georgia Tech's research guides—Know What We Know: Find It in LibGuides!—establishes the overarching goal of the research guides' site.

FIGURE 14.3
Georgia Tech Library, International Affairs,
http://libguides.gatech.edu/intatop

Courtesy of Georgia Tech Library

The guide author conveys the resources to the audience utilizing an information hierarchy that makes topical information easily accessible. Although the information conveyed is comprehensive, the LibGuide user is not overwhelmed by the content. LibGuide users can easily navigate to related guides or choose their desired information medium.

The simplicity of the site allows the patron to focus on how well the information has been organized; however, the guide fails to utilize color to draw the user to key information. Dynamic content, such as RSS feeds, ensures that the content is consistently new, encouraging repeat visits.

Top Three Public Library Choices for Exceptional Technical Design of LibGuides

San Antonio Public Library, San Antonio, Texas

San Antonio's website demonstrates how easy it is for nontechnical librarians to create informational LibGuides. If you need information about upcoming events,

FIGURE 14.4
San Antonio Public Library, Welcome to LibGuides,
http://guides.mysapl.org

Courtesy of the San Antonio Public Library, San Antonio, Texas

book recommendations, or special needs services information, just look on the LibGuides site. The hierarchy of information appears to conform to Dewey or Library of Congress standards. Each page has a Welcome box, which addresses the intended audience. While the purple color is a little harsh on the eyes, the selection of visual images allows the user to grasp the overall LibGuide content within seconds.

Burlington County Library System, Westampton, New Jersey

In a public library with a diverse population, it is difficult to create LibGuides that appeal to everyone. Therefore, many LibGuide authors tend to provide an extensive amount of information. Burlington County Library System actually has only a focused amount of information, which refers their patrons to the necessary resource. By limiting the amount of available information on each page, Burlington County Library LibGuides authors increased the accessibility and usability of the guide. LibGuides that require a more extensive amount of information are still categorized so that the number of tabs does not grow beyond what a LibGuides site could support.

FIGURE 14.5
Burlington County Library System, The Research & Information Center, http://explore.bcls.lib.nj.us

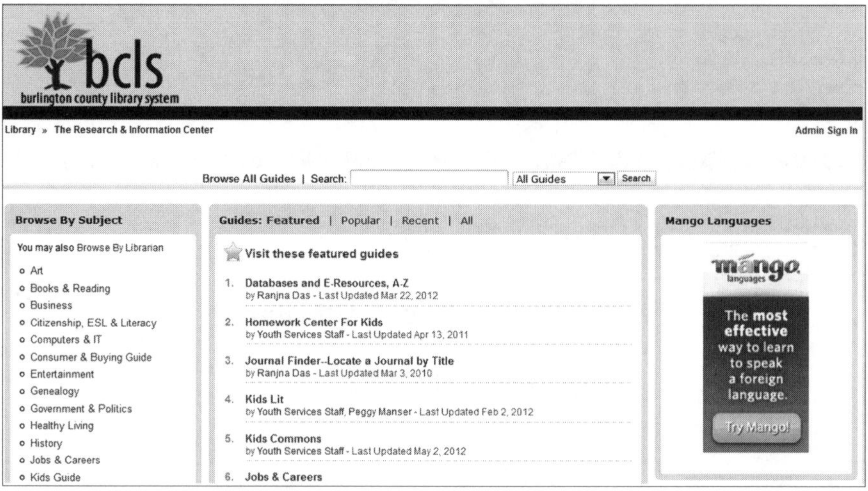

Courtesy of Burlington County Library System

Yet, in order to increase readability of a LibGuides site, Burlington County Library LibGuides authors could consider decreasing the amount of text on each page and consider trying to add more visual components to each page. Access to Help could also be more available.

Westerville Public Library, Westerville, Ohio

Westerville LibGuide authors tease LibGuides users with exactly the right amount of topical information. The simplicity of each guide allows the user to quickly skim the content. Patrons know that if more information is needed, librarian help is a click away. Westerville also uses Flickr images to further indicate to the users the LibGuides' content. Westerville provides several different methods to navigate through the LibGuides site—click on a tag word, click on a topic, or perform a keyword search to find a desired LibGuide for an issue.

While the main peach color relaxes the user, Westerville may want to reconsider the use of gray as a background color. The black text seems to blend into the gray on occasion. Westerville may also want to make their Contact Us link more prominent so that LibGuides users could more easily contact them with questions regarding content.

FIGURE 14.6
Westerville Public Library, Explore @ the Westerville Library,
http://explore.westervillelibrary.org

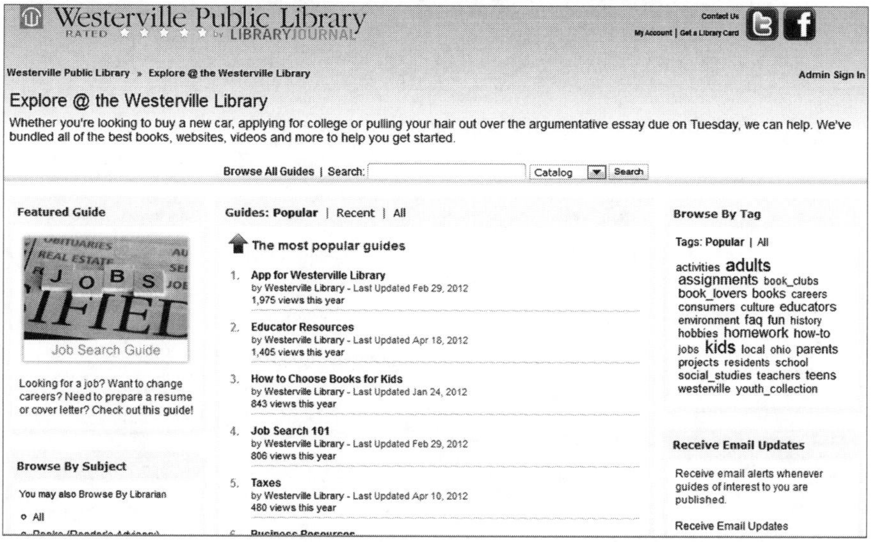

Courtesy of Westerville Public Library

Top Three K–12 School Library Choices for Exceptional Technical Design of LibGuides

GBS Library, Glenbrook South
High School, Glenview, Illinois

This is overall a vibrant LibGuides site bound to catch the attention of teens at Glenbrook South High School, whose librarians have created a LibGuides site that utilizes various information hierarchies. LibGuides users can access information based on the information medium, subject, or course. The use of text color draws attention to key elements that students must know while using the library. By utilizing images and videos, the librarians are employing the characteristic generational needs of their intended audience. Here the librarians have found a balance between visual and informational content.

Although not easily accessible, the Class & Homework Help Guide creates content for the specific needs of a course. The collection of resources is easily decipherable, and the links are easy to follow. One detrimental element of the guide is that Help may only be accessed from the LibGuides home page. Students

FIGURE 14.7
Glenbrook South High School, Welcome to LibGuides,
http://gbslibguides.glenbrook225.org

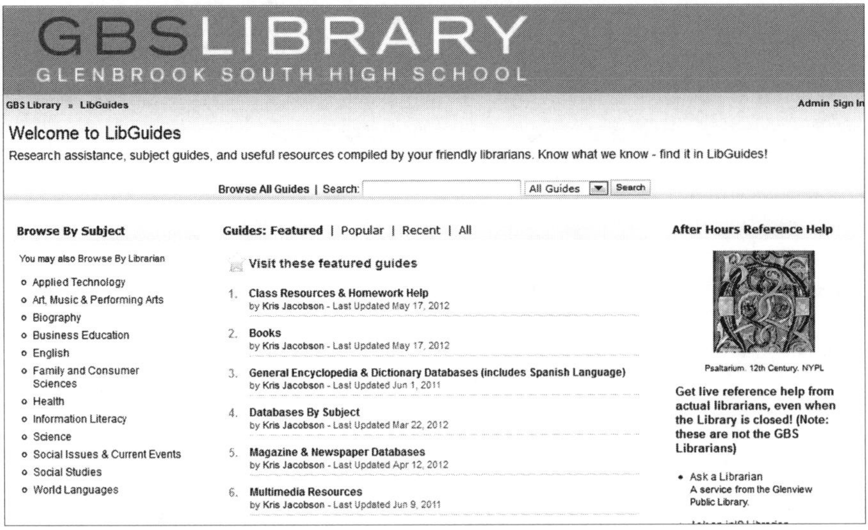

Courtesy of Glenbrook South High School, created by Kris Jacobson

should easily be able to seek help without navigating away from the individual LibGuides page.

Creekview High School, Canton, Georgia

These librarians' guides are like no other guides. They use media and visual images to attract the attention of Creekview High School students. The use of media, visual images, and hyperlinks allows these authors to have dynamic LibGuides that clearly identify the intended audience—teens.

Creekview librarians do not confine LibGuides to library instruction. They have expanded the content of their LibGuides to answer questions that the user may have about certain emerging technologies. Their apparent excitement about their profession is evident in each created LibGuide. These guides display a very simplistic information hierarchy. The LibGuides address the users' topical needs. Students are not inundated with information that may not be relevant to their research needs. Need help? Simply send an e-mail. One minor observation—the dark blue links on the top navigation toolbar blend into the light blue toolbar color.

263

FIGURE 14.8
Creekview High School, Welcome to LibGuides,
http://theunquietlibrary.libguides.com

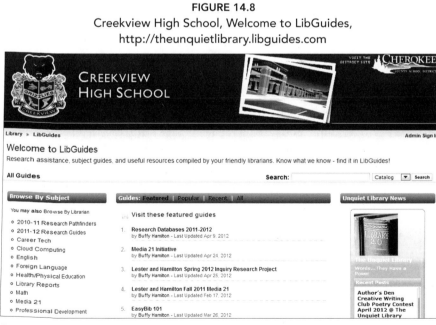

Courtesy of Creekview High School Library, created by Buffy J. Hamilton, School Librarian

FIGURE 14.9

East Lyme High School, Welcome to the Frances Hart Ewers
Memorial Library, http://eastlymehs.libguides.com

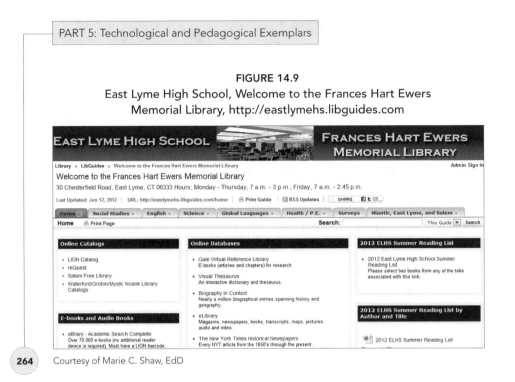

Courtesy of Marie C. Shaw, EdD

East Lyme High School, East Lyme, Connecticut

Technologically, the East Lyme High School LibGuide site is designed well. It is easy to use and attractive because of the simplicity of its uncluttered layout. The site has consistent coloring and the links are easily identifiable. Browsing for information is straightforward since the information architecture of the site is clearly defined. The hierarchy is easily discernible and the appropriate LibGuide can be found using any of the headers. Subtabs are used with the main headers, thus allowing information to be found, but keeping the main page tidy.

The East Lyme High School LibGuide assists students to find their desired information, although an easily recognizable Help! box would give students a way to query the library staff with specific questions.

Top Three Special Library Choices for Exceptional Technical Design of LibGuides

Metropolitan New York Library Council, New York, New York

When first exploring METRO LibGuides, they appear not to deviate from the original LibGuides design elements; however, this LibGuides site is actually a gem.

FIGURE 14.10
Metro LibGuides, Welcome to LibGuides,
http://libguides.metro.org

Courtesy of Metropolitan New York Library Council

The simplicity of the design allows the LibGuides authors to focus on the content and the information organization.

Each guide has a Welcome box, which gives general information on the intended audience and discusses how the LibGuide is divided. The user can simply click on one of these links or click on the topical tab to access information. To keep the information provided current and pertinent to the user, METRO LibGuides authors use RSS feeds, video, digital books, and other multimedia elements. The addition of SlideShare presentations changes the LibGuides from plain pathfinders to instructional tools.

Although the content and information delivery is the most crucial element for LibGuides authors, METRO's LibGuides may benefit from strengthening their brand by moving from the generic LibGuides template to one more exciting.

Memorial Sloan-Kettering Cancer Center Library, New York, New York

Designing LibGuides for a public audience may be a challenge, but with a well-defined topical hierarchy, the public can navigate to their desired information.

FIGURE 14.11
Memorial Sloan-Kettering Cancer Center Library, Welcome to LibGuides,
http://libguides.mskcc.org

Reproduced with credit and permission of Memorial Sloan-Kettering Cancer Center Library

The librarians at Sloan-Kettering understand this. With a simple list of subject headings, the public user knows exactly the intention of the created LibGuides. If the simplistic subject headings are not enough to assist in determining if this is the right guide, the Welcome box clearly identifies the intended LibGuides audience. The navigation of each LibGuide is simple and easy to utilize. After perusing the LibGuide, if users require additional help or information, they may click Ask a Librarian for further assistance.

Kaiser Permanente Libraries, California

Kaiser Network utilizes LibGuides as the main portal for their library. The hierarchy of the tabbed navigation clearly establishes the main services of the Kaiser Network libraries. Click on LibGuides to navigate from library services to individual LibGuides. Individual LibGuides are subsequently broken into the type of resource. LibGuides users may contact the LibGuides authors by leaving feedback, comments, or by utilizing the Ask a Librarian form.

Kaiser Network LibGuides authors have selected visually appealing images that direct users to a particular resource. However, Kaiser could increase their effectiveness by using color to attract users to key information.

FIGURE 14.12
Kaiser Permanente Libraries home page,
http://kplibraries.libguides.com

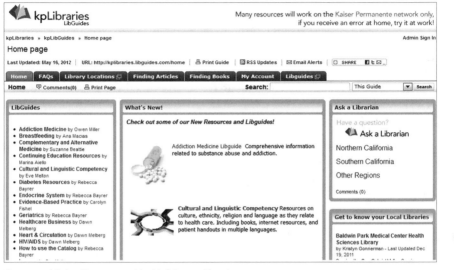

Courtesy of Kaiser Permanente Health Sciences Libraries

BEST PRACTICES IN PEDAGOGICAL DESIGN

The evaluation of guides on the basis of pedagogical design considered the use of LibGuides for reference and instruction. Given the technological ease with which guides may be created, the time and energy gained by LibGuides' relatively short learning curve should be spent carefully examining desired user outcomes as planning for content proceeds. With each LibGuide, the librarian is establishing a virtual connection to the user by providing an alternative and, in some cases, possible enhancement to both in-person reference desk assistance and classroom instruction. The review of websites, therefore, was based on library standards and guidelines, such as the Reference and User Services Association's "Guidelines for Behavioral Performance of Reference and Information Service Providers" (www.ala .org/rusa/resources/guidelines/guidelinesbehavioral), particularly those for remote service, and "Guidelines for Implementing and Maintaining Virtual Reference Services" (www.ala.org/rusa/resources/guidelines/virtrefguidelines). As well, the Association for College and Research Libraries' "Information Literacy Competency Standards for Higher Education and Guidelines for Distance Learning Library Services" (www.ala.org/acrl/standards/guidelinesdistancelearning) were equally relevant. The teaching and learning analysis also considered how people learn, together with current educational strategies, such as blended learning, evidence-based practice, constructivism, and scaffolding.

After completing a LibGuides literature review and studying the standards and guidelines, the ideal characteristics for reference/instruction were summarized into eight major categories (see table 14.2). Individual LibGuides were then evaluated to see how many of the criteria each guide met. Those in each library category with strong pedagogical features were collected for a second review. In the final evaluation the contenders were compared and contrasted to determine the best examples.

The "Major criteria for reference/educational evaluation of LibGuides" (see table 14.2) provides a checklist to aid in the review and improvement of LibGuides. Creating a Web 2.0 guide, which is both attractive and interactive, to be that point-of-need resource for users is a worthwhile endeavor. Collaborating with fellow library authors will produce learning objects, boxes, and entire pages that may be shared with a little tweaking to fit the subject discipline or guide topic. Ideally, fewer well-planned, high-quality LibGuides are more beneficial than many cookie-cutter LibGuides, which are unwieldy to maintain and can't offer responsive authoring to keep the LibGuide fresh and engaging. Static content is reminiscent of the paper pathfinder. Course guides get many hits around the time of library instruction, but subject guides appeal to a broader audience. Course tabs may be added to a subject guide. The subject guide used in instruction will generate more usage in the end.

The solid instructional design elements of a LibGuide considered for inclusion in this chapter, and outlined in table 14.2, are

- Presentation/interest
- Access to resources
- Research skills
- Information literacy

- Scaffolding
- Blended learning
- Follow-up
- Assessment

Further explanation will be provided as each LibGuide chosen is described in the next sections. Chapter 7 of this book, as well as chapter 5, discusses these pedagogical principles in greater detail.

TABLE 14.2

Checklist of major criteria for reference/educational evaluation of LibGuides

Criteria	Definition	Characteristics
Presentation/ interest	The overall look of the guide adds positively to its instructional value.	• User is attracted to the page • The point of the guide is clear • First page of the guide provides an overview • The user knows what to do next
Access to resources	The guide takes advantage of available technology (embed-ded media, widgets, etc.) to help guide patrons through library resources.	• Search tips and other aids are available for those who are using a resource for the first time • Use of media to address multiple learning styles • Options to obtain immediate assistance are available
Research skills	The guide considers current practices in the discipline for the guide's intended audience, such as evidence-based learning.	• Users can succeed at research based on resources included in the guide • Resources appropriate to the discipline and the nature of the inquiry are provided • Elements of the entire research process are present
Information literacy	The guide provides evidence that the user is guided to effectively finding, using, evaluating, and citing information.	• User can readily identify poten-tial sources of information • Search strategies are evident • Source evaluation criteria are available • Assignment related to the guide is clearly described • Citation guidance is available
Scaffolding	Information on the guide is presented in a logical, connected sequence to support all learners.	• Evidence that learning occurs in context and builds on prior knowledge • Examples provided are relevant • Audience is clearly defined
Blended learning	The guide supports other forms of instruction at the institution, including the involvement of other departments or services.	• Professor, course, or department is recognized, when appropriate • Needs of both on-campus and off-campus users are recognized
Further assistance/ follow-up	The guide includes convenient links to help from staff.	• Additional help is clearly available • Library lingo has been eliminated
Assessment/ feedback	The guide uses web forms, etc., to gather information/statistics/ feedback to provide assessment.	• Evidence of feedback tools to facilitate user input

Top Three Academic Library Choices for Exceptional Pedagogical Design of LibGuides

ASU Libraries, Arizona State University,
Tempe, Arizona

Each page is visually appealing to a range of viewers. Different learning styles are addressed by the use of widgets, tutorial videos, RSS feeds, chat, and a poll to gather feedback. A Citing Sources tab promotes information literacy.

A link to the Department of Chemistry and Biochemistry at ASU demonstrates librarian/department collaboration. The Course Guides tab displays single-page guides specific to the information needs of each course. The Getting Started tab is helpful, as students often report their greatest research difficulty is knowing how and where to begin. Users are not overwhelmed by the number of tabs directing to information resources.

Strong evidence of learning outcomes and information literacy objectives/activities are evident on the Course Pages; however, it is not clear if these are generated solely by the librarian or done in the context of a course assignment.

FIGURE 14.13
Arizona State University Libraries, Chemistry & Biochemistry,
http://libguides.asu.edu/chemistry

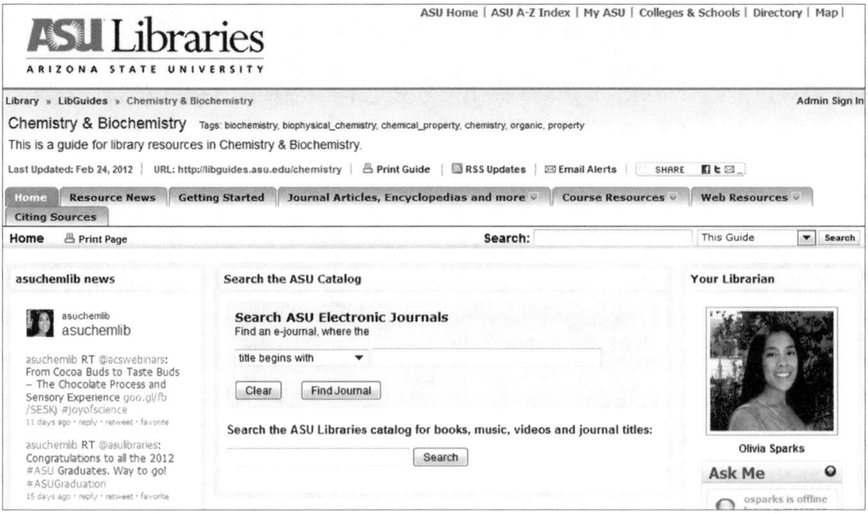

Courtesy of Arizona State University Libraries

Northwestern University Library, Evanston, Illinois

The user first encounters a clean, organized presentation. The clever use of subpages provides access to additional resources without the cluttered look of multilayered tabs. The guide contains a well-rounded collection of information sources for research in African American studies, including excellent campus resources (guides, handouts, tutorials, and faculty publications) and a comprehensive news collection for current information. Web 2.0 tools include chat and Twitter. Guides for Specific Courses are located on the Getting Started page. This wealth of information sources is a boon to anyone doing research, both on and off campus. In order to better promote autonomous learning, some guidance on research strategies would make this guide ideal.

FIGURE 14.14
Northwestern University Library, African American Studies, http://
libguides.northwestern.edu/content.php?pid=39921

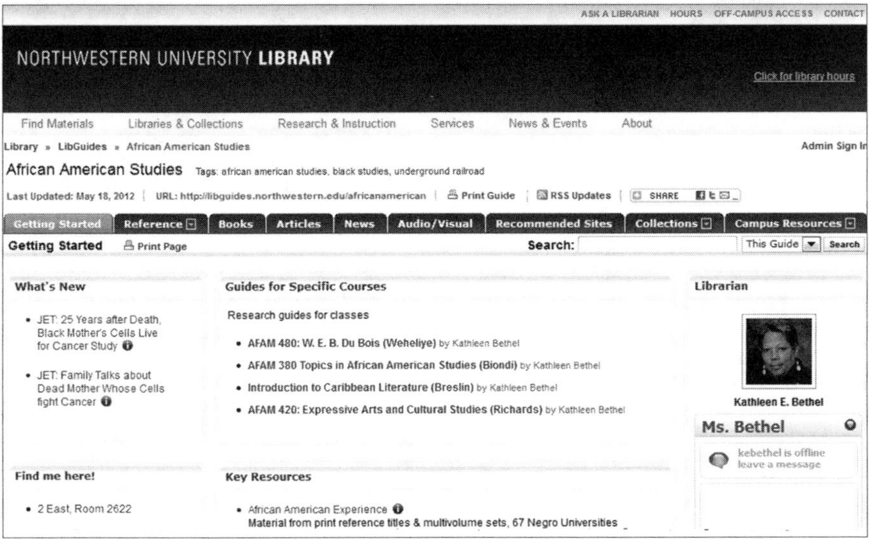

Courtesy of Kathleen Bethel, Northwestern University Library

McCain Library, Agnes Scott College, Decatur, Georgia

This colorful guide has great eye appeal. It provides an easy overview of the resources supporting the reading program for incoming freshmen. The tabs plus the subpages under Refugee Issues & Services certainly make clear the significance

FIGURE 14.15
Agnes Scott McCain Library, Outcasts United: 2010–11 Common Read,
http://libguides.agnesscott.edu/OutcastsUnited

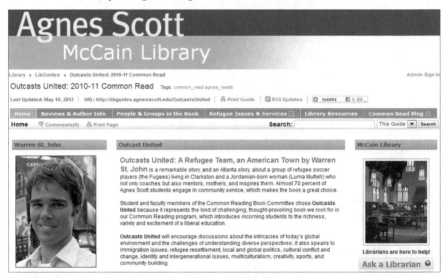

Used by permission of McCain Library, Agnes Scott College

of the reading to the campus community and beyond. Through a collection of book reviews, articles, and media, the author has demonstrated what good research looks like to students before they arrive on campus and how librarians and library resources can enrich the learning experience. There is no evidence of faculty collaboration or that feedback is being gathered, nor does the home page state the purpose or intended audience.

Top Three Public Library Choices for Exceptional Pedagogical Design of LibGuides

Anne Arundel County Public Library, Anne Arundel County, Maryland

This guide expertly leads students (and their parents) to homework help in a variety of content areas: Biography, Current Issues, History, Math, Science, Countries, and Literature. It uses graphics for interest without being overwhelming. A PowerPoint presentation on the home page gives the user an introduction to the Homework Center. Multiple opportunities exist for further assistance. Explanations, which

FIGURE 14.16
Anne Arundel County (Maryland) Public Library, Homework Center,
http://libguides.aacpl.net/Homework

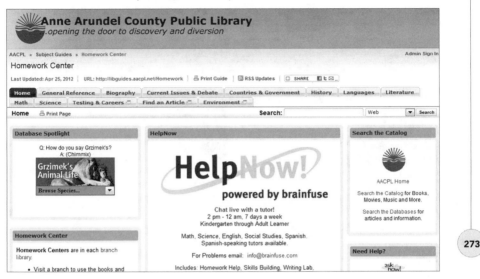

Courtesy of Anne Arundel County [Maryland] Public Library

promote independent learning, are free from library lingo. In the case of database lists, a link is always provided to a page that defines databases and their purpose in great detail. Website suggestions state that they have been evaluated by Anne Arundel County librarians. Citation resources are provided. Although the term *information literacy* is not used, the librarian authors surely had it in mind when creating this homework resource. The Homework Center supports a variety of learners and proves itself to be an online educational resource to which parents may confidently send their chilren. It is not clear if any assessment is being done on the learning outcomes of the Homework Center. A form could be added to gather user feedback.

Vernon Area Public Library District, Lincolnshire, Illinois

This genealogy LibGuide does an excellent job of presenting information in a logical sequence, deftly blending library materials together with those of local genealogical societies and agencies and genealogical resources generally available online. The home page instantly attracts users with a colorful presentation of a variety of media: book covers, links to handouts, tutorials, blog links, and a box

FIGURE 14.17

Vernon Area Public Library District, Genealogy,
http://guides.vapld.info/content.php?pid=41967

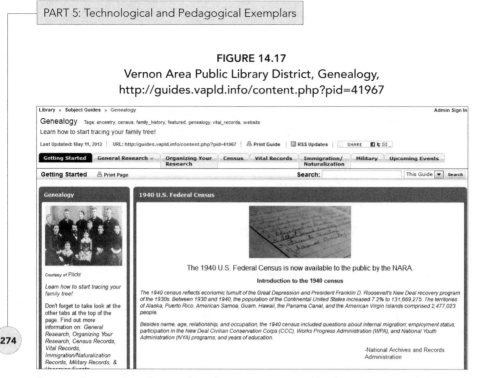

Courtesy of creators Diane Presta and Lisa Greene, Vernon Area Public Library District, Lincolnshire, IL

devoted to the current prime-time television program on tracing family history. Subsequent pages treat each major aspect extensively and provide valuable, point-of-need resources. For instance, the page titled Organize Your Research offers links to free forms and charts and a video with advice from The Beginning Genealogist. In addition to general research tips, sub-level pages provide assistance with specific areas of family research. Both beginners and experienced researchers benefit from the wealth of links, videos, tutorials, and forms. This guide methodically addresses a common research need by integrating library services with outside resources and saves library patrons a great deal of time searching for and evaluating websites. Once they discover this LibGuide, Vernon Area Public Library patrons will have no problem growing their family trees.

High Plains Library District, Erie, Colorado

The Business Resource Center gets high marks for stating its purpose and audience on the home page: "This resource guide was designed specifically to help you answer questions and ease your through any business related impasses that may come your way. Whether you are a budding entrepreneur just starting up your

FIGURE 14.18
High Plains Library District, Business Resource Center,
http://highplains.libguides.com/business

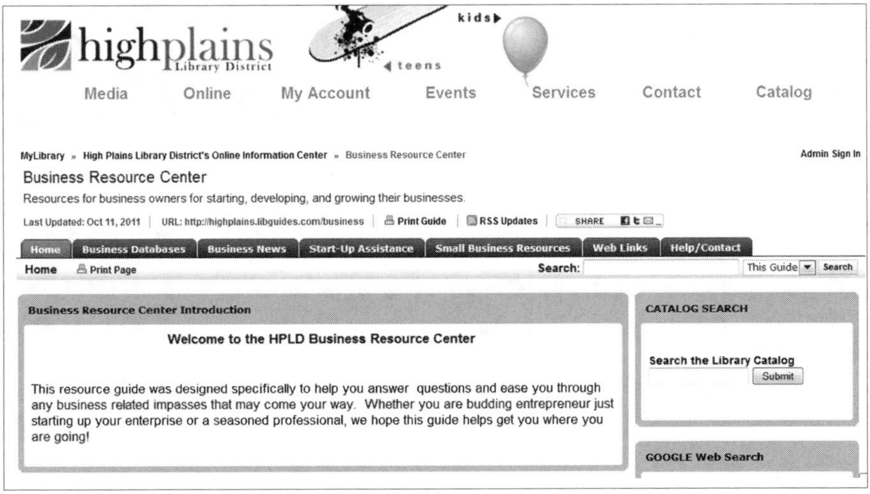

Courtesy of High Plains Library District

enterprise or a seasoned professional, we hope this guide helps get you where you are going!" Users know what to expect and why they should use the guide. The presentation is not confused by many little boxes per page, but is simplified by two columns per page, rather than the typical three. The Help/Contact tab makes it obvious how to follow up, if desired. The recommended websites are neatly organized using an A-Z directory. The user is guided in the research process by such features as the annotated databases page, which also includes an explanation of how to access the databases. Regional and national news sources and news feeds are nicely displayed. This LibGuide not only provides access to resources, it also fosters independent learning and understanding of available resources and technologies.

Top Three K–12 School Library Choices for Exceptional Pedagogical Design of LibGuides

Seattle Academy of Arts and Sciences
Library, Seattle, Washington

This guide is an exciting example of librarian/teacher collaboration involving "student-created resources for renewable resources." It models the integration of library services into the classroom curriculum. Several science classes created

FIGURE 14.19
Seattle Academy of Arts and Sciences, Renewable Resources,
http://guides.seattleacademy.org/ScottA

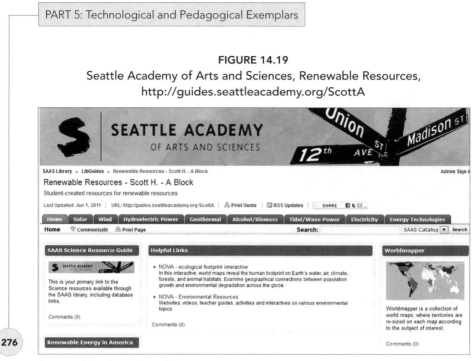

Courtesy of Seattle Academy Library

LibGuides on the topic of renewable resources. Students selected text and graphics to demonstrate a range of energy sources, such as solar, wind, hydroelectric, and so on. Creating an information product as the outcome of research is clear evidence of information literacy as described in the American Association of School Librarians' Standards for the 21st-Century Learner. Individual authors are not named and credit is often not given for content or images used; nonetheless, students spent time reviewing material to include in the guides and created an information resource for their classmates using a new technology. It is evident that students experimented with interactive features and embedding media to make the guides both colorful and educational. The students must have been inspired by the Web 2.0 features modeled by the librarian on the Guides home page and on the LibGuide titled "Science Resources." To bring the project full circle and maximize the pedagogical benefit of the LibGuides assignment, students could be encouraged to include (and acknowledge) library resources, in addition to websites.

Palo Alto Unified School Libraries, Palo Alto, California
This LibGuides homepage states, "PAUSD teacher librarians and teachers create LibGuides to support class assignments and research and to guide and promote reading." The elementary, middle school, and high school libraries in this district

FIGURE 14.20
Palo Alto Unified School Libraries, *To Kill a Mockingbird,*
http://libguides.pausd.org/mockingbird

Courtesy of Palo Alto Unified School Libraries

have joined together to produce this mission statement and the resulting LibGuides. The easy-to-navigate LibGuides home page (http://libguides.pausd.org) lets users choose from over ninety guides by school type, subject, and author. As an example, the LibGuide entitled "To Kill a Mockingbird" provides users with links to "primary sources, digital books, articles, journals, newpapers, videos and more." Information resources specific to the book are interspersed between well-crafted how-to pages on topics such as citing sources and evaluating information. The pages on Boolean searches and Google searching, which may be found under the Finding Information tab, contain very useful pedagogical features. Both pages describe themselves as modules and provide learning objectives and instructions on how to proceed through the material on the page. The page on Primary Sources could benefit from a similar treatment to aid the novice user in understanding what qualifies the items listed as primary sources. Additional contact information is needed for students to follow up. It would also be helpful to clearly state the relationship between the LibGuide and the course curriculum or assignment it supports.

Boyden Library, Deerfield Academy, Deerfield, Massachusetts

This United States history guide supports assignments given by several classroom teachers. It is clearly organized and visually appealing. It does not overwhelm

FIGURE 14.21

Boyden Library, United States History: 20th and 21st Centuries,
http://libguides.library.deerfield.edu/history

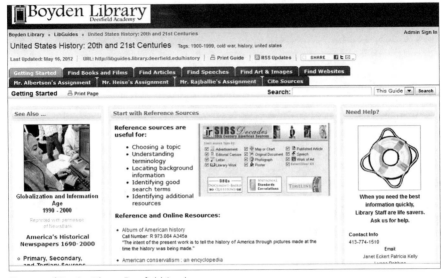

Courtesy of Boyden Library, Deerfield Academy

the user with the extent of the content or the use of bells and whistles. The guide contains little embedded media, although there is a PowerPoint presentation on how to use NoodleBib. This guide presents the resources in a logical sequence. Getting Started introduces reference works and explains their purpose. The first page also contains links to other LibGuides on the research process and related LibGuides on decades of the twentieth and twenty-first centuries. Users have a clear overview of the available options. The Find Books & Films tab not only provides access to the catalog, but it guides the user through examples of keyword and subject searches. The Find Articles and Find Websites pages are equally well-constructed. There is no advice provided on how to evaluate websites, but perhaps students are not encouraged to use websites other than those vetted by the teachers and librarians. The addition of a user input box would help the authors gather feedback.

Top Three Special Library Choices for Exceptional Pedagogical Design of LibGuides

NATO Multimedia Library, North Atlantic Treaty Organization, Brussels, Belgium

The NATO Welcome LibGuide provides users with a thoughtful, general introduction to the scope and purpose of LibGuides. It also offers an explanation for why its LibGuides exist. "NATO LibGuides have been created for topics that are of current interest to NATO's mission." Access issues are clarified up front. Many aspects of good instructional design are apparent—consideration of the learner, stating objectives, and selected use of media and materials. The individual guides—for example, Women, Peace and Security—have Feedback pages, which allow the user to enter comments or suggest an additional link or resource. The LibGuides follow a consistent template. The links and videos provided for each resource type are comprehensive, but not excessive. The first page of each guide provides places to start and additional keywords to aid in searching. Together the guides are a great educational tool for NATO researchers. They provide coherent access to a wealth of materials a typical user would not readily identify alone.

FIGURE 14.22

NATO Multimedia Library, Women, Peace and Security, http://natolibguides.info/women. All NATO LibGuides are available at http://natolibguides.info. Nato's website is www.nato.int.

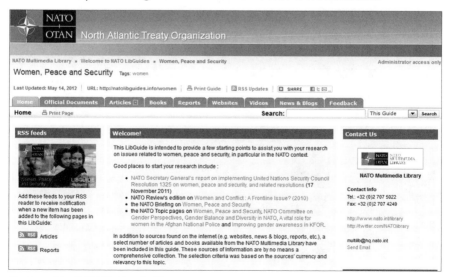

Courtesy of the NATO Multimedia Library

Library of the Marine Corps, U.S. Marine Corps, Quantico, Virginia

This special library states, "The mission of the Library of the Marine Corps (LoMC) is to support study and research throughout the Marine Corps. . . . It provides worldwide patrons with access to an extensive collection . . . in order to support professional military education." These librarian-authored LibGuides aptly support the library mission. An example of an individual guide is the Gettysburg Staff Ride. The definition provided states, "A staff ride is a case study, typically of a military battle or campaign, conducted on the ground where the event happened." The librarian-selected resources are extensive and geared specifically to this course event/field trip. The Gettysburg Staff Ride Briefing Book is posted as further proof of the integration of the LibGuide and course curriculum, although it is not clear which resources are required for the class. Exhaustive book resources are presented, as are many links for online collections and media. Any Civil War researcher will appreciate the detailed pages for Day 1, Day 2, and Day 3 of the battle.

Students are apparently not expected to complete a research project, because no instruction for or links to the library catalog, journals, or databases are included on the LibGuide. The author included interactive quizzes on most pages.

FIGURE 14.23
Library of the Marine Corps, Battle of Gettysburg Staff Ride, http://guides.grc.usmcu.edu/staffrides-gettysburg

Courtesy of Rachel Kingcade, Chief Reference Librarian, USMC Research Library

McLean Library, Pennsylvania Horticultural Society, Philadelphia, Pennsylvania

The Pennsylvania Horticultural Society has thirty-two resource guides. The Philadelphia Gardening Guide states, "Use this guide to learn where to buy plants, what to grow, how to connect with other gardeners and where to learn more." This guide is a pleasure to use. It gets high marks for visual presentation and organization. The author does an excellent job of teaching the user all there is to know about gardening in Philadelphia. Guide pages include Organizations, Good Reads, Watch, Listen and Learn, Plant Sources and Recommendations, Where to Get Help, and Events. This guide makes appropriate use of available technology to bring resources to the library users. The blog feeds and embedded video never overwhelm. The blog feed which answers research questions submitted to the Horticultural Society is especially interesting. Excellent contact information is provided for those who would like to follow up and a box is provided to submit additional links.

FIGURE 14.24
McLean Library, Philadelphia Gardening Guide,
http://pennhort.libguides.com/PhiladelphiaGardeningGuide

Courtesy of Pennsylvania Horticultural Society

BEST LIBGUIDES OVERALL

As previously mentioned, it was our intention not only to provide technically excellent LibGuides and pedagogically solid LibGuides in each of the four library categories, but also to present one LibGuide site from each library type that combines excellence in both characteristics in one LibGuide. The following are our top choices.

Academic Library: Kraemer Family Library, University of Colorado, Colorado Springs, Colorado

Design Features
Bright, vivid colors attract information seekers to the University of Colorado, Colorado Springs (UCCS) LibGuides site, but it is the content layout and navigation that keeps them coming back. Each UCCS LibGuide begins with consistent text welcoming the user to the LibGuide and explaining the purpose of the LibGuide. The use of subpages creates a consistent information hierarchy that allows the LibGuide user to navigate to their desired information resource. UCCS has also chunked information into memorable segments that provide the user with

FIGURE 14.25
Kraemer Family Library, Welcome to LibGuides,
http://libguides.uccs.edu

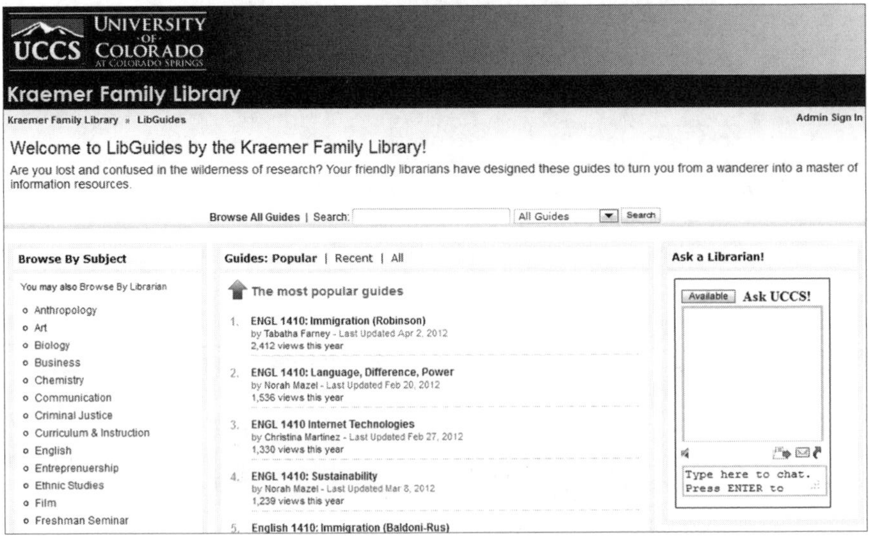

Courtesy of UCCS Kraemer Library

retainable information. Users are encouraged to leave feedback or to seek help utilizing the chat window.

Although the selected pictures are relevant, there is a prevalent lack of visual media on the majority of the LibGuides. Although each LibGuide has a consistent look, layout, and navigation, each LibGuide author's personal style is reflected in his or her developed LibGuide. The LibGuide authors do not seem to be bound by a restrictive template.

Pedagogical Features

Using one LibGuide as an example—Class Guide: ENGL 1410 Food Production and Food Culture (http://libguides.uccs.edu/engl1410_hemenway)—its Welcome to the Guide box does an outstanding job of identifying the purpose, including a numbered list of information outcomes from the course. The box entitled Before We Get Started is an especially user-friendly feature that advises users what steps are necessary to access library resources and services. In addition to lots of contact information with encouragement to use them, an annotated link to the library tutorial is included. The Reference Resources page contains not only a list of reference books with covers, but boxes explaining why they help and how to find them. The Finding Books page is very much geared toward independent learning. Keyword vs. subject searching is covered, but this guide goes further, even including a box that explains what to do if the book is not on the shelf, and how to use the local public library. The page would be perfect if it provided some linked subject headings pertinent to the course topic. All the pages are well-crafted but could use some customization to establish collaboration between professor and librarian. The author makes creative use of the Comments feature in LibGuides. On the interactive Resource Sharing page, users are asked to post article, book, and website recommendations to the comments. All in all, this guide is a great model from a teaching perspective.

Public Library: Montgomery County Public Libraries, Montgomery County, Maryland

Design Features

Although Montgomery County Public Libraries has only published thirty-eight LibGuides, the authors seem to address many of the informational needs of their public community. From arts to computers, there seems to be a guide for every topic. Yet, a visitor to this LibGuide site does not feel overloaded with information.

The LibGuides authors consider their intended audience when selecting the content and the visual images. For example, the Readers Café LibGuide gives a brief list of literary databases, but also discusses upcoming events; the Teen Site utilizes brighter colors, more visual content, and social media to attract their audience to utilize their information.

Controlled color is another method that the LibGuides authors utilize in order to draw attention to certain informational or visual content. The LibGuides authors have also chunked information in a way that it is easy to remember the content after leaving the page. Chunking also allows for the text to be read and ingested quickly. Help is only a click away. Montgomery provides an instant messaging widget, but also utilizes pictures of their librarians to allow their library users to identify the creator of the LibGuide.

Pedagogical Features
The LibGuide, Readers Café (http://montgomerycountymd.libguides.com/readers cafe), makes excellent use of technology to introduce patrons to resources in the library and beyond. The Tell Us What You Think box solicits feedback and an entire page is dedicated to gathering patrons' book suggestions, which are then annotated

FIGURE 14.26
Montgomery County Public Libraries, Subject Guides & Electronic
Resources, http://montgomerycountymd.libguides.com

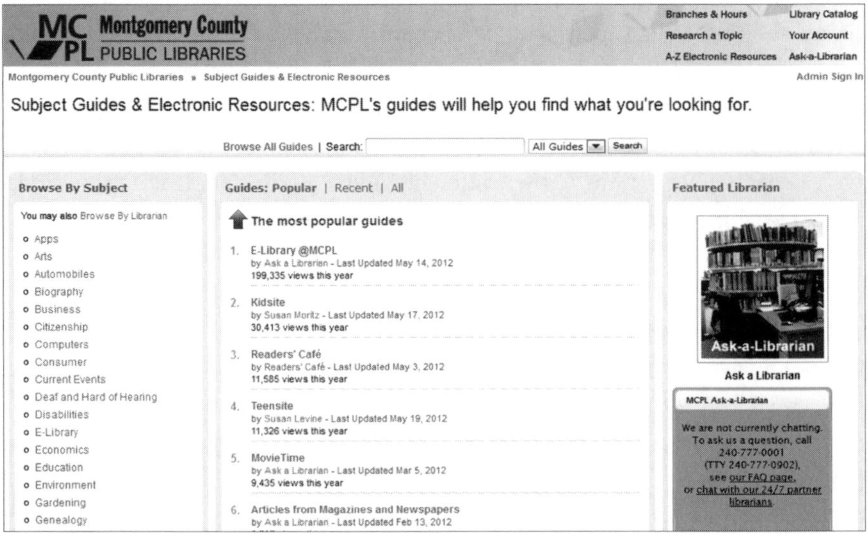

Courtesy of Montgomery County Public Libraries

and displayed. The guide is further interactive in that it provides quizzes, links to RSS feeds, library newsletters, and more. The subpages are logical and eliminate the need for layers of tabs. The content of this guide certainly lives up to the great visual interest it demonstrates and will not disappoint either the novice or the expert. What a fantastic marketing (and educational) tool for the branch book clubs, as well as the libraries themselves!

K–12 School Library: Wheeler School, Providence, Rhode Island

Design Features

The Prescott Library LibGuide is an excellent example of the guide authors considering their audience. With sharp, clear graphics, the guide authors lure their young audience to use library resources and get librarian help. Each LibGuide has a "Schedule an Appointment" widget located on the right column. This allows students to clearly see how they can obtain help from the guide author. Also, each guide author incorporates a variety of media objects to explain their topic further.

FIGURE 14.27
Wheeler School, Prescott Library, Welcome to LibGuides,
http://wheelerschool.libguides.com

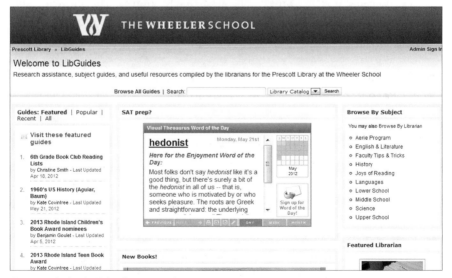

Courtesy of Wheeler School, Prescott Library

The Prescott Library LibGuides look very cutting edge. They are designed to be functional and get students excited about library resources.

Pedagogical Features

The Impact of World War I: Political & Social History (http://wheelerschool .libguides.com/wwi) is one example of Wheeler's exemplary LibGuides. The guide clearly describes its support for a "tenth grade project examining the impact of World War I on various aspects of the arts and society." The guide is visually bright and appealing using the school colors. The eye can readily scan the home page because resources are presented in many boxes, rather than as long lists. The home page immediately greets the user with numerous interactive features, such as an appointment scheduler to work with the librarian in person, an option to submit a website for inclusion in the guide, and search boxes directly to the recommended resources for getting started. The user is guided through each major area of the assignment by tabs. Each of these top-level pages has multiple subpages to assure the user covers all necessary topics. On each page a box called "Questions to Consider" reinforces the connection between the class assignment and the guide, while fostering critical thinking. Page content is appropriate for its audience in that it is thoughtfully put together using both school and carefully selected web resources, yet is not overwhelming by its quantity. The subpages under the Search Tips tab make excellent use of SlideShare presentations and YouTube videos to instruct about the research process and how to cite sources. This engaging and educational LibGuide must certainly attract upper-school students to seek out the library, its resources, and the librarian who authored it.

Special Library: Arnold Library, Fred Hutchinson Cancer Research Center, Seattle, Washington

Design Features

Fast access to pertinent information is the goal of every special library. The Fred Hutchinson Cancer (FHC) Research Center has surpassed that goal. Simply click on one of the seventeen LibGuides to access information on citation management, author's tools, or grant funding. The FHC Research Center authors use only the search box and tabs for navigating through the LibGuides. The tabbed navigation uses clear, evident language that allows for the most novice researchers to find their desired information. Videos and images assist further in aiding researchers.

FHC LibGuides authors have chosen to use a soft, muted color that allows the textual and visual information to be the highlight of the LibGuide. The

FIGURE 14.28
Arnold Library, Welcome to LibGuides,
http://libguides.fhcrc.org

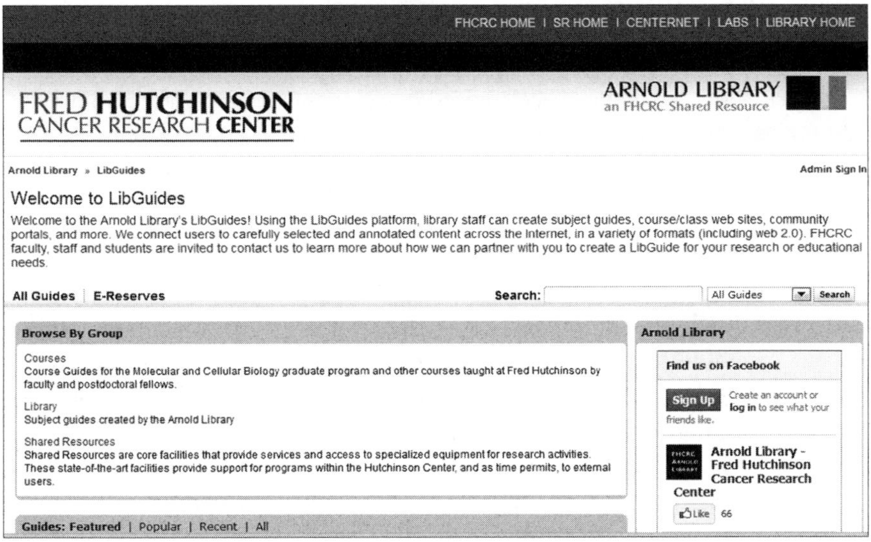

Reprinted by permission of Fred Hutchinson Cancer Research Center

selected visual graphics supplement the text rather than detract from the informational message.

Pedagogical Features
The LibGuide entitled Author's Corner (http://libguides.fhcrc.org/authors) provides "Writing, publishing and sharing resources for FHCRC authors." The user is able to get a quick overview by the inclusion of an introduction to the individual guide pages on the home page: Writing Resources, Publishing Resources, NIH Public Access Compliance, Sharing Your Work, and Copyright & Reuse. Users are invited to discover how the library can help them in the writing process from start to finish—citation management tools, journal citation services, the institutional repository, obtaining an ISBN or DOI, and much more. Future authors are led through scaffolded online resources that guide them each step of the way.

CONCLUSION

This final chapter has displayed the tremendous pool of talent shown by guide authors as they apply their individual technological and instructional design skills to LibGuides—a common platform from which to launch a web presence. The foundations of this chapter are the two checklists devised by the authors that actually represent a practical summary of this entire book. The Checklist of Major Criteria for Technical Design Evaluation of LibGuides (see table 14.1) represents the best practices that should be followed when creating a usable LibGuide. The Checklist of Major Criteria for Reference/Educational Evaluation of LibGuides (see table 14.2) is based on the most current instructional theory, discussed in chapter 7 of this book, which should be considered when creating a teaching LibGuide. This chapter exhibits, more than any other in the book, the tremendous talent and skill librarians display as they create an attractive and useful web presence.

After reviewing over 500 LibGuides websites and applying the technological and pedagogical criteria, self-analysis of our own LibGuides has become easier. An outcome of this research was the formulation of a LibGuides Standardization Working Group at our library, which assists in the recommendation and application of both the technological and pedagogical design features.

Springshare continues to make modifications to LibGuides, in an effort to build an even easier tool for the creation of interactive and dynamic resources for library patrons. However, usability, findability, and teachability are concepts over which the LibGuides' author has sole control. Using the design criteria in this chapter, institutions may evaluate current LibGuides and plan future LibGuides.

Given the large number of LibGuides and the accelerated rate at which new institutions are adopting LibGuides, it was not possible to visit LibGuides websites for all libraries. The examples in the chapter are meant to provide a starting point, not to exclude any outstanding LibGuides. Certainly additional examples of well-executed LibGuides exist in both technological and pedagogical design.

To see more examples of LibGuide best practices, browse the Springshare's LibGuides Best Practices website (http://bestof.libguides.com). Recommendations for excellent LibGuides examples are welcome there and may be submitted to Springshare on that page.

APPENDIX D

LibGuides for Special Purposes

As we were evaluating LibGuides for this chapter, we occasionally discovered a guide that we felt would be particularly useful to display as a sample of the broad-ranging environment that LibGuides could represent. Following are the URLs for these specially purposed guides.

Guide Area Activities and Attractions

Art Center College of Design, James Lemont Fogg Memorial Library, Pasadena, California (Art Center College of Design, Guide to Pasadena and Los Angeles, http://artcenter .libguides.com/content.php?pid=184745).

LibGuides Tutorial

Ashland University Library, Ashland, Ohio (Ashland University, Learn about Our LibGuides, http://libguides.ashland.edu/libguideshowto).

Supporting Faculty Teaching

Curtin University Library, Bentley, Australia (Curtin University, Supporting Your Teaching, http://libguides.library.curtin.edu.au/supporting-your-teaching).

LibGuides Used as a Complete Website

Marysville Public Library, Marysville, Ohio (Marysville Public Library, Welcome, www.marysvillelib.org).

Staff and Department Directory

Massachusetts Institute of Technology, Libraries, Cambridge, Massachusetts (MIT Libraries, Staff and Department Directory, http://libguides.mit.edu/content .php?pid=110460&sid=1057503).

Teacher-Authored LibGuide

Mesa High School, Mesa Public Schools, Mesa, Arizona (Mesa High School, AP Literature and Composition, http://libguides.mpsaz.net/mhsap).

Mobile Applications

UCLA School of Law, Hugh & Hazel Darling Library, Los Angeles, California (UCLA School of Law, Mobile Applications for Law Students & Lawyers, http://libguides .law.ucla.edu/mobilelegalapps).

About the Editors and Chapter Contributors

EDITORS

Aaron W. Dobbs

Aaron W. Dobbs is systems and electronic resources librarian and assistant professor at Shippensburg University of Pennsylvania. He received his master's degree in management from Austin Peay State University and his MSLS from the University of Tennessee. Dobbs is heavily involved in the American Library Association as councilor-at-large on the ALA Council, chair of the ALA Website Advisory Committee, and as an ACRL legislative advocate. His current professional interest is in creating student-centered library websites, particularly with LibGuides. He can be contacted at awdobbs@ship.edu.

Ryan L. Sittler

Ryan L. Sittler is the instructional technology / information literacy librarian at California University of Pennsylvania. Ryan holds an MLS from Clarion University, an MSIT from Bloomsburg University, and is ABD in communications media and instructional technology at Indiana University of Pennsylvania. Sittler has coedited two other books with Doug Cook: *Practical Pedagogy for Library Instructors* (2008) and *The Library Instruction Cookbook* (2009). He is also part of a team that developed the educational information literacy game *A Planet in Peril: Plagiarism,* which won the Caspian Learning 2010 Serious Games Challenge. He can be contacted at sittler@calu.edu.

Douglas Cook

Doug Cook is an instruction librarian and professor at Shippensburg University of Pennsylvania. He received his MLS from the University of Maryland and DEd from Pennsylvania

State University. He has recently coedited five books: with Tasha Cooper, *Teaching Information Literacy Skills to Social Science Students and Practioners* (2006); with Ryan Sittler, *Practical Pedagogy for Library Instructors* (2008) and *The Library Instruction Cookbook* (2009); with Lesley Farmer, *Using Qualitative Methods in Action Research* (2011); and a children's book with Carolyn Cook, *A Hike on the Appalachian Trail* (2010). His current research interests are web-centered pedagogy and real-world definitions of information literacy. He can be contacted at dlcook@ship.edu.

CONTRIBUTORS

LESLIE ADEBONOJO is the undergraduate student services librarian at East Tennessee State University. As a medical and academic librarian, she has presented at national conferences and published a number of articles on library management and the use of educational technology. She received an MSLS from Case Western, and an MEd from East Tennessee State University. She can be contacted at adebonol@mail.etsu.edu.

NEDDA H. AHMED is the arts librarian at Georgia State University. As the liaison to the School of Music, the School of Art and Design, and the Moving Image Studies program, Nedda prepares artists, filmmakers, musicians, and scholars to conduct effective research. She has served as the website editor for the Arts Libraries Society of North America (ARLIS/NA) since 2005 and has taught several workshops (including two on designing LibGuides) at ARLIS/NA conferences. She can be contacted at nedda@gsu.edu.

JUDITH ARNOLD is coordinator for user engagement and outreach at the Wayne State University Library System, where she provides reference, instruction, and serves as liaison for English, Linguistics, Classics, and the Honors College. She received her MLS from Kent State University and master of English from Vanderbilt University. She is the coauthor of *Research Writing in the Information Age* (1998) and has written articles for the *Journal of Academic Librarianship*, *Research Strategies*, and *Internet Reference Services Quarterly*. She is a member of the Library Instruction Round Table's Program Planning Committee, an Editorial Board member of *Reference and User Services Quarterly*, and co-instructor of the ACRL e-learning course "Learning Objects: Creating Instruction to Go." She may be contacted at ay4047@wayne.edu.

JULIE LEE ARNOLD is the course manager for UCSP 611, Introduction to Graduate Library Research Skills, a required graduate school course at the University of Maryland University College. She is also a reference and instruction librarian. She received her MLS from the iSchool, University of Maryland, in 1998. She has published and presented on virtual reference and web conferencing in distance learning. Among her articles are, with Neal Kaske, the highly cited "Evaluating the Quality of a Chat Service" (*portal: Libraries and the Academy*, 2005), and with Barbara J. Mann, "Breaking Out of the Asynchronous Box: Using Web Conferencing in Distance Learning" (*Journal of Library Information Services in Distance Learning*, 2009). She may be contacted at julie.lietzau@umuc.edu.

LORA BALDWIN is the distance learning librarian at Indiana University East in Richmond, Indiana. She holds a master of library science and a master of educational psychology, both from Indiana University. She has eclectic research interests and has presented at national conferences. She can be contacted at mcclell@iue.edu.

REBECA BEFUS is the mathematics librarian and part of the Information Literacy unit at Michigan State University. She has been involved with information literacy and first-year experience since 2009. She has presented on topics including first-year experience, information literacy instruction, and design/development of online tutorials. She received her MSLIS from Syracuse University and an MEd in instructional technology from Wayne State University. She can be contacted at befus@msu.edu.

VERONICA BIELAT is a user experiences librarian, the instruction services coordinator, and library liaison to the College of Education in Wayne State University's Library System. In addition to her involvement in information literacy initiatives on campus, she co-teaches the course Instructional Methods for Librarians through the Wayne State University School of Library and Information Science. She has presented and published several times on the topics of faculty/librarian collaboration, course-integrated information literacy instruction, and integrating technology into information literacy teaching. She received her MLIS from Wayne State University. She can be reached at vbielat@wayne.edu.

KATHY CAMPBELL is head of reference at the East Tennessee State University Library. Her prior experience includes academic, public, and school libraries. She holds an MLS from the University of Tennessee and has published in both national and state journals. Her research interests include the use of educational technology in reference and library instruction, e-learning, and library management. She can be contacted at campbeka@etsu.edu.

CLAIRE CLEMENS is an education librarian at the College of New Jersey (TCNJ). As a certified public school teacher, Claire works to ensure ready access to library resources and services, including special collections for teacher education, for all users in the School of Education. She is currently a member of the LibGuides Standardization Committee at TCNJ and a member of the Shared Information Literacy Committee of the Virtual Academic Library Environment of New Jersey. She holds an MLIS from the University of South Carolina. She can be contacted at clemensc@tcnj.edu.

STEPHANIE DELANO DAVIS is the coordinator of information literacy at Northwestern Michigan College. She received a master of librarianship from the University of Illinois, Urbana-Champaign, and also holds an MBA from Spring Arbor University. She is passionate about information literacy and enjoys helping students learn research skills, whether through face-to-face instruction or through online tools, such as LibGuides. Her essay "Will Graphic Novels Redeem Comics?" appeared in the book *Understanding Evangelical Media: The Changing Face of Christian Communication* (2008). Contact her by e-mail at sdavis@nmc.edu.

MARK ELLIS is the documents/law/maps librarian at East Tennessee State University (ETSU). He was formerly head of reference at ETSU. He holds a PhD from the University of Illinois, and an MSLS from the University of Kentucky. He has presented at national and international conferences. His research interests include the changes in government publication, e-learning, emerging library technology, and medieval literature. He can be contacted at ellism@etsu.edu.

JENNIFER EMANUEL is the digital resources and reference librarian at the University of Illinois. She is focused on integrating online tools into public services, as well as being a public service voice in technology projects. She has worked extensively with next-generation discovery systems as well as usability testing of various tools, and is particularly interested in how library users utilize library tools in different ways to benefit their research. She received a master of science in information science from the University of North Carolina at Chapel Hill, and is pursuing her EdD in educational leadership from the University of Missouri. She can be reached at emanuelj@illinois.edu.

TABATHA FARNEY is the web services librarian for the Kraemer Family Library at the University of Colorado, Colorado Springs, where she helps build, customize, and maintain the library's website and other online tools, including LibGuides. She earned an MLIS from the University of Illinois at Urbana-Champaign and is deeply engaged with web development. Her research interests include web analytics, open source technologies, and the implementation of technologies in libraries. She is coauthoring a forthcoming LITA Guide with Nina McHale called *Web Analytics Strategies for Libraries* (2013). She can be contacted at tfarney@uccs.edu.

LAURA WESTMORELAND GARIEPY is the assistant head for instructional services at Virginia Commonwealth University. She leads the instructional services team and oversees teaching and learning endeavors at James Branch Cabell Library. She also collaborates with faculty to incorporate information literacy skills and concepts into the university curriculum. Her research interests include teaching and learning, assessment, and library administration and policy. She holds a master of science in library science from the University of North Carolina at Chapel Hill. She can be contacted at lwgariepy@vcu.edu.

RICH GAUSE is the government information librarian at the University of Central Florida Libraries in Orlando, where he supervises the maintenance of the U.S. and Florida Documents Collections. He also coordinates the library's LibGuides installation. He is collection liaison for the Theatre Department. Gause has done numerous workshops at professional meetings, including several on LibGuides. He holds an MLS from Florida State University and an MBA from New Hampshire College. He can be reached at Rich.Gause@ucf.edu.

KATHY GAYNOR is currently the interim university library director at Thompson Rivers University in Kamloops, British Columbia, Canada. She has presented extensively on Web 2.0 technologies and their uses in libraries at conferences in British Columbia. She holds an MLIS from McGill University. She can be reached at kgaynor@tru.ca.

BETH LARKEE KUMAR is the electronic resources and serials librarian and the liaison librarian to the College of Education at the University of Colorado, Colorado Springs. She uses LibGuides both as an administrator and content creator for instruction sessions for the four departments in the College of Education. She earned her MSLIS and EdM from the University of Illinois. Two of her research interests are the marketing of electronic resources and working with online students. She can be reached at bkumar@uccs.edu.

295

KENNETH LISS As of September 1, 2012, Ken Liss was a member of the Community Engagement division of Springshare, LLC—the producers of LibGuides. While working on this book he was the coordinator of digital user services at the Boston College (BC) University Libraries. He served as subject librarian for Communication Studies and also led and managed Boston College's LibGuides and virtual reference services. Before coming to BC, Liss spent eight years as a business librarian at the Harvard Business School and the Kirstein Business Branch of the Boston Public Library. He was the founding editor of *HBS Working Knowledge,* an online magazine at Harvard. He can be reached at ken@springshare.com.

BARBARA J. MANN serves as the assistant director for public services, information and library services, University of Maryland University College, where she leads and oversees a robust instruction program and a busy reference service. She also serves as an adjunct associate professor teaching the graduate-level required, noncredit course Introduction to Graduate Library Research Skills. She obtained her MLIS from the University of South Carolina. She has coauthored several publications pertaining to research and information literacy instruction, as well as coauthoring the book, with Andrea Morrison, *International Government Information and Country Information: A Subject Guide* (2004). She was recently awarded the 2012 ACRL IS Miriam Dudley Instruction Librarian Award. Her current research interests are information literacy in the distance learning environment and leadership styles in the workplace. She can be reached at barbara.mann@umuc.edu.

EMILY S. MAZURE is the biomedical research liaison librarian at Duke University's Medical Center Library. In this position, she provides targeted support and services to biomedical researchers in the Duke community. Previously she held the position of education and research librarian at Virginia Commonwealth University's Tompkins-McCaw Library for the Health Sciences, focusing on developing and providing instruction for faculty, staff, and students. She holds a master of science in information from the University of Michigan. She can be contacted at emily.mazure@duke.edu.

JENNIFER A. MCDANIEL is an education and research librarian at the Tompkins-McCaw Library for the Health Sciences, Virginia Commonwealth University. In this role, she is involved in the development of educational content that integrates library collections and services into courses and curriculum, and the advancement of faculty and student academic success. She received her MSLS from the Catholic University of America. She can be reached at jamcdaniel@vcu.edu.

SUE A. MCFADDEN is an emerging technology librarian at Indiana University East, Richmond, Indiana. She received her MLS from Indiana University. Her research interests are varied and include Web 2.0 tools for online research and learning. Sue has presented at national conferences on library instruction, collaboration, and Web 2.0 tools. She is active in ALA/ACRL sections. She can be reached at smcfadde@iue.edu.

JOSEPH RAWSON is the 24/7 services coordinator librarian at the University of Maryland University College. He oversees the programs that provide library services to the university community 24 hours a day, seven days a week, year-round. He teaches LIBS 150 for the School of Undergraduate Studies. Previous to working for UMUC he was a reference librarian at the main branch of the Providence Public Library in downtown Providence, one of the largest libraries in the state of Rhode Island. He received his MLIS from the University of Rhode Island. Prior to his career as a librarian, he spent many years as an education, event, and member services director for builder and realtor trade associations running educational programs, conventions, and working with faculty to develop course curriculum. He can be contacted at joseph.rawson @umuc.edu.

AARON TAY is a reference librarian with the National University of Singapore. He received a master of information studies from Nanyang Technological University. He has written and presented papers on mobile interfaces, library guides, and online library marketing. Tay was named a Library Journal Mover & Shaker for 2011. More recently, he was named the Library Association of Singapore's Outstanding Newcomer. His research interests include the use of social media and mobile phones for libraries and bibliometrics. He blogs regularly at http://musingsaboutlibrarianship.blogspot.com and can be contacted at aarontay@gmail.com.

ERIN R. WHITE is the web systems librarian at Virginia Commonwealth University Libraries. She leads a small team that is responsible for the libraries' website, staff intranet, mobile website, and other public-facing web interfaces and applications. Her research interests include emerging technologies in libraries, project management, and user experience design. She holds a master in information science from the University of North Carolina at Chapel Hill. She can be contacted at erwhite@vcu.edu.

SHARON WHITFIELD is the emerging technologies librarian at the College of New Jersey. In this role she gets to experiment with new technologies with the goal of getting others excited about technology's use in the library. Prior to becoming a librarian, Whitfield held the position of trainer in the field of information technology. This experience helped her to understand how users think and interact with technology, resulting in the creation of user-centered websites and technologies. She holds a master of library and information science from the University of Pittsburgh. She can be contacted at whitfies@tcnj.edu.

Index

3m

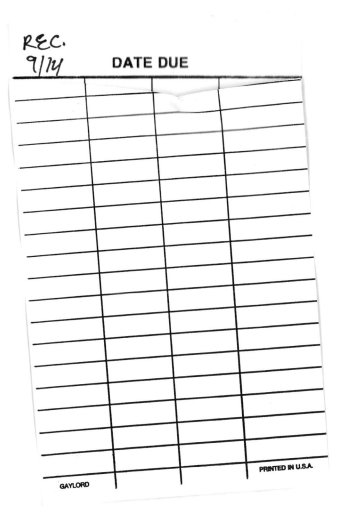

REC.
9/14   **DATE DUE**

GAYLORD   PRINTED IN U.S.A.